IN
DIFFERENT
WORLDS:
FROM POW TO PHD

DANKWART KOEHLER

Bridgeway Books

In Different Worlds: From POW to PhD
Published by Bridgeway Books
P.O. Box 30071
Austin, Texas 78755

For more information about our books, please write us,
e-mail us at info@bridgewaybooks.net, or visit our web site at
www.bridgewaybooks.net.

LCCN: 2010925636

ISBN-13: 978-1-934454-41-1
ISBN-10: 1-934454-41-9

This book is written with the intent of being as accurate as
possible. It is based upon how the author remembers events
and experiences.

10 9 8 7 6 5 4 3 2 1

To my wife, Christa;
our three children, Birgit, Steffen,
and Kirsten;
and our five grandchildren, Cory,
Sasha, Annika, Emeline, and Leyli.

My special thanks go to Cathy Priest,
as well as to the editors at Bridgeway
Books, for their extensive and thor-
ough review of the manuscript.

Contents

Prologue vii

Part I

1. Ebingen, 1926 1
2. Early Years in Heilbronn 7
3. Hitler Becomes Chancellor of Germany 18
4. Growing Up 21
5. World War II 57
6. Prisoner of War 95

Part II

7. Beginning a Second Life 153
8. Exchange Student in America 180
9. Back in Germany 202
10. Atlanta, Georgia 221

11. Bell Telephone Laboratories 234

12. Switzerland 254

13. Return to the United States 268

14. Photography 290

15. Three Years in Belgium 300

16. Back Again in New Jersey 308

17. Retirement Life 313

Appendix A: Personal Thoughts on Selected Topics 317

Appendix B: Summary of *Zeugen des Abendlandes*
(Witnesses of the Western World) by Franz Goldschmitt 322

Bibliography 324

Prologue

This book is the story of my life, a life that began in one world—which itself underwent certain transformations—and then led me into a totally new world. These notes are written for two purposes. One is to provide a documentary for our children and their children; to tell them about their roots. The other is to describe the unusual political circumstances under which I grew up and how my eighty-year life has evolved from there. This book is not meant to be a political book. Yet my description of growing up in Germany during the Third Reich, under Hitler, will undoubtedly evoke political feelings and emotions in many readers. I hope my book may impart a message of human understanding.

The post-World-War-II generation that followed me in Germany can confirm that there was—and still is—a complete communication gap between them and their parents. The older generation was ashamed and often did not even try to understand their own past, nor did their children dare to ask how almost the entire population of Germany followed Hitler, and how the worst crime against humanity in recent history became possible. Even in schools in postwar Germany, the issue became taboo, and not just officially. Every teacher was afraid to expose him or herself, or to voice an opinion that might be misconstrued as a defense, or even an endorsement, of the criminal regime of the Third Reich. Yet we need an answer to the question of how it was possible for a nation to follow a dictator who led it—or misled it—to destroy the lives of millions of people.

I can say that I enjoyed a happy and safe childhood—even though my later teenage years were harshly, and in a life-changing way, affected by World War II. You can lead a happy life under a dictatorship, provided that you don't belong to any group the government considers to be an "enemy." Maybe these pages contribute to one of the less discussed, but perhaps most important, dangers of a dictatorship: the seduction, or blinding, of a people to become followers. Much has been written about the "results" of Hitler's dictatorship. But how much is understood of how it got there? Having lived inside the Third Reich, as well as in postwar Germany, and now in the United States, I might perhaps be able to contribute to that understanding from an angle that outsiders cannot.

Holocaust studies are offered today at many institutions. The field serves the extremely important purpose of preserving the memory of these crimes against humanity and of the human suffering resulting from them. But I have the impression that Holocaust studies often neglect a second aspect: the thorough examination of the causes. The first aspect looks back, but the second is essential if we want to look to the future and work toward overcoming bias and hatred in the world.

If you want to teach your children not to follow strangers, would you only show them images of what happened to abducted children or would you explain to them what motivated these children to follow the criminals? Similarly, we might find an analogy in military history, going back to the time of Romans. A successful strategy requires knowing not only your enemy's weaknesses, but, equally importantly, their strengths, in order to be able to defeat them.

It is difficult for today's younger generations to envision life at a time when the extensive forms of communication of today, which we take for granted, did not exist, e.g., TV, Internet, mobile phones, and a free press. Dictatorial systems have always enforced and thrived on a lack of communication. We appreciate the freedom we have today, especially in the United States, and we take it for granted. But even the concept of freedom is relative. You don't know what you are missing until you have it. Imagine, for example, a utopian society on another planet where personal ownership is totally unknown; you would not expect the creatures on that planet to complain about a lack of freedom in this respect.

When I now look back at the earlier part of my life, I realize that I learned many lessons about human relationships. One is the need to understand other peoples, their cultures, and their feelings. It happened, and still happens throughout the world today, that certain ethnic groups felt superior to other groups and engaged in acts of suppression. In some cultures, men feel and act as if they are superior to women. Only time—combined, of course, with communication, education, and new experiences—can overcome these biases. To feel that your own country is the best of all countries, however, seems to me a very normal attitude, and as I grew up, I felt that way, too.

It is easy to hate a country or an ethnic group as long as you don't know its people as individuals. This reminds me of an analogy. Soldiers struggle with learning to kill an enemy in combat at a close range, where they can see the enemy's eye. Many find this almost impossible to do. Yet firing a shell at the unknown enemy from a distance does not create as personal a dilemma.

I found that you also can hate a country as a political institution, while still respecting or loving its people. You can find a similar spectrum of people in other countries as in your own; some of these people you like more, or even make friends with, and others you like less. Once you develop a friendship with specific members of that group or country, the generalized hatred often begins to fade away. This process of overcoming past hatred is lengthy and often requires a new generation to grow up. It is especially difficult when religion, and especially religious extremism, is involved. When young Germans today drive into France for the weekend to meet with friends, or vice versa, it is inconceivable that they will ever go to war against each other again.

Communication has certainly made the world smaller. It is less and less possible to isolate a people from the outside world. I see the fall of Communism, for example, as having primarily three sources. One derives from the fundamental flaws of its original basic ideology, such as the lack of adequate pay incentives for people who work harder than others, and the restriction of personal property. Another is the impossibility of totally planning and controlling the supply and demand of the market. But very key causes to its demise are the increasing means for exchanging information, both internally and with the outside world, which have broken the communication isolation that Communism uses to control its people.

As a result of my personal experiences, I have come to the conclusion that a war should not be a solution to a political problem. Are there exceptions? Probably, but only if the threat is immediate, as it is, for example, in an attack. However, people's opinion will differ about where the threshold is. If one can understand the consequences of WWI, and especially WWII for Germany or France, one can also better understand the antiwar positions of these two countries with respect to the Iraq war in 2003.

I do not claim to be a historian. The following remarks are my personal experiences and impressions, and hence largely subjective.

There is talk in some U.S. newspapers today about Germans beginning to feel like victims of their past. The question of whether this is true or even justified does not make sense. Germans do not and cannot deny the crimes of the past. At the same time, hundreds of millions of human beings, men, women, and children, experienced unimaginable hardships and sufferings during the war, be they Germans or citizens of another nation. Their experiences cannot be hidden. If only we could learn from the experiences of the past!

In writing this book, I depended primarily on my recollections. For the period of my captivity, I am fortunate to have in my possession a complete collection of all the letters that I wrote home. Occasionally I've included a brief history to contextualize my experience.

PART I

1

Ebingen, 1926

May 19, 1926

One day in 1926, Klara Köhler was pushing a baby carriage through the small town of Ebingen in southwestern Germany on the Schwäbische Alb, not far from the Black Forest. A woman stopped her and said, "Wow, you have twins. That's a lot of work, isn't it?"

Klara, my mother, responded, "But it is also a joy." I was one of the twins; the other was my sister Ursula. To my parents' surprise, Ursula appeared ten minutes after me. I always pointed out that I was ten minutes older, especially when people remarked that Ursula was—in the early years—taller than I. Our birth, on May 19, was about six weeks ahead of normal expectations, and, in those days, our survival was not guaranteed. Ursula weighed less than four pounds and I weighed barely five. As our parents later told us many times, after our birth, our mother kept asking my father continuously whether her little girl was still alive. We both made it.

As another of my mother's stories goes, we became aware of each other when I did my baby stretches in the crib and hit Ursula in the face. That sealed our partnership. Until the age of about sixteen, when the war sent us our separate ways, she was my constant companion. Even in my dreams later in life, she often appears as my companion, especially since many of my dreams keep going back to my childhood.

Parents

My father was born on June 8, 1890, and was given the magniloquent name Paul Friedrich Georg August Köhler, though he went by August. His father, a very gentle man, had the respectable position of head cashier at the main post office in Heilbronn, Germany. His mother, for whom we grandchildren did not have the same warm feeling as we did toward our grandfather, was the former lady-in-waiting of the Princess of Waldenburg. The picturesque castle of the Duke of Waldenburg can still be seen on a mountaintop not far from Heilbronn. We only remember our grandmother dressed in black, as it was apparently customary for "elderly" ladies.

My father's parents wanted him to become a Protestant minister and sent him to the theological seminary in Schöntal, and subsequently to the seminary in Urach. A few years later, my father felt somewhat "overexposed" to theology and decided to study philology instead. His prime interests were languages, including Latin, Greek, French, English, and Hebrew, which were part of his seminary education. But before beginning his studies, he had to do a year of military service in the 122nd Infantry Regiment.

His studies of new philology at the University of Tübingen in southern Germany also led him to London for one semester, and Grenoble, France, for another. This impressed us children, since very few people we knew had ever been outside of Germany. Father finished his studies with a Doctor of Philosophy. Throughout his life, he was always known as Dr. Köhler. In Germany, "doctor" is a title not only used by medical doctors, but also by those with other doctoral degrees. The formal address is "Herr Doktor," followed by the person's name.

Very often the wives are similarly addressed as "Frau Doktor," even though, according to correct etiquette, they are not entitled to use their husband's title. My mother told our butcher not to address her in this way, since she did not have a doctorate. However, the butcher continued just the same. German storekeepers like to greet their entering clients with such titles especially loudly, in order to let other customers know what a distinguished clientele they have. Here in the United States, we often see designations of businesses like "Lawn Doctor" or "Doctor Fix It." This would be against the law in Germany, where the title is legally protected.

By the time my father finished his studies in Tübingen, World War I had broken out. He was drafted and fought in the trenches of the Western Front in France. By 1915, he developed severe paratyphoid, for which he was disabled from service on the front. However, he still had to serve in the military until the end of the war, at which time he was discharged as a reserve lieutenant.

He became a lecturer in the seminary of Blaubeuren, and in 1921, having passed the necessary government exams, he became a *Studienrat* in Ebingen. Studienrat is the name for a first-level permanently employed high school teacher. Unlike in the United States, a teacher in a German public school or university is always a government employee, enjoying a steady salary and corresponding benefits.

My mother, Klara Sophie Jäger, born on November 19, 1896, was the daughter of the rector of the middle school in

Heilbronn. My grandfather was quite progressive and followed his conviction that girls should also have an education. Following her basic education, my mother studied at the teachers' seminary in Markröningen. Grandmother Jäger was a perfect complement to her husband: very gentle, warm, and loving.

In 1939, my father had to research his ancestry. The government required their employees to prove that they were of pure Aryan descent.[1] The good news for my father was that it became an interesting project in itself, regardless of the original motive. He could trace his own ancestry as far back as 1785, and, in one case, even to the year 1684. All of my ancestors lived in the Swabian southwestern part of Germany, the "Schwabenland," where the local dialect is Swabian, or *Schwäbisch*. My forefathers were mostly teachers, ministers, farmers, winemakers, or craftspeople like carpenters, blacksmiths, shoemakers, bakers, and stonemasons.

I don't think my father could find anyone who practiced the profession of a *Köhler*. Köhler is the name for the old profession of making charcoal by incomplete burning of woodpiles in the forest. A few Köhlers still existed in Germany when I was a child.

The families of our ancestors were big. One reason for this was that people were aware of the high death rate of babies and children. Yet many of my later ancestors lived a long life. All of my grandparents, as well as both of my parents, lived almost exactly to the age of eighty.

My father first took notice of my mother when she visited the parents-in-law of her sister Julie Rittman, who lived in the same house as my father's parents. My father later arranged to meet my mother "by accident" a few times as they traveled on the same train from Heilbronn to the university in Tübingen.

---

1. I heard from a Swiss friend recently that during the war, Switzerland, when they were afraid of a German occupation, also required certain government employees to search their family history for proof of "Aryan descent."

Our parents told us children the story of how, after they got engaged, on one of those train rides, my mother happened to clumsily drop something. Upon seeing this, my father said "you little sheep," which in southern Germany is a term of endearment. However, my mother took offense and seriously pondered whether she could engage in a marriage on such shaky ground. Fortunately, she forgave my father and they were happily married on August 18, 1921. The wedding was performed in a church in Heilbronn and the reception festivities were held at the house of Grandfather Jäger in Heilbronn. I can't remember my parents ever bickering or arguing, at least not in front of us children, and I can even imagine that they never really did.

In 1922, their first son, Uli, was born. We children later secretly calculated that he was born nine months and six days after the wedding and not a day sooner, which was important in those days. My brother Volker followed Uli two years later and my sister and I came two years after that. Since my father was a teacher of German, the choice of names for his children was strongly influenced by his background. He chose very modern names. Volker, and my name, Dankwart, are from the old German *Nibelungenlied*, or "Song of the Nibelungs," a saga written toward the end of the twelfth century. Dankwart is the brother of the hero, Hagen, in that saga. The name means a protector (*Wärter*) of others through his thinking (*denken*). Whereas the names of my siblings became quite popular and modern names in Germany in the following years, my own name died quickly in the name book. The reason was that the advent of cars in the nineteen twenties created the new profession of the *Tankwart* (filling station attendant). On countless occasions, people thought it was funny to call me Tankwart, but I could not agree with this attempt at humor.

Throughout his career, my father taught primarily German in the last grades of high school, but also some English and French. The old languages, Latin, Greek, and Hebrew, were more or less a hobby for him. Other interests he cultivated were meteorology, graphology, geology, and photography.

My parents stayed in Ebingen for eight years. I remember very little from that time. My father's photographs captured some family events, and, as is often the case with photographs, they helped me keep at least some faint memories. Seeing a photograph reinforces the even weak memories that we have from a given time or event. Thus, the difference between remembering an event and remembering its photograph may be indistinguishable. There is one non-photographic event that I do indeed remember, even though I was only about three years old. I locked myself in a room by playing with the dead bolt on the door. I pushed the little lever and could not open it afterward. My parents tried to teach me from the outside how to open the lock, but to no avail. After a while, I saw a strange face appear in the glass panel above the door of the ten-foot-high room; I became scared. He was a craftsperson that my parents had called to resolve the emergency. The man cut out the glass panel and climbed down into the room; I was saved.

2

Early Years in Heilbronn

Move to Heilbronn

As our father gained some professional seniority, he applied to the ministry of education for a transfer. Where else would he want to go than to his and his wife's hometown of Heilbronn? Not only did it become a reality, but he also came to teach in the same school and building that he once attended as a child. For his family, he embarked on building a single-family home within a few hundred yards from where the town ended and the farmers' fields and vineyards began. Today, this is a prime location, as it is now considered to be right in the city and is within walking distance from the center of town. Unfortunately, the builder did a little switching around and my parents wound up in a two-family house, next to the originally promised single-family house. In 1929, our family moved into the new house on Solothurnerstrasse 21. The family that moved into the single-family house became our very good friends.

Heilbronn lies on the Neckar River, about halfway between Stuttgart and Heidelberg, where the Neckar enters the Rhine River. The origin of Heilbronn goes back to the year 741 when the Villa Helibrunna was first documented, the first basilica was built, and St. Kilian was said to have been baptized at the Heiligbronna. In 1265, it got its first constitution. In 1371, it became a *Freie Reichsstadt,* or "Free Imperial City." This meant, simply, that it belonged to the emperor, who was Karl IV at the time, rather than to the king or the Duke of Württemberg. To protect it from the potentially hostile country that surrounded it, Heilbronn, like other Free Imperial Cities, had a wall encircling the entire town. Its status as a Free Imperial City lasted until 1802, when the Duke of Württemberg was allowed to occupy all free cities in his territory as a compensation for yielding land on the left bank of the Rhine to France.

Heilbronn's Gothic cathedral, the Kilianskirche, and a picturesque town hall, whose construction was completed in 1580, characterize the center of the town. Other than the few main through streets, the streets in downtown consisted of very narrow alleys. On these alleys, the houses were built so that every floor extended one or two feet further out than the one below it. If you lived on the top floor, you could almost shake hands with your neighbor. These narrow streets in the center of town were always a bit of a mystery to us. We felt a bit uneasy going there, yet it was perfectly safe. The families on these streets have lived there for many generations, if not centuries.

The big *Marktplatz* (market square) is in front of the city hall. Its name alludes to the markets that have been held there for centuries. A monument on the square features Robert Mayer who is considered one of the most famous citizens of the town. My father was a city guide at various times of his life, especially for English- and French-speaking groups. He once overheard another guide explaining the monument to his tourists, saying, "Here sits Robert Mayer, who invented heat and energy." Robert Mayer was not quite that presumptuous, but he was the first to publish and mathematically define the law of conservation of energy between heat and mechanical energy in 1842.

Our state, Württemberg-Baden, has always been well-known, not only for its cuckoo clocks, the Black Forest, and its wine, but much more so for its mechanical industry. Heilbronn is no exception with several factories relating to precision engineering. On the northern outskirts of town we had one of the best-known bicycle factories, which has since become an Audi car factory. We also had other factories in town during my childhood, like soap and sugar factories, some of whose chimneys spewed soot that often landed in our plates when we ate on our deck. I find it amazing today when I see old photographs that feature smoking chimneys and other smoke-filled sceneries admiring the industrial progress. Even my father wrote a poem glamorizing this progress.

Our father enjoyed a decent and guaranteed income as a teacher and government employee, but we never considered ourselves rich. We lived sufficiently well and led a happy life. My oldest brother Uli once wore a white shirt to school. His schoolmates remarked that he must have a rich father since he came to school in a white shirt, whereupon my brother said, "If you saw my father's bank account book, you would not say that."

Our father liked mathematics without ever having had an in-depth education in higher mathematics. He was completely nontechnical. Our light switches at the time had a set of spring blades that determined the jumping motion from the "off" to the "on" position, and vice versa, as you rotated the switch. Every once in a while, the springs would wear out and break. My father would have the electrician come by to repair the switch—until I took over as a teenager. It took a screwdriver and less than five minutes of time to insert a new spring set, without any danger of electric shock.

Our favorite shoe store was in the middle of town, right behind the city hall. With a fair amount of shock now, I recall the day the shoe store installed the latest "progress of technology": an X-ray machine. Its purpose was to see in the fluorescent display how well a shoe would fit. We kept going over to the machine, sliding in one of our feet, and watching the screen as we wiggled our toes. We did this for many seconds at a time. The radiation exposure must have been ten or hundred thousand times more than when you have an X-ray taken by your doctor today.

Another dangerous game occurred when one of our thermometers broke and we would play with the mercury balls on the table. Nothing was known at the time about the danger of mercury vapors.

The Economy

Having good employment in the twenties was a significant blessing. The man who was later to become my father-in-law was under similar circumstances as my father. Having finished his engineering degree, he was lucky to find employment with the federal railroad system. I remember a commonly quoted satirical rhyme about people who worked for the railroad, which said, "He who is nobody and knows nothing goes to work for the post and railroad." However, in the post-war economy of the twenties, it was a privilege to be offered employment by the Reichspost or Reichsbahn, provided that you passed the stringent employment entry examination given for the higher government services. Germany's economy went into a downspin on account of war debt and reparation costs, and suffered a hyperinflation in 1923.[1] My father would later tell us of the days when the cost of a pretzel had risen to a few hundred reichsmarks and subsequently to a million, showing us some of the useless million reichsmark bills. At the peak of the inflation, it took 4.2 trillion reichsmarks to buy a single American dollar.

Other than the stories we heard from our parents, we children were too young at the time to feel affected by the economic situation. My father had secure employment. We led a happy life. A few things exemplifying the difference in technology between then and now still stick in my memory. For example, Tuesday was wash day in our family. Our mother certainly did not wash her laundry in the river, but she had a big kettle, located in the laundry room, which was called the *Waschküche* (washing kitchen). A wood stove formed the bottom part of the kettle, heating the water above. Somehow the heat caused the cylinder to undergo a back-and-forth motion, moaning under the load of the heavy work. In the room next to the washing kitchen in the basement was the ironing stove. It had an octagonal form and stood in the middle of the room with an exhaust pipe leading to the outside. On one of the eight sides was the door for the burning wood. The irons were placed against the seven other flat metal sides to be heated. The hottest iron was picked up with a wooden handle for ironing and replaced by a new one when it was no longer hot. The name "flatiron" comes from this type of pressing laundry. Wash day was an all-day activity for my mother, which did not allow her time for preparing the usual lunch. Instead, she prepared a soup and one of her delicious apple pies the day before, which we liked even more and made us always look forward to wash day.

---

1. Robert Selig, "Armseliges Deutschland: War Defeat, Reparations, Inflation, and the Year 1923 in German History," German Life, October/November 1998, http://www.germanlife.com/Archives/1998/9810_01.html.

Elementary School

In 1932, Ursula and I were enrolled in first grade of elementary school. Our school, the Rosenau Schule in Heilbronn, was in an old sandstone building, a five-block walk from our house. The left wing was for girls; the right wing was for boys. But how can you separate twins? After some negotiations by my parents, an exception was granted for my sister. She became the only girl in a class of fifty-two students. The only time the big class was split was for the subject of religion, which was taught in two sections, Protestant (which meant Lutheran) and Catholic, which was the smaller section. Other religions were not represented, at least not in our class. Ursula and I received a good education and liked going to elementary school for the four years.

My parents knew the teacher, Herr Bessler, who befriended my aunt. His interest in her became more and more obvious, as I was often asked by him during class time to take little notes to Fräulein Jäger,[2] who was a teacher in the girls' section. A few years later, this correspondence culminated in marriage. This was the second for Uncle Gottlieb, as we came to know Herr Bessler, and the first for Aunt Lia, who married fairly late since she had been taking care of her parents. It was quite common, and often expected, in those days for one daughter to look after her parents, with a silent wish by the parents that a suitor did not appear on the scene too soon.

One of our aunts lived just across the street from the school. My parents arranged with Herr Bessler for us to go across the street to use the toilet of Tante Helene, since the facilities in the school building were not up to my parents' standards of hygiene—nor to anyone's standards today.

---

2. The designation Fräulein (Miss) was used at the time for all unmarried women, regardless of age. Today, it is no longer used for unmarried women above the age of about eighteen; they are addressed as Frau (Mrs.).

Ursula felt quite at home in the huge class of boys, and looked to me as her protector. The more you go back in time from today, the more discipline in school was written in capital letters. The teachers had their little bamboo sticks of which they made occasional use, especially in the form of a whip on the fingertips, called a *Tatze*. Ursula remembered an episode where the class was late coming in from the break. As we marched two-by-two into the classroom, Herr Bessler hit everybody walking on the right side on the lower backside. As my sister realized she was on the wrong side, she quickly pushed me over to change sides with her. However, the teacher reduced the intensity somewhat as I walked past him.

On our birthday, Ursula and I always found two chocolate *Maikäfer* (May bugs), or cockchafers (similar to the June bug in the United States, but slightly bigger and more ornate) on our desks. The other pupils did not get such a birthday greeting, but they did not object; it was obvious that my sister was "special" in our class.

When learning the ABCs, we were taught that there are eight vowels in German, namely *a, e, i, o, u, ä, ö,* and *ü.* The latter three were simply different vowels with different sounds and we did not call them "umlauts," a designation that actually has a much broader meaning.[3] Those two dots or two little strokes are leftovers from the letter *e* that used to be printed or written over the respective vowels in former times. Many immigrants dropped the umlaut, instead of using the equivalent ae, oe, or ue. I am quite sure that the name of the famous bathroom fixture maker, Kohler, was originally written "Köhler" way back in the old country.

Anglophones usually have difficulty pronouncing *ö* and *ü.* As we grow older, the connection between the sounds we want

---

3. The change in vowels in English when going from the present tense, "I give," to the past tense, "I gave," would be another example of an umlaut.

to make and the constellation and sequence of controlling our muscles in our sound-producing organs becomes more and more automatic, and the ability to create new sounds becomes more and more difficult, hence we may speak with an accent. I would say that up to the age of eighteen or twenty, children can learn new languages, usually containing totally new sounds, without an accent, but this ability disappears gradually. The accent becomes stronger as the age at which a person learns a foreign language increases. This is not to say that with constant effort and training we cannot somewhat reduce our accent, but it takes a pronounced effort. When I took English in school, our teachers, who tried to teach British English, had strong accents themselves. I was twenty-seven when I first lived in the United States and thirty-four when I immigrated; hence I never could eliminate my accent completely. I was eighteen when I learned French beyond some initial high school knowledge; therefore, I have less of an accent in French than in English, yet I am significantly more fluent in English.

My Grandparents

It was an important asset in our childhood that all of our grandparents lived in town. Both grandparents lived in old four-story sandstone buildings. I don't remember my father's parents being anywhere else but in their apartment. On Easter, we would have the Easter egg hunt in their living room. Grandfather Köhler had a respectable white mustache and we were more comfortable with him on our visits than with our more reserved and less affectionate grandmother. Grandfather always considered it funny to scratch our face or hands with his mustache, but we did not share that particular pleasure with him.

One thing that I clearly remember in their apartment was the toilet. It consisted of a board with a hole in it. Next to it was a neatly cut stack of newspaper to serve as toilet paper. It was only much later that the hole was replaced with a flush toilet and the room was converted into a "water closet." The abbreviation "WC," for water closet, is still in common use today in public places like restaurants, as you may find out quickly when traveling in Germany.

As I am thinking about those days and the visits with our grandparents, I remember the many French words that were in use in Germany at the time and are almost unknown in today's use of the language. These words, like *plafond* (ceiling), *trottoir* (sidewalk), *chaise longue* (couch), *porte-monnaie* (wallet), *souterrain* (basement), *wasch-lavoir* (washbasin), and *pot-de-chamber* (chamber pot), were leftovers from the days Napoleon had occupied this part of Germany on his way to Russia. The Swabian word *ade*, used as a good-bye, is a short form of the French *adieu*.

We found visits with our maternal grandparents usually more interesting and colorful. My grandfather was a stern but just man. He demanded a lot from his six children. It was the rule in those days that the children help very actively with the family chores. Grandfather Jäger lived just three blocks from our home, but he also had a garden about a mile away, which had a romantic aura for us. At the entrance gate was a birch tree, into which grandfather inscribed the names of all his grandchildren, eventually reaching the number thirteen. The bulk of the garden consisted of fruit trees and bushes, with some vegetables in one section. The older grandchildren were called upon to help from time to time with some of the garden chores. Naturally, we preferred the eating part and had our favorite trees, which were not always the same as the ones grandfather had given us permission to eat from. We liked being in the garden more than walking on the country road to get there. Our grandfather always went to his garden with his handcart, a *Leiterwagen* (ladder cart). It was like a miniature horse cart whose sides were made of ladder-like struts. Grandfather always carried a shovel on his cart, so he could pick up the horse manure from the many horse-drawn carriages of the farmers and winemakers that kept entering and leaving the town.

A few years after he died, the town newspaper published a series about distinguished people in the town, one of which featured our grandfather as the former rector of the middle school. Describing him and his life, the article said that he was known as the Horse Manure King. This enraged our aunt, his daughter, so much that she complained to the newspaper, but to no avail. It was already out. The rest of the family just got a giggle out of the nickname because it was how we remembered him, too.

Another interesting attraction for us grandchildren at our grandparents' house was a large burlap bag filled with sugar in the hall outside the kitchen. Grandmother needed sugar in large quantities for preserving the fruits and vegetables from the garden in glass jars. We could not pass by without reaching in and were surprised by Grandmother who scolded us, but, in reality, had fun catching us. Grandmother Jäger was an excellent cook and baker. We enjoyed eating at their house and I can still hear her saying in the Swabian dialect "Nehmet no, esset no," which means "Do help yourselves and do eat."

As was quite common, our parents also had a hand-drawn cart, although it was smaller than the one our grandfather had. One use of the cart was to carry the luggage of visitors that we picked up at the train station. Another use, which we children dreaded, was for going to a farmer in one of the villages, some five or more miles away, to buy fruit or vegetables for filling our own glass jars for the winter.

I clearly remember the death of all of my four grandparents. They all died within a few years of each other when I was in my teens. When the first of my grandparents died, it was the first time that I was confronted with death and saw a dead human being, which was something I had not even seen in a picture before.

The Wine of Württemberg

As soon as you pass the last houses of Heilbronn, you are surrounded by vineyards. The wine from this part of the country, Württemberg, has its own taste, quite distinguishable from any other wine. It is fairly mellow with a distinguished bouquet, yet not as acidic or metallic as, say, a Rhone wine. Its red color is not as dark as most other red wines. Once you get used to "our wine," or if you grow up with it, it is likely to become your preferred wine. Württemberg wine is not well-known outside Germany, and you may have real difficulties finding it in the United States. As the locals say, "our wine is too good to be exported—we drink it all ourselves." Theodor Heuss, the first president of the new Federal Republic of Germany after World War II, who was an alumnus of my high school, wrote his doctoral thesis about wine growing in Württemberg.

Before the destruction of the city in 1944, many of the winegrowers lived and had their business in the center of the city, on the narrow little streets that were characteristic of these old medieval towns. Today, the winegrowers live more on the outskirts of the town and many of them have formed cooperatives. When we were children, we would see the horse carts carrying the grapes from the vineyards into town. Occasionally we would ask the farmer to give us a grape as they drove past us—but the request was not always honored.

3

Hitler Becomes Chancellor of Germany

Hitler Seizes Power

Catching a cold was quite frequent in our family, especially in winter. Sometimes, the cold made the rounds in the family. I remember one such time. It was January 30, 1933. My three siblings and I were sick in bed. Emma, who was my mother's maid, our governess, and a servant—all-in-one—came up the stairs and told my parents that Field Marshal Paul von Hindenburg had formed a new government with Adolf Hitler as the new chancellor. Being not quite seven years old, this did not mean very much to me. The reaction from our parents indicated that they welcomed the news. As we children grew older, we learned and were taught why this was, or at least seemed to be, a positive event at the time.

As the party name indicated, the declared mission of the National Socialist German Workers Party (NSDAP) was to restore national pride and social welfare. Gone were the turbulence and fights between parties. As we know, the party did this by setting up dictatorial control of police and government offices. Hitler declared emergency laws that "temporarily" eliminated the Weimar Republic, and forbade trade unions and many other organizations, like student fraternities, that did not fit into the new concept. After January 1933, the opposition was silent, or at least invisible.

To understand why the wide majority of the German population embraced the new government, it is necessary to take a look at the political and economic situation of post-WWI Germany.

The Treaty of Versailles at the end of WWI—with its loss of German-speaking territories, colonies, occupation, and its reparations—came as a big shock to Germany who had expected a lenient treaty.[1] This was followed by years of economic disaster and political turmoil. The main political parties, the Communists, Social Democrats (Sozis), and National Socialists (Nazis), engaged in constant and often bloody fights, raiding each other's meetings. It was because of these fights that the party supported their most active members, the storm troopers, called the SA for *Sturm Abteilung* (storm division) with a new elite troop, the SS—the infamous organization that would later be responsible for the terror in the concentration camps. SS originally stood for *Saal Schutz* (room guards), but the name seems to have later been changed to *Schutzstaffel* (protective squadron).

In 1930, NSDAP became the second strongest party in the country, and three years later, won the majority in the election. Hindenburg did not have much choice but to accept Hitler as chancellor, and thought he could control him. Hitler seemed to have received financial support from some Anglo-American sources who hoped he might engage in a war with Russia which would weaken both countries to the point that Germany could

---

1. What a difference this was to the Marshall Plan at the end of World War II, which turned Germany into an ally and friend instead of a potential future revengeful enemy!

be attacked and destroyed. The German population at large welcomed the promise of bringing Germany back on its feet, enacting social reforms, and "temporarily" suspending the Weimar Constitution with its unrest.

Our father, who was still an admirer of the kaiser, was taken by Hitler and his ideas of restoring Germany's pride and power, and of putting our economy back on its feet. Father was never interested in politics; avoided conflict, both personally and politically; abhorred violence; and believed wholeheartedly in the goodness of man. We could never visualize our father in a physical fight with anybody. He joined the SA, but after attending a few meetings, left, because he found most people there to be uncultured and rude. He told us never much about the meetings. I assume they were primarily social get-togethers, political discussions, and rallies.

His world was spiritual and deeply embedded in poetry. He was an admirer of Goethe with all his heart. A cast of Goethe's head taken on his deathbed was on the wall next to my father's desk.

Both of my parents became members of the NSDAP, which was commonly referred to as "the party" since it was the only one. Membership did not require participation in any activities, but was more or less a declaration of allegiance. For my father, this was, to some degree, an implied obligation within his profession as a teacher, but he saw no conflict in it. Many years later, our father even offered his services to the city to help in the organization of city festivities with the hope of infusing more culture into the city's public events.

4

Growing Up

Family

Our family led a peaceful and quiet life. Our parents were not rich, but sufficiently well off, as you would expect from a middle-class family where the father had a good and stable occupation. Life for us children centered around family, school, and, in later years, the Hitler Youth. Our parents instilled in us the values of honesty, trust, respect of others, and a diligent work ethic.

Of course, there was no TV at the time, and, for a long time, we did not even have a radio. I shared my school life and leisure time with Ursula. Volker, being two years older but only one grade above us, was close to both of us. However, Uli, with his four year age difference, was truly the older brother. We looked up to him. He introduced us to the experiences that were ahead of us. When he said he hated something, be it an event or something to eat, we automatically hated it too. Still today, I dislike certain food and I know it goes back to when Uli told us that he ate something in camp and it was "terrible."

Street Play

We all did our school homework more or less quickly, without too much coaching or pushing from our parents, and then it was off to the street. Our playground was our own little street where we usually played with the neighborhood kids, especially the Nietzers, who lived next to us in the one-family house. In the other half of our two-family house lived the Stahls, a family with which we were not on particularly good terms. Some of our mutual animosity originated from the acoustic transparency of the walls between our living rooms. The Stahls did not like to hear us play the piano, and we did not like to hear their son play the piano. Hence, we came to a musical "truce" with the Stahls. We, as well as their son, would not play the piano from 12:00 p.m. to 2:00 p.m., or after 8:00 p.m. This restriction surely took some of the pleasure out of learning an instrument.

The cold war with the Stahl family next door also affected us whenever we played *Fussball* (soccer) in the street. Playing in the street was no problem from a traffic viewpoint since only two families on our block had a car. All the houses on the street had a four-foot-high wooden picket fence facing toward the street. As was bound to happen, once in a while we kicked our ball over a fence. When we did, we would quickly run through the gate into the neighbor's yard to get the ball back, or, if the gate was locked, climbed over the fence. Our biggest fear was that the ball would land in the Stahl property, in which case, we had to be careful and quick to get the ball back. Very often, we saw Frau Stahl hiding behind her curtains, waiting for this to happen. We did not like the barrage of words that would hit us following such an event.

Birthdays and Holidays

Naturally, I had my birthday together with my twin sister, Ursula, on May 19. Uli's was a week later and two weeks after that, on June 8, was the double birthday of my father and Volker. These double-birthdays called for special celebrations. If the weather was right, we had a birthday celebration with some of our cousins and neighborhood children in the garden. The highlight usually was homemade ice cream. My mother and Emma would alternate turning the handle on the ice-machine bucket until the creation was complete. This was all the more meaningful for us since we did not indulge in the habit of visiting Dall'Asta, the prime ice cream store in town. My father usually documented these special birthday events photographically; we still treasure the pictures in our family photo collections.

Christmas was celebrated in the German tradition, which we still maintain with our own family here in the United States. The "Christmas Child" (*Christkind*) comes on Christmas Eve. When the little bell rang in the Christmas room, we were allowed to enter. There, the Christmas tree was lit with candles. The lights on the Christmas tree were real candles, made specifically for the tree and placed in special candleholders. The tree was always quite fresh and its branches were untrimmed, and thus quite open so there was enough space around each of the roughly twelve candles. The tree candles were only lit three or four times: Christmas Eve, New Year's Eve, and when we had guests. Whenever the tree was lit, everybody watched the spectacle. I never heard of anyone, among the people we knew, having a fire caused by the Christmas candles. The only exception was, many decades later, in a cathedral in Ulm, where a branch caught fire. Everybody watched with one eye as the custodian put out the burning branch while the service continued.

Underneath the tree, the model train ran its rounds and the presents were spread out. After listening to the Christmas story from the Bible and singing one or two Christmas carols, we were treated with Mother's famous Christmas cookies and anxiously awaited the opening of our presents.

Like our birthday presents, our Christmas presents were fairly simple. Except for some special situations when we really needed something big, like a new bicycle because the old one was too small, the presents usually consisted of very practical things: a pen and pencil case, a new school bag, a pair of nail clippers, a new pair of pajamas, new handkerchiefs, and so on.

Easter, or to be more precise, the Easter egg hunt, was a triple celebration for us. First we would celebrate with our family, either indoors or in our small outdoor garden, depending on the weather; then we would have an Easter egg hunt with the grandparents Köhler in their apartment; and finally, we'd join our cousins, in Grandfather Jäger's large fairytale garden, for an egg hunt.

In addition to the traditional holidays, we had political holidays, primarily Hitler's birthday on April 20, the anniversary of the seizure of power on January 30, 1933, and Labor Day on May 1. We enjoyed not having school and occasionally seeing a parade on these days, and later even participating with the Hitler Youth. Most houses showed the German black, white, and red flag and/or the Swastika flag on those days.

Sunday Walks

As is still the custom in Germany, on Sunday afternoons we usually went for a walk in the woods. Practically all woods in Germany were, and still are, maintained by the respective forester. Many walkways lead through the woods and are frequented by people going on their Sunday afternoon stroll. For us children, the walks were more interesting when we could take a ball with us and kick it along as we walked. For many people, the walk culminated in a visit to a local restaurant for cake and coffee or lemonade. For us, coffee and cake was taken at home. The four o'clock coffee and cake was, and probably still is, in Germany, what the five o'clock tea is in England.

From time to time, the walk, or *Spaziergang*, took on the form of a one-day hike. Beautiful rolling hills and forests surround Heilbronn. With a five- or ten-mile hike, you are in this pleasant scenery. On these longer hikes, our parents rewarded us with a visit to a country restaurant. The little villages in the country still had their old charm. Usually in the middle of the village was the traditional fountain where farmers led their cows and horses to drink. My father was once drinking some water from such a fountain when he heard a woman open her window and yell, "Here, they drink water from the fountain, and over there, they could get the best *Viertele*." Viertele, a "little quart," is the name for a quarter liter of local wine.

Cuisine

As you would expect of any mother in the southwestern part of Germany, our mother was a good cook. Her cuisine was what we call good *schwäbische Kost* (Swabian cuisine). It has remained my favorite food, and I am happy that my wife, Christa, who comes from the same part of Germany, does it equally well. Cooking skills are handed down through generations from mother to daughter. Boys, or men for that matter, were not involved in learning the art of cooking in those old days.

While we were growing up, we were not exposed to non-Swabian food, be it from northern German or any other country. Even though I have since expanded my taste somewhat, I still follow, to a small degree, the Swabian doctrine, "What the farmer does not know, the farmer does not eat." The only time my siblings and I were exposed to a different, i.e., North

German, cuisine was when we were sent to a summer camp in northern Germany. More about this is to follow later.

The ultimate in Swabian cuisine are spätzle. They are a form of homemade dumplings. The purists make them by scraping the dough from a wooden tapered board, called a spätzle board, into boiling water. The more common procedure for making them, however, is to use a special spätzle press. Some ten years ago, when a large percentage of foreigners came to live in Germany, one of them wrote to the German magazine *Der Spiegel*, commenting that spätzle are nothing but a glue of flour without any taste; he could not understand why the locals were so excited about them. Over a hundred responses arrived on the editor's desk defending the insulted national Swabian honor. However, one has to understand that spätzle are just a type of noodle, albeit the best type in my opinion, depending on how many eggs are used. Their secret lies in their irregular shape and thus large surface which can hold the essential flavors of a meal, which is usually meat gravy. Spätzle and goulash are at the very top of my own list of favorite foods.

Many food items that are common today in Germany were either unknown or at least very rare and often expensive when I was growing up. We had never heard of vegetables like zucchini or broccoli, or of fruits like mangoes or kiwis. Similarly, the use of garlic was unknown at the time. We only heard of garlic and its smell in the context of anti-Semitic remarks, especially with respect to Eastern European Jews. Because of Germany's strides to be as independent as possible from foreign imports, items like coffee, bananas, and oranges were considered a luxury. Only when we were sick, were we sometimes given oranges as a special treat. My mother regularly ate something very exotic, grapefruit, when it was available. She needed it, so we were told, as a medical supplement against her gallbladder problems. In a sense, we felt sorry for her to have to eat something as bitter as that.

We rarely drank anything with our meals, not counting a glass of wine for our parents on very special occasions. Drinking with a meal was considered to be somewhat unhealthy and thought to reduce your appetite. Emptying your plate was a given. It came as a surprise to me when I later heard that in the American South, some people consider it impolite as a guest to empty your plate since the host might interpret it as not having offered you enough.

There was another myth that we heard as children, namely that it would be dangerous to drink water after eating fruit containing pits, especially cherries or plums. The myth seems to be related to microorganisms that might ferment the fruit's sugar, and thus generate carbon dioxide in the stomach, an effect that, even if it exists, is totally negligible within the environment of all the other chemical processes occurring in the stomach.

Vacation

Vacation has always played an important part in German life. You don't ask your coworkers *whether* they went on vacation, but you ask *where* they went on vacation. This may not be surprising when you consider that the minimum vacation in the German workplace today is six weeks. Unlike the States, the trade unions in Europe have always included bargaining for vacation as an important issue in their contract negotiation.

The next question regarding vacation is how the weather was. In western and central Europe, sunshine is an event to be treasured and thus talked about. My thought is that in Germany, you have about one day of sunshine for four days of cloudiness or rain, while in the New York area, where we used to live, it is just about the opposite.

For our family, our vacations were always pleasant occasions. We went either to the nearby mountains east of town, to the Black Forest, or to the German or Austrian Alps. We stayed in a simple guesthouse or rented rooms from local families. Many local farmers rented out rooms during the summer, often restricting themselves to living more or less in their kitchens. Our vacations consisted of going on hikes or swimming in the local lakes. The lower mountains at the edge of the Alps were about as far as our vacations ever took us. Middle and northern Germany was not under consideration as a vacation destination for us. Not only was it too far and perhaps more expensive, but there was never a desire for it. We had no relatives or friends there. The mountains in the south were always the biggest draw.

My parents always had stories about us that they told our friends. One of them went as follows: on one of our vacations, we had just hiked, for the first time in my six-year life, across the Austrian border. We wound up in torrential rains, which led to local flooding. I was quoted as saying, "This is the greatest flood that I have ever seen in Austria."

I remember how, on a much later vacation in the Black Forest, we tried to teach our mother how to ride a bicycle. She did master it, but never acquired her own bicycle. That was in contrast to my teenaged siblings and me, who would barely go any place in town without using our bikes.

Summer Camp

When I was about nine years old, we had a vacation that left nothing but sour memories with us children, as well as our parents. My twin sister, my older brother, two children of friends, and I were to spend six weeks on the fabulous island of Sylt, near the northern border of Germany, in a children's camp organized by a Lutheran church organization. Going to northern Germany was for us as foreign as it might be for an American child today to go to Europe.

We had been looking forward to bathing in the ocean. Instead, all we were allowed to do was form a circle with the other children and bounce up and down in shallow water. The worst part was the food. It was a cuisine that we were not used to, and we were not brought up to eat or try unknown food. My sister was the worst off. She vomited several times, and a few times was forced to eat what had landed on her plate.

One of the punishments for talking at night was that the counselors made you stand in the hall with a blanket. Several times it happened that the counselors, who partied somewhere else in the building, forgot about the child, and left him or her standing there for an hour or longer.

Even though our letters home were censored, we succeeded in getting word to our parents about our situation. They immediately contacted the organization and were allowed to pick us up and to take us home after two weeks. We later referred to this camp as the "children's concentration camp." This was, of course, before we learned of the term's ultimate horrific meaning.

Music and Its Secret

We were not a musical family in the strict sense, but my parents were anxious that we all learn an instrument. Uli played the violin, while Volker, Ursula, and I took piano lessons with Fräulein Fröschle for about six years. We practiced what we were instructed to play, and were happy when an assigned piece of music was checked off, allowing us to move on to the next one. I could not say that we played with great joy. To my later dismay, Fräulein Fröschle never taught us anything about harmony or how to play by ear while adding our own harmony to the basic tune. The joy of playing changed only after we all returned from the war, when we began playing the latest popular music. Both Volker and I continued with playing the piano. I played classical music along with contemporary light music. One of the highlights of my musical endeavors was when I performed Schubert's A Minor Impromptu for Piano for my mother's eightieth birthday in 1976. Uli continued playing the violin all his life, and became a music critic for local newspapers during his retirement.

Thinking of music reminds me of a beautiful movie that I saw as a teenager. It was called *Sie tanzte nur einen Sommer* (She Danced Only One Summer). At one point in the film, a music teacher tells a young girl that he discovered the secret of music: repetition. Over time, I have thought a fair amount about this statement. There is some truth to it, but I believe we could be a bit more precise and modify it. I would say that the secret of music lies in anticipation and fulfillment.

We anticipate the notes that follow what we hear. We sometimes even sing or hum along with the music, even if only in our minds. We become uneasy when the expected notes don't follow. The reason for the uneasiness is the deviation from our expectations, either in the form of a purposeful disharmony in the composition, or as an error in the performance.

So-called easy music is music that is simple enough in composition that we can anticipate what notes will follow next. Hearing a piece of music repetitively will help us learn what to expect, what to anticipate. Repetition thus becomes simply a tool for building up our expectation toward fulfillment, and therefore increases our enjoyment of music. We consider music difficult when we initially lack this sense of anticipation; we can only acquire it through repetition and learning. The more difficult the music is, the more learning is needed, but, most likely, we will then arrive at a deeper level of enjoyment.

One interesting element of anticipation is the rhythm of the music. With a strong rhythm, we can at least anticipate the beat of the music.

Roller-skating

The intersection between the Südstrasse and our street, the Solothurnerstrasse, was also the center of another activity:

roller-skating. In the corner house lived Fräulein Gräfer. Fräulein Gräfer organized an unofficial mini roller-skating club of neighborhood children and taught us how to roller-skate. Our practice took place right in the middle of our street and even in the intersection with the larger Südstrasse. Since this was not quite legal, one of us was usually assigned to look up and down the Südstrasse to see if a policeman was in sight. When an alarm was given, we would quickly disappear in the basement of the corner house. If the policeman showed up and asked about roller skaters, someone would tell him that there were none around.

Fräulein Gräfer founded the Ice- and Roller-Skating Club of Heilbronn. She organized a demonstration with us, through which we requested the city to provide the club with a home. Many years later, this became a reality; shortly thereafter, the club produced a German roller-skating champion.

We also played soccer in the streets. My brother recently showed me a police ticket that he received in 1936 at the age of fourteen with a fine for one reichsmark, stating that he had played soccer in a certain street.

The Weather Station

Our father had a telephone with the number 2873. It was initially one of only two telephones on our block of about thirty families. The neighbors used our phone when they had an emergency.

The impetus for having a telephone came from an interest my father pursued ever since he was a child: the weather. After moving to Heilbronn, he volunteered to run a weather observation station. One of the standard white weather stations was installed in our backyard. Three times a day, at 7:23 a.m., 2:23 p.m., and 9:23 pm, some twenty observations had to be taken, including "dry" and "wet" temperatures, barometric pressure, wind strength, cloud formations, and blueness of the sky. We also had recorders for temperature, humidity, and barometric pressure, whose paper strips had to be changed weekly and sent to the federal weather bureau.

A later addition to the station consisted of a sunshine writer. A glass ball, acting like a magnifying glass, burned the time course of sunshine onto a strip of specialized paper as the sun proceeded through the sky. Since our rooftop was not easily accessible, this particular instrument was on the rooftop of my grandparents' house, three blocks away, creating an additional chore for the evening. Every morning at 7:30, we received a phone call from the central weather agency to transmit our daily readings. Of course, having the weather station required that someone had to be available every day at the appropriate times. My father found one or two people who could substitute when we were on vacation. We children also started to help take the weather data as we grew older. My father's observation station contributed to my continued interest in weather and climate.

High School

Entering fifth grade is a big change and requires a significant decision by a German student. This is the point when a child has three choices: either stay in the most basic form of school, the *Volksschule*, for four more years; enter middle school for typically six more years; or go to what in Germany is referred to as high school, for eight or nine more years. The idea behind this separation is that these forms of secondary school prepare the child optimally for a future career path.

The concept of a four-year secondary education beyond the four years of elementary school goes back to the century-old tradition of learning a trade. At about the age of fourteen, i.e., after eight years of schooling, a child can begin an apprenticeship in a chosen trade. This apprenticeship, which used to take four years, but nowadays takes three, typically includes two years of continued part-time schooling at a trade school, where the instruction focuses entirely on the specific trade. This intensive form of education is the reason why trades have been respected professions for centuries. You were not a baker, mason, carpenter, or even a salesperson in a specialty store, without having had such training. In many medieval towns in Europe, you can still admire the beautiful architecture of the old, respected, and often very rich, trade guilds.

The next level of schooling, the middle school, opens the door to additional professional careers, including certain civil service positions. The high school option was, and to some degree still is, the only education that opens the door to later academic education. Going from middle school, via additional high school training, to a university was a rare exception and is still difficult to do today. On the other hand, you can learn a trade after having completed middle or high school, in which case the trade training is usually reduced from three years to two.

The drawback of this school system is that it involves entering a one-way street at an early age, determined to a large extent by the intelligence and knowledge of the child displayed at age ten. The school system was recognized after World War II as socially unjust and led to some efforts toward revision. The main difference between then and now is that it is now easier to transfer between the three branches. On the other hand, the advantage of the system, especially with respect to the high school option, is that it provides an advanced level of education, and is thus excellent preparation for college. In mathematics and physics, the education goes to levels that are typically taught in the United States in the first or second year of college. German math, for example, includes differential calculus and an introduction to integral calculus, and German physics includes the Heisenberg "uncertainty principle." Some German organizations and even consulates in the United States claim that a German high school diploma is equivalent to two years of college in the United States. I can accept that claim for the American college freshman year, but not much beyond, especially not for specialized academic fields like my own field of engineering.

To be accepted to high school at age ten, we had to pass an entrance exam. In the larger cities, you often had a choice of the type of high school you could attend. The type I went to was called a "gymnasium." The term may sound confusing unless you go back to its Greek origin, and understand the concept of the *gymnasion*, which was an open place where men held physical exercises, usually naked (*gymnos* is the Greek word for "naked"). Bathing rooms and instruction rooms where the philosophers lectured were part of the Greek gymnasium, following the theme of "a sound mind in a healthy body." In the German gymnasium type of high school, you learned Latin in the first year, i.e., fifth grade. This was followed two years later by Greek. Today, the term "gymnasium" has broadened in meaning and is used for all forms of high school, the classic form of which is now called the "humanistic gymnasium."

Thus, I was subjected to seven years of Latin instruction. While I don't consider it practical to learn that much Latin, it proved to be an excellent basis for the other languages that I learned later or became interested in. At the point where we were supposed to start with Greek, we switched to learning English instead. Hitler had issued a directive in 1938 that most gymnasiums had to teach English instead of Greek, since he felt it was more important in the new world. In our state, Württemberg, only three classic, or humanistic, gymnasiums were left after Hitler's directive. The others, including ours in Heilbronn, were converted to general high schools. A little joke made the round in those days. What is the shortest unit of time? The answer is one Rust. This being the time it took for Hitler to give an order and for our state's minister of education, Herr Rust, to execute it.

In our earlier school years, our parents would often speak French at the dinner table whenever they wanted to talk about something that we children were not supposed to hear. This was especially the case when my father was telling my mother something related to his work at the school. We always had great fun when we understood a word or two—such as the name of one of our teachers—even though we did not understand the context. As we began to learn French, however, my parents had to be more careful with their conversations.

Throughout the German education system, everybody in a class took the same courses together. Some branching existed, say between a language and a mathematical direction, whereby a class was split into two sections, but otherwise, you were always together with the same students. It turned out that most of the better math students in my class opted for the language branch rather than the math branch since learning French was something new and interesting. Thus, I began to learn French two years after learning English, and it later proved to be very useful.

A love of languages was definitely in our family, with much of the inspiration coming from our father. In addition to languages, our father was also interested in mathematics, but his seminary and academic training never included an education in higher math. So his love of mathematics was concentrated on arithmetic rather than algebra and calculus. I still remember a book that my father once gave me, either for my birthday or Christmas. It was called *Im Zaubergarten der Mathematik* (In the Magic Garden of Mathematics). It contained well-illustrated mathematical facts and curiosities. The book fascinated me and stimulated my interested in mathematical and scientific things.

In math at school, I was definitely better than my siblings. We once had my brother Volker's math teacher as a substitute. Volker was not very good in math. When I was in about eighth grade, I could solve the quadratic equation:

$$ax + bx + c = 0$$

The solution for the equation is:

$$x = \frac{-b \pm \sqrt{b^2 - 4ac}}{2a}$$

Upon seeing this, Volker's math teacher exclaimed, "If you continue like that, you'll be better than your brother."

The subject I was not particularly good in was physical training. Our family was not very athletic and I also felt somewhat disadvantaged by being the smallest boy in class. I made up for my small stature somewhat in disciplines that required endurance, such as rope climbing and long-distance (3,000 meters) running, where I was usually in the top group.

Just as in elementary school, I still shared classes with my twin sister Ursula in high school. While the town had a high school for girls, it had no humanistic gymnasium specifically for girls; therefore, our gymnasium was coed. We had seven girls in our class. I still remember when, some three or four years later, after our school was converted to a regular high school, all of the girls came back from the president's office in tears, having been informed that they had to leave and attend the girls' high school in town.

Since schools were located in the densely populated areas of cities and towns—there was no suburbia at the time—there was no need for school buses. I had never heard of school buses until I came to the United States. Our high school was just about three-quarters of a mile from our home; hence, like my brothers, Ursula and I walked to school. For lunch, we walked back home. Lunch was, and in most families still is, the main meal of the day in Germany and schools stopped from 12:00 to 2:00 p.m. Mothers usually stayed home to feed their children.

For students that lived farther away, the large lunch break often was a problem. Those who took the streetcar could still go home for lunch, but it was not a solution for the students who came to the city from one of the villages outside the city. They took the train to school, followed by the streetcar, or walked from the train station. Usually the public transportation system was, and still is, quite good, not only in Germany, but pretty much throughout Western Europe. However, cars have filled towns and cities today to the point that parking is a major problem everywhere.

When I was about eleven years old, my school friend Ernst Reibel taught me how to ride a bicycle. Soon thereafter, I had my first bike. I believe my parents bought it from Ernst or even got it for free. As we became older, our bikes were our means of transportation. Our parents often commented that we would use our bikes just to go some 300 yards. Our bikes were simple: one gear, a luggage carrier for a school bag, and a light, which was compulsory to use at night.

For our parents, walking and riding the streetcar were their means of transportation. Yet, using the streetcar was still a rare event. If you had to go to another town you used the train. To call a taxi was reserved for real emergencies, like going to a hospital. Even though the streetcar was not expensive, we children considered it a challenge to ride without paying. I must confess that, in little things like this, cheating sometimes was a game; however, on the larger scale, honesty was a given. When I later came to the States as an exchange student in Atlanta, I was impressed to see, for example, how newspapers were sold in the street. People took a paper from a stack, dropping money into an attached box. Similarly, it was a surprise for me to learn about the honor system in U.S. colleges where students take quizzes without the professor being present.

The crime rate in Heilbronn, as in the rest of Germany, was very low and practically invisible to us children. There was no place in town where we felt endangered. We read very little about serious crimes in the newspapers. Penalties for crimes were very harsh. During the war, severe penalties were extended even to small crimes; later during the war, the death penalty was threatened for any theft of government property. This absence of public crime is one of the few, or perhaps the only, advantage of a dictatorship. The horrible political crimes that happened behind the scenes of the criminal dictatorship, to what were considered the "enemies of the state," were carefully kept invisible and secret to the population at large.

Skiing

We admired our neighbor, Frau Nietzer, when she came back from her ski vacation in the Alps with an incredibly deep tan. We heard from her that they even had ski lifts in those resorts. For us, skiing was a much simpler undertaking. When we had a snowfall of five or ten inches, which might happen once or twice a winter, we would put on our skis, ski to some little meadow a mile or two outside of town, and ski up and down the small hills. We would build a little jump, ten inches high, and had fun going over it. We took our regular boots to the shoemaker who nailed leather straps over the heels to hold the ski binding. The skis were wooden with a spring binding that would go over the heels above these straps. The boot was held in the ski only at the front, similar to today's telemark skis. Even though I did not take up real skiing until about twenty-five years later at Great Gorge in New Jersey, our minimal childhood ski practice gave me a good feel for standing and moving on skis.

Hitler Youth

I still remember the day when, in 1936, shortly before I was about to join the Hitler Youth, Uli came home in tears. It was announced that membership in the Hitler Youth was to become compulsory. Up to this point, he had enjoyed the meetings with like-minded friends. Now, the new organization would include many who did not want to be a part of it, which would take out much of the fun. While the new law was not immediately enforced, it became fully effective in 1939.

The Hitler Youth consisted of two sections: boys from ages ten to fourteen were in the Jungvolk, which might be translated liberally as "Young Scouts"; older boys, from fourteen to eighteen were in the Hitler-Jugend (HJ), or "Hitler Youth," proper. Similarly, girls joined the Bund Deutscher Mädchen (BDM), the "League of German Girls," of which the younger section was called the Jungmädel, meaning "Young Girls."

Of course, the Hitler Youth was set up by the government to politically educate—or brainwash—the youth. But we did not see it that way. The weekly meetings were the occasions when we met our friends. We liked being together, singing songs, doing sports, and playing games. It is interesting to note that it was only ten to fifteen years later that we started thinking about the text of the songs that we sang in the Hitler Youth, and later, in the military. Those songs, for example the murderous pirate songs, sounded good to us at the time since we never reflected much on their words. We also enjoyed marching to music on special holidays, especially when accompanied by the fanfare bands that were part of the Hitler Youth. We did not see any connection to politics in these activities at the time. But our views changed.

After the war and the end of the Nazi regime, we would have found it ridiculous and out of the question for high school students to participate in public marching; the same attitude was prevalent in other countries in Europe as well. It was only when I later came to the United States that I saw the youth marching again. However, it was connected to sports and public parades and not an outgrowth of political or pre-military activity.

Our meetings and activities in the Jungvolk section of the Hitler Youth became a focal point of our non-school activities. We even wore our uniform at our confirmation in the Lutheran church, where our uncle was the minister. I was good at some of the Hitler Youth activities and therefore liked those, but, in others, I was not skilled and therefore hated them. Sometimes we had orientation rallies in the country, where we had to find a destination using a map, watch, and compass. I particularly enjoyed these exercises. Throughout my life, I've liked maps. Today, my wife has taken over map reading when I drive, since she rightfully feels that my reading the map while driving, as I occasionally did in the first years of our marriage, is not a particularly good idea.

I was also good in target shooting, which we occasionally did with small-caliber rifles. What I often disliked, on the other hand, were the Hitler Youth camps, including the food, sleeping in a tent, and especially the night excursions. Occasionally, another troop would steal our flag in the middle of the night and we had to get up and get it back, often by fighting, since the flag was sacred. Being one of the smallest members of the group and having not been brought up in an environment where we would physically fight with other children, this was not my cup of tea.

My brothers, sister, and I stayed in the Hitler Youth sections for the ten- to fourteen-year-olds, the Jungvolk, after we reached age fourteen. You could stay there as a leader if you were promoted to a level of leadership. The camaraderie was much better in the Jungvolk than in the Hitler Youth proper. It turned out that in my high school class, all but one student stayed in the Jungvolk.

One of my leaders in the Hitler Youth later had an accident with a rifle while in the military and studied law instead of serving in the army. Many years later in his career, he became the

Prosecutor General of the Federal Republic of Germany. Since this was during the 1970s, the period of activity of the German Red Army Fraction terrorist group (RAF), his house was guarded by tanks for many years.

Another of my leaders, who was at the fifth level in the Hitler Youth and was in charge of all the youth in the city, was half Jewish. He kept it a secret, yet his superiors knew it. Early after joining the army, he was also wounded in an accident and was sent home, allowing him to begin his studies at the university. After the war, as an attorney, he became very active in the prosecution of former Nazis.

All through my school and Hitler Youth years, I suffered under the fact that I was quite small. I remember when my good friend Hans-Günther Bunz and I were sent by our teacher to make a reservation for the class in the botanical garden. Teachers usually sent their better (or best) students for such errands. HaGü, as we still call him today, was the tallest, and I the shortest, in the class. Our teacher was afterward told by the garden manager that "a young man and a school boy" were there to make the reservation.

Being small also affected my athletic abilities, compared with the other children. I was not good at throwing balls, for which I almost missed making the Hitler Youth *Sportabzeichen*, a certain sports level that was expected in Hitler Youth, and a requirement for promotion. Unlike in the States, baseball was not a known sport on the European continent and we children would rather kick a ball than throw it. As is the case in many dictatorial societies, a big emphasis was placed on sports, both in school and in the Hitler Youth. One of the results for the importance placed on sports education was the chance for a good supply of German athletes in the Olympic Games. Hitler took advantage of that in the 1936 games in Berlin. It is said that he was furious that Jesse Owens, a black man, won the one-hundred-meter dash and set a new world record. We kids, on the other hand, were fascinated by the one-hundred-meter race and played Jesse Owens in the street.

The town of Heilbronn had a very good theater. It held special youth performances for the Hitler Youth. Maliciously, these youth performances were always scheduled for Sunday mornings to create an ideological conflict with going to church. Since the Swabians in general are not only known to be stingy with their money, but also with their applause in the theater, the theater actors preferred to perform for the youth, by whom they were much better received. With the help of my brothers, who were also leaders in the Hitler Youth, we always managed to get the best theater seats. During those years, I attended at least twenty operas and operettas.

In addition to the theater, the movie theaters also had many special screenings for the Hitler Youth. In addition to a few propaganda movies, such as Leni Riefenstahl's famous film of the 1936 Olympic Games, *Olympia*, and her film of the 1935 Nazi Party congress, *Triumph of the Will*, we saw many excellent films. Visual and verbal violence was absent from these films; when the content required it, it was only alluded to.

Political Indoctrination

The party ruled the country. All opposition was suppressed and hence invisible to the general population. Our local newspaper was the main source of public information. In the early years of the party's power, my parents still did not have a radio. My grandparents had one of the new radios, called a *Volksempfänger* (people's receiver). They were put on the market so everybody could receive the party line. The message was always the same: progress has come to the country; the economy is healthy; you can again be proud to be German. The history books were rewritten, as were many other things, including children's games, some of which I remember featuring Hitler as a "friend of the children," "friend of the animals," and so on. It may be interesting to note that even *Time Magazine* voted Hitler "Man of the Year" in 1938.

The saying in Heilbronn was that Hitler would never visit us because in the late 1920s, someone wanted to throw him into the Neckar River. No one could confirm whether any of this was true or not. One day, around 1936, the word spread that he would visit the town in the afternoon. But after the streets filled with people awaiting the Führer, nothing happened. Another word went around that it was a word-play hoax, "Between three and five comes the *vierer*." In the local Swabian dialect, *vierer* (four) sounds like *Führer*.

It may be difficult to envision today that we were happy at the time, and accepted a political system that would later commit such horrible crimes against humanity. Today, as we are flooded with information from newspapers, radio, TV, and travels abroad, it is particularly difficult to understand how people could be influenced by such one-sided and completely biased information. Yet even now, many people—and even politicians—have difficulty understanding foreign cultures. Unless you have direct personal experience with other cultures through your family or friends, or have any contradicting inside knowledge, you will likely treasure your own country and believe that it is the best place in the world. This is especially true if it is the only place you know and if you've never set foot outside of it. A Turk is proud to be a Turk and an Italian is proud to be an Italian. Both are likely to think that their country is the best in the world. (I am not talking about people that might be persecuted in their country for one reason or another.)

With very few carefully worded exceptions, our teachers in school did not present any ideas contrary to the party line. For the most part, other than the Nazi greetings at the beginning of a class, school instruction stuck to academics without discussing politics. One exception to this was our chemistry teacher, Herr Vosseler. Despite the directives from the ministry of education to no longer credit Jews for their scientific achievements, Herr Vosseler very pronouncedly stated on the appropriate occasion that such and such a chemical process was, until recently, named after a certain Jewish inventor. "I say it even though he is a Jew," became a frequent "humorous" quote among us students. Herr Vosseler's anti-Nazi position went back to the Weimar Republic years when he had been a Sozi, a member of the socialist party.

In contrast to Herr Vosseler, we had one teacher, Herr Mozer, who taught a course called "Weltanschauung," which literally means "view of the world." It was our official and only national-socialist education. In a sense, it was meant to be the replacement for the religion courses we still had in elementary school. Catholics and Protestants had separate instruction; everybody fell in one or the other category.

Weltanschauung with Herr Mozer was almost a joke. Practically everybody in class went along with the general ideology of the government, but this teacher's instruction was so exaggerated that we considered it hilarious. He bashed everything about Germany before 1933 and criticized everything non-German. He made very denouncing comments about an organization that my mother belonged to in the twenties, the Wandervogel, which was dedicated to hiking and the outdoors.

I remember another incident where Herr Mozer told us sixth or seventh graders about the new degenerate nylon stockings in France. He told us that the French introduced it so "the ladies of the night in Paris can better pursue their trade." I wondered for a long time why wearing stockings would be of any help in this trade.

Herr Mozer also taught us Latin and physical education. He did not look like a sporty type and apparently did not like teaching sports. Very often after our arrival in the sports gymnasium, he would look for some excuse that we had done something wrong, like talking when we were not supposed to. "Sport is cancelled today—you will have a quiz instead," we heard. So we would go to our classroom and after a few minutes heard the words, "Back to the sports hall." This way, almost half of the period was killed.

A major propaganda statement that we repeatedly heard in Hitler's speeches, which was later used as one of the main justifications for World War II, was "Germany demands the unification of all Germans according to the right of self-determination of all peoples." This demand for reunification not only referred to areas like Alsace and Lorraine that had a mixed history and culture, but also to the areas in the east that had originally been German in culture and language, but had been separated from Germany as a result of the Treaty of Versailles.

Other propaganda demanded the return of the four African colonies that Germany had held until the Treaty of Versailles after WWI. I still have an essay that I wrote in school with the title: "Deutschland fordert seine Kolonien zurück" (Germany Demands Its Colonies Back). My essay reflected our indoctrination at the time: Here is an excerpt of what I wrote:

> In the second half of the nineteenth century, German pioneers negotiated the acquisition of the four German colonies in Africa. They were acquired by negotiation and not by brutal force and blood as the British did. The colonies gave us some of the natural resources that Germany needed. In contrast to the British, Germany received the trust of the Negro tribes, and the territories flourished. Yet in WWI, Germany was attacked in Africa, and in the Treaty of Versailles [after WWI], the colonies were stolen from Germany. The Germany of Adolf Hitler fights for the heritage of industrious and courageous Germans. In this fight, the German colonies will become German again.

In school, I knew only a few students who made pointed negative remarks about Hitler and the party, especially in the later war years. As I analyze these cases today, I realize they each had some source of information that we did not have in our family. For example, one student's father was in an opposition party before the Nazis came to power, and his personal opposition had not disappeared. Another student, who sat next to me throughout my high school years, had a grandfather who immigrated back to Germany from the United States and certainly provided his family with a different political perspective and insight than the German party line. But the grandfather did not and could not make his voice heard, other than through some occasional non-party line remarks by his grandson. Otherwise, this schoolmate was also a leader in the Hitler Youth.

Within our own family, I had two uncles who were not fully aligned with the party. One was a minister; the other had been a prisoner of war in WWI in England, and for many years, managed to subscribe to a British newspaper. This gave him a different perspective on the world. Today I ask myself why our father did not look for a similar source of information, given the fact that he had studied briefly in England and France. I can only try to explain his support of the system with his total lack of interest in politics and especially in any form of personal conflict. His world was in poetry and literature and he believed in the goodness and honesty of man. Unlike our uncle who read the British newspaper, our father was not a businessman.

It is also important to recognize that, as a result of personal threats and the government control of the press, the voices of the minority—those that opposed the system—were not heard publicly. As the system became more and more criminal, people who were insiders in the execution of the crimes, or were knowledgeable about what went on in the concentration camps, either as guards or as prisoners, knew their lives were in danger if they talked to anybody about it. Knowledge stayed confined to their closest family members.

The press was not only controlled politically; other unwritten rules also existed. No picture of a dead person appeared in any newspaper, magazine, or other form of publication. Sex and sexual language were equally taboo. I remember how we children discovered, with great curiosity, little notes in the newspaper that someone was arrested for "violation of paragraph 175." The newspaper would not say anything more, but section 175 was the paragraph of the legal code that made a homosexual act a crime. If someone of the same sex touched you too closely, you would say as a joke that you were not born on 17.5, i.e., May 17. In France, the similarly quoted number was sixty-nine since their corresponding law, making homosexual acts a crime, was section 69.

Our Political and Geographic Isolation

Hitler classified the peoples of the world in his own pecking order. Germany was of course "the best country in the world." Next were other Western European countries, like England and France. Then came Eastern Europe, Asia, Africa, and finally America. Until the war, the United States was basically an unknown to the German population at large. We never read anything in the paper about life in the United States. As children we only had two images of the United States: the American Indians and the Jewish financiers who "tried to control the world and were responsible for the economic misery after World War I."

According to our indoctrination, the Jews were not directly within this pecking order. The Jews were our enemies. They were dangerous to our society, we were told. A difference was made between the "more cultured" and more intelligent western Jews and those in Eastern Europe. The party published a newspaper uniquely dedicated to the hatred of the Jews. It was called *Der*

Stürmer, which means "the stormer." Neither my parents nor any of their friends or relatives subscribed to this paper.

On a similar note, to this day, I have not met anybody in Germany who has read Hitler's book *Mein Kampf* (My Struggle), which he wrote in 1925 while imprisoned. We did not study it in school or in the Hitler Youth. Unlike Mao Tse-tung's *Little Red Book* in China, *Mein Kampf* was not our party bible. Later, in postwar Germany, it was forbidden to sell the book. I have still not held a copy in my hands.

Our image of the American Indians was largely created by the German author Karl May. He wrote some eighty books in the late 1890s and early 1900s. The stories of Winnetou, the Apache chief, and Old Shatterhand, left every German boy spellbound. May's books are still popular today. He traveled extensively, but never made it to the States. Some of this imagery of American Indians obviously played a role when the postwar German travel industry began to advertise travel to New England in the fall as travel to the "Indian Summer." Their use of the term related to the red fall colors and not to the occurrence of mild weather.

I don't recall having met a foreigner while I was growing up, except when visiting my school friend whose grandfather used to live in America, and earlier, on another occasion, when we had guests from Switzerland in our house. I was about eight years old at the time. My father was active in the organization Verband für das Deutschtum im Ausland (VDA) or the "Association for German Culture Abroad." It was founded in 1881 and is still in existence in some form today. Through this organization, a sports group came to our town from Solothurn, Switzerland. We still have a picture of our father giving a speech on the huge market square—without a microphone—to welcome the Swiss group.

Since our street's name was Solothurnerstrasse, it was natural that our family, as well as others on our street, offered quarters to the Swiss visitors. It was quite common at the time for the local population to offer private quarters when there was a public event that drew people from out of town. Similarly, when personally traveling, you would not go to hotels, but stay with friends and relatives. In our minds, hotels were for the rich.

The few times during my childhood that I saw a black person was always at the circus, where a black man was displayed as a curiosity in the tent's entry. Our isolation against meeting and knowing foreigners had its equivalent even within the different parts of Germany. Germans tended to stay in the area where they grew up and rarely traveled much outside that area. We lived in the southwest, and all of our relatives were in the southwest or south. Our limited family travel always took us south toward the mountains, and thereby once or twice into Austria, but never to the north. The only exception was our summer camp experience on the island of Sylt.

Thus, the north of Germany was almost like a foreign country for us. Our own family had no relatives or friends anywhere north of us. The north Germans spoke either High German or a different local dialect. During my time in school, there was only one person in my brother's class who spoke High German. Our conversational language was *Schwäbisch*, our Swabian dialect. Almost none of our teachers spoke genuine High German but rather an approximation of it with a Swabian accent. We, the students, also were supposed to speak High German, but, like our teachers, we did so with a fairly strong Swabian accent.[1]

---

1. The word "dialect" is usually reserved for a language that is basically different from the official language. The languages spoken in the various parts of Germany, like Swabian, are somewhere between an accent and a somewhat different language. Swabian has its own grammatical deviations from High German, similar to Bavarian, Swiss, or Yiddish. I might mention that the latter is more closely related to Swabian than to High German or to any of the other variations. Thus, the word "dialect" is not inappropriate. However, when a Schwabe tries to speak High German with limited success, it becomes an accent. As is the case in most countries, dialects and accents are stronger in the countryside than in the cities. Unlike in northern Germany, speaking dialect is not a sign of poor education in southern Germany or Austria. This is even more so the case in Switzerland. Their dialect is called Schweizerdeutsch, or "Swiss German." It is the commonly

Anti-Semitism

Even though Hitler's crimes against the Jews count among the most hideous genocides in human history, anti-Semitic doctrines were not a new invention by Hitler, but go back as far as ancient Roman times. Unless you had personal connection with Jewish people, you did not pay much attention to this aspect of the party propaganda, which, especially during the early years of Nazi power, came only occasionally into the open. Anti-Semitism did not shake the average citizen.

It is always easier to hate a group of people or a whole country if you see the entity rather than its individual human beings. I don't remember having ever talked to a Jewish person until after the war, even though at one time we had two Jewish families living on our street. Their children never played with us. We thought they were somewhat weird, as we were taught they would be, when in reality they probably were rather shy and even afraid. My father told us children that during World War I, he once was in a synagogue to administer the military oath to Jewish soldiers in the German Army. To us, this was a memorable story.

I never had any Jews in my class, which does not mean that there were no Jewish students in my school. My father once had a Jewish boy, Marschall, in a class that he taught. His classmates picked on him. My father told the class that Marschall was a good student, both academically and in sports, and that they should pay him the same respect as any other boy in class. Somebody denounced my father and he was cited to appear before the

---

accepted language in the street (in the German-speaking part of Switzerland), whereas the Swiss look at the German that they learn in school almost as a foreign language. It is called "written German," in order to stress that it is a Swiss language and has nothing to do with Germany. Since the end of World War II, the dialect picture in Germany has changed drastically. With millions of refugees coming into the south and other population movements within Germany, speaking "good" German, i.e., High German, has become widespread. Today, parents in the south often still speak Schwäbisch, whereas their children speak an impeccable High German, and so do many teachers.

county party boss. Kreisleiter Richard Drauz told my father that he should never again make such a statement if he valued his family and his professional position.

The system tried to tell us that the Jewish people were responsible for our past misery and dangerous to our future. Not only were the Jews, especially the American Jews, blamed for the financial ruin that fell upon Germany as a result of the Treaty of Versailles—usually referred to as the "Versailles Dictate"—but they were also blamed for the Great Depression, the resulting rise of Communism, and the ruin of many German individuals, particularly farmers. We were told that, especially after World War I, many farmers were exploited and ruined through loan-sharking by the Jews. German propaganda told us that it was part of the Jewish religion and philosophy to not only support each other, but to not have any qualms about hurting non-Jews.

Decades later, during an affirmative action workshop at Bell Laboratories I attended in the 1980s, our instructor told us about a dangerous new form of anti-Semitism in the Midwest. She explained that some Midwestern farmers had recently made similar claims of exploitative loan-sharking by Jews.

Borrowing money was not part of the German culture. Still today, many Germans avoid accruing any debt. Most Germans dislike using "plastic cards" for purchases, except for debit cards that deduct money directly from their bank accounts. A big day in our parents' and grandparents' lives was when the mortgage was paid off; paying interest on a mortgage was perhaps the only form of interest a good citizen should ever pay. When lending money within a family became necessary, considering interest was, at least in the days when our grandparents and parents grew up, inappropriate. Hearing a comment in those early days like, "Only Jews would do that," was not that unusual. What this all means is that the hate propaganda against Jews was cleverly designed to find some resonance among German non-Jews.

Even after the war, the attitude toward interest changed only gradually, as the following little story from my own family illustrates. Saving was a low priority for my brother, Volker, and his wife, which did not please my parents. Therefore, to encourage him to own a home rather than rent an apartment, in the early 1960s, they gave him a quarter of the value of their house as an advance of his later inheritance. It was meant for the sole use of a down payment for a small house.

After my mother's death, twenty years later, my sister and her husband, who had been living in our parents' home, took over the house. According to my mother's will—my father had died several years earlier—my twin sister was to pay me my quarter share of the house. The house had naturally increased in value over those twenty years. Hence, I proposed to my sister and her husband that we either reassess the house for its current value or agree on a certain interest rate, like 4 percent, to be applied to the 20,000 reichsmarks Volker had received twenty years earlier. My brother-in-law said that it would not be right to pay me more than my brother had received. I had a hard time convincing him that, even within a family, considering interest is not immoral, but fair. He finally agreed to a payment in accordance with the current estimated value of the house, which amounted to exactly the same value as a 4 percent interest increase.

To stimulate anti-Semitism, German propaganda invented stories during the latter part of the war about increasing sabotage in Germany, especially in the war factories. The newspapers and speeches said that the sabotage was largely organized and financed by the Jews. No explanation was given as to how they could even accomplish this.

Some people in the United States may see the persecution of the Jews in Germany as the prime goal of Hitler's coming to power, or even the reason for his success. Hitler did not come to power because he wanted to kill the Jews. He came to power and was accepted by the population at large because he promised to restore Germany as a nation. During the early years of Hitler's power, we saw the bashing of the Jews as one of many aspects of the political propaganda—rhetoric to which we did not devote much attention.

However, the persecution of the Jews came clearly out into the open in 1938. On November 10, my sister and I saw a building burning on the way to school. It was the Jewish synagogue. Twelve years old, we did not know what to think. The newspapers had said that the Jews wanted to destroy Germany and its newly won power and self-respect. But what good would it do to burn down a building?

The next day, following what became known as Crystal Night (*Kristallnacht*), we read in the newspaper that Jewish stores, like Woolworth, had their front windows smashed. Signs were put up at the stores, reading, "A German does not buy from a Jew." In the weeks that followed, we heard that in order to "isolate our enemies," Jews had been arrested and put into confinement on the Asperg. The Asperg is a small mountain near Stuttgart with a prison on top. As young children, we had always heard the joke that the Asperg was the tallest mountain in Germany because it takes twenty years to go up and down. As for the Jews that were sent there after Crystal Night, we later heard that they were actually sent to a concentration camp in Dachau, near Munich. The rumor we heard was that they had to do hard labor, shoveling rocks from one side of the road to the other and the next day back again. We did not know much about these camps, which were set up in 1933—for political and so-called antisocial prisoners, like homosexuals—"to protect the people," as the party said.

But from that time on, we, in our southern part of Germany, heard very little about Jewish suffering until after the war.

This may be hard to believe in today's age of communication. There was practically no communication other than the party line that you could read in the newspapers and heard on the radio. We did not see or hear of any torturing or killings of Jews, criminals, or other so-called enemies of the state. The system maintained absolute secrecy about what happened behind their closed doors. The facts about Auschwitz and the other extermination camps were not publicized within Germany. Anyone who was ever released from a concentration camp—there were very few—was told in no uncertain terms that his or her freedom would be short lived if any details were leaked. This required secrecy also applied to the SS troops that were assigned to the concentration camps.

And even if the truth about these crimes had been known to the population at-large, would you have demonstrated in the streets if you knew for certain that you would either be immediately executed or join those in the concentration camps?

It is interesting to note that information about the extermination of Jews in concentration camps did not get to the Allies until mid-1944, when two escaped prisoners from Auschwitz, Rudolf Vrba and Alfred Wetzler, reported to the Allies.[2] Prior rumors about mass killings in concentration camps had been dismissed by the Allies. It was in 1944 that U.S. Secretary of the Treasury Henry Morgenthau wanted to bring the new knowledge about the concentration camp at Auschwitz out into the open.

I recently helped a former neighbor of ours in New Jersey digitize his yet unpublished memoir on the computer.[3] In the book, he describes his service in the German RAD and the army. In June 1940, he was expelled from the army because he had a Jewish grandmother. In the later period of his adventurous life, without proper papers, he hid with his family in southern

---

2. Rudolf Vrba, *I Escaped from Auschwitz* (Fort Lee, NJ: Barricade Books, 2002).

3. Richard Hillebrand, "Mach's gut, mein Junge: Lebenserinnerungen," to be published.

Bavaria. His grandmother was eventually taken to a concentration camp. In February 1945, his family received a letter saying his grandmother had died of pneumonia. He says in his memoir, "We believed it, at the time."

A few months ago, I heard a radio program about photographs that were found showing German administrators at a concentration camp celebrating Christmas and having fun among themselves. The program brought up the question: how was it possible that a country like Germany could commit the unspeakable crime of mass murder and still go on with its daily life? The answer does not lie in a national urge for killing. It lies in the successful teaching and indoctrination of bias and hatred. Enhanced by interpersonal competitiveness, humans are always receptive to teachings which say they are superior not only to other people, but, what is more tragic, to other races, nations, or religions. Throughout history, people have killed because they felt superior—be it white people going on religious crusades, or killing black people or American Indians. What was different in the Holocaust, however, was the incredible extent of the crime and the systematic way in which it was executed.

We must look at the horror of the crime to preserve the memory of its victims, and we must look at the cause to learn how to prevent such acts in the future, and overcome bias and hatred.

The Anschluss and The Sound of Music

Another political event happened on April 10, 1938: the Anschluss, or the connection of Austria to Germany. More than 95 percent of Austrian voters voted in favor of joining the German Reich. While it is quite possible that some vote counters changed the numbers a bit, it remains clear that the large majority of Austrians voted in favor of the Anschluss. Whether the final number was 85 or 95 percent is immaterial. The Austrians saw that Germany was well off—economically, socially, and politically—and felt they might benefit from it. After all, they spoke the same language. After the war, however, you could not find a single Austrian who admitted to having voted for the Anschluss in that 1938 election.

Of course there were groups in Austria who opposed the Nazi rule. The Austrian nobility was one such group. This is illustrated in the story of Baron von Trapp, who decided, with his family of seven singing children, to emigrate from Austria and move to the United States. Like many in the Austrian nobility, they were uncomfortable with the new political system and took the big step of leaving their homeland.

On a trip to Vermont in March 1979, my family and I visited the Trapp Family Lodge near Stowe and enjoyed a chat, in German, with the real Maria von Trapp, who was in the souvenir store signing copies of her book. Our children had performed the musical in their high school two weeks earlier and the group had written to her, which made our visit especially memorable. We bought Maria's book in which she describes her family life in Austria, their flight to Switzerland in 1938, and their subsequent move to the United States in 1939. Maria told us that the departure from Austria was not as dramatic as in the musical, where the family flees directly from the stage into the Austrian mountains and on to Switzerland. On another trip to Vermont, we did some cross-country skiing in the ski area adjacent to the Trapp Family Lodge. It was maintained by one of Maria's sons who was born after the family's settlement in the United States. The lodge was destroyed by a fire in December 1980, but was later rebuilt. Maria van Trapp died in 1987, forty years after her husband.

5

World War II

The War Breaks Out

One of my uncles, my mother's brother Hans Jäger, was without question the favorite among our relatives. As the top manager and assistant to the owner of a factory, he lived in a house directly behind the factory. The factory manufactured wafers used for cooking and as hosts in religious communion services. Among all our relatives, he was the only one who had a car—albeit a business car. Uncle Hans was an avid mountain climber and an equally avid bachelor until he met his future wife, Finny, while mountain climbing. The story made the rounds in our family that he once asked Finny to wait for him on a desolate spot along the hiking trail. After waiting not far from where she stood—to see how she responded to the hardship—he emerged a few hours later. She passed the test and they got married. Needless to say, Aunt Finny became our favorite aunt.

Even more so than his father, my grandfather, Uncle Hans was very strict with his own five children. As they tell us today, they envied the affection we, their cousins, received from their father, as he hid his feelings toward them behind critiques and demands for achieving excellence.

Uncle Hans's house had a big garden behind it. The visiting nephews enjoyed sleeping in a tent in the backyard; it was more fun than sleeping in the house. We also liked to sneak into the factory stable where we found burlap sacks with the leftover sheets from which the circular wafers had been punched out in the production process.

It was the end of August 1939. My brother Volker and I, together with a cousin, made the 140-kilometer journey by bicycle for a visit with Uncle Hans in Günzburg, Bavaria. At the same time, our oldest brother, Uli, had the rare opportunity to undertake a trip to Bulgaria. Political tension was in the air. General mobilization was declared in Germany while we were in Günzburg. We immediately packed up and began our bicycle trip home. As we passed through many small villages, we saw farmers taking their horses to be turned in to the military, and people packing up to report for service. Once home, we heard that our father, age forty-nine, was called up to report for military service in a nearby factory that was converted to a garrison. It would take Uli another couple of weeks to return home from Bulgaria.

The news during these mobilization days talked about the possibility of a war caused by the increasing threat to and oppression of the German people in Poland, who lived in a section of Poland that had been separated from Germany as part of the Treaty of Versailles.

A few days later, on the morning of September 1, 1939, Hitler came on the radio. Even though I was only thirteen at the time, I still remember his voice and his words, "Since five o'clock this morning, we are shooting back." Germany invaded Poland. Was it going to be a quick occupation to reconnect East Prussia, which was separated from the rest of Germany by the Polish Corridor and given to Poland as part of the Treaty of Versailles? Hitler claimed that the German population in the corridor was oppressed by Poland and recently attacked. Or was it going to be a more lengthy war with France and England participating?

Nobody could imagine that a war had begun that would cost the lives of over fifty million people in the world, half of them civilians. The uncertainty and fear of the unknown future was overwhelming, yet we still had hope for a quick ending. More recently, on September 11, 2001, I relived that feeling of uncertainty and fear when I saw and observed the burning and collapse of the World Trade Center towers both on television and directly from our house in Holmdel, New Jersey.

War Years at Home

It looked initially like a blitzkrieg: Germany invaded Poland. Seventeen days later, the Soviet Union invaded Poland from the east and concluded a German-Soviet friendship treaty. By the end of September 1939, Poland was totally occupied. France, Great Britain, and Canada declared war on Germany. Half a year after the war began in the East, the war also started in the West.

Life at home continued, although changes were beginning to take place. For a few months, Father was in a temporary garrison only about four blocks from home. We continued going to school and had our Hitler Youth meetings as before. But as the war intensified, our lives were more and more affected by it. In May 1940, the war on the Western Front began, and one year later, on June 22, 1941, Hitler started his so-called campaign to increase Germany's *Lebensraum*, or "living space," by attacking Russia.

The news reported on the progress of the German army. To glorify the success of the German forces, the radio prepared its listeners with the announcement: "In a few minutes we shall bring a special communiqué of the Grossdeutscher Rundfunk (Greater Germany radio system)." This was accompanied by the main musical theme from Franz Liszt's Symphonic Poem No. 3, also called *Les Préludes*. We children would open the windows when the music came on, so our neighbors could also get ready to listen to the news.

Listening to foreign radio, on the other hand, was something most people, including my parents, did not dare to do. It was illegal to listen to it and the penalties were severe. If your neighbors or someone else reported you to the police, you could wind up in a concentration camp. The BBC news was introduced by the famous first four notes from Beethoven's Fifth Symphony. Because of our strained relationship with our neighbors, the Stahls, we were afraid that they might hear the foreign broadcast through the walls if we were to play it, and we thought they would only be too happy to report us.

A major hardship during the war was that many daily goods, like butter, meat, milk, cheese, sugar, bread, and eggs, became extremely rare. During the first two years of the war, a person received about three pounds of bread, one pound of meat, and a quarter pound of cooking oil or margarine per week. People performing heavy work and pregnant mothers received special supplementary allocations.

As the war went on, rationing became tighter. Very often, the allocated food was not available on the market. For example, instead of a pint of fat-free milk each week, you might just get the equivalent amount in milk powder, or dried eggs as a substitute for real eggs, or potato powder instead of real potatoes. Everything imported, like coffee, disappeared quickly from the shelves of the food stores. Coffee was replaced by ersatz coffee. Our ersatz coffee was also called "malt coffee," since it was made from roasted barley.

Much of the scarcity of food was a result of the fact that male farmers were drafted into the war, and women had difficulty running the farms by themselves. A shortage of gasoline also existed, but was not felt by the general population because only a few rich or select people had cars. The military certainly had the highest priority when it came to receiving scarce commodities. Some of the ersatz foods actually tasted quite good, in particularly the ersatz honey. But rumors had it that some other replacements, such as certain sausages, were made of sawmill dust. No one knew whether this was true or not.

Instead of getting the *Mutterkreuz*, or the "Mother's Cross," decoration from the Third Reich for having four children, our mother, like most mothers, should have been decorated for her ability to feed us during the war. It still amazes me how our mother managed to put a meal on the table every day with the little we had. She practiced the art of cooking different meals with basically the same simple ingredients. Once in a while, we had a chance to visit farmers we knew outside of town, and we could pick up a few gems, like eggs, cooking fat, or even some meat. In several of the war years, the fruit trees in the country were full of apples, pears, and other badly needed fruits, yet no one was available to harvest them.

All in all, there was no serious starvation among the German population. As we can read today, a good part of this was at the expense of the occupied territories in the East.

Given the scarcity of food, absence of cars, long walks, and other forms of exercise, "obesity" was an unknown word during and after the war. To a large extent, obesity is still not considered a problem in Germany today, let alone an "epidemic," as it is occasionally referred to, here in the United States.

A few times, our school class was sent out to the countryside to help with the harvest for a few weeks, in particular during the pea and the canola harvests. My brother Volker also spent a few weeks with his classmates helping with the wine harvest in Haberschlacht, a small village not far from our town.

In addition to the rationing of food, clothing was heavily rationed. To buy clothing, you needed special allocation coupons (*Bezugsscheine*). As the war went on, it became more and more difficult to obtain any coupons, or even to buy the merchandise for which you had coupons.

Introduction to Photography

Photography played an increasingly important role in my life, beginning in my teen years. I still have the glass negative of a photograph my father took at his own wedding in 1921. It was taken with a camera that you might consider to be a consumer version of professional graphic cameras. My father's camera was the source of a large number of excellent and treasured family pictures. The camera used 9-by-12-centimeter (3½-by-4¾-inch) glass negatives. On sunny days, our father would make prints by placing photo paper under the glass negatives and placing them in a frame for twenty to thirty minutes in the sun on the windowsill. I understand that the procedure is called "printing-out paper," since it uses the sun's energy for the development process, which is also the reason why it takes so long. I think my father had to fix them afterward; otherwise they would not have kept so well over the decades. The prints had the brown colorcast that old prints are famous for, and that was later simulated by sepia-toning conventional prints.

When I was a teenager, my father introduced me to his camera and to photography in general. Since my father's glass-plate camera was simple in concept, I used it to study the basic physics of photography, such as the effect of the lens opening (the f-stop) on depth-of-field and the variation of the bellows extension according to object distance. An exposure meter was still a thing of the future. Instead, my father had a chart where you would look up a sequence of numbers for the season of the year, time of day, cloudiness, brightness of the object, and film sensitivity. Adding up these numbers would lead to a final number that determined the f-stop for a given exposure time. The film speed in those days was given in Scheiner, which was later replaced by DIN and is nowadays ISO.

When my father was called into the military, I took over the camera. I have many memorable pictures that I took around 1941, when I was fifteen years old, such as pictures of our mother to send to our father in the service, or reproductions of documents and other photographs. Photographs were quite expensive at the time. Developing one glass plate cost one reichsmark, which, in terms of purchase value, may equate to perhaps five dollars today. This gave me a lasting education to think twice before clicking the shutter. Later I relaxed my thinking in accordance to what we said in photographic circles—film is the cheapest part of photography. And with digital photography today, clicking the shutter is practically free; yet a bit of self-discipline still helps even now.

Prior to the arrival of the American occupation troops, my parents buried the camera in the garden, stamping the earth over it. Indeed, the occupiers requested the population to turn in all cameras, together with weapons and radios. Our camera did not take the treatment too well. After the war, it needed extensive repair. I still have the camera today, now with an additional back for 120-type film, and I have used it occasionally in recent years, primarily for experimentation.

School

School basically went on as it did before the war, but there were some differences. The most important one was that all the younger teachers had left for the battlefield. Some of the older teachers who had retired were called back to teach. I must confess that we did not have much understanding of the situation the returning teachers were in, and we were not always nice to them. Herr Rapp was a case in point. Even though discipline was probably much stricter then, than it is nowadays in many schools, we gave Herr Rapp no chance. One day in May, someone who had collected a box of May bugs brought them to school. During class, we produced an admiring "aah," similar to what you hear in a crowd watching fireworks, whenever a bug took off toward the window. In his despair, Herr Rapp declared, "You can set the bugs free to fly, as long as you don't yell 'aah.'" However, there was one thing we had not accounted for: in the subsequent hour, we had Herr Heck as a teacher, whom we all feared. Rumor had it that he had been recently transferred to our town from a school where he had lost all control over his students. Obviously he had decided to start his new position on a different foot from the very beginning, and successfully did so. What if we did not collect all the bugs between classes and some started flying in Herr Heck's class? They did—and we caught hell.

Herr Setz was another teacher whom we did not treat fairly, as we realized later in life. He taught Latin, a subject for which we did not have much enthusiasm, to say the least. When we were not sufficiently quiet, Herr Setz would read his Latin text in a whispering tone until the end of the class hour. Occasionally he would make just a brief remark. One of these remarks became a standard quote among us: "Kühner, I know you will be a U-boat commander soon and therefore don't give a damn about old Setz." My grades in Latin, which started off in my lower grades as As, gradually turned into a C after about seven years. That grade was still near the top of the class, but Herr Setz remarked, nevertheless, that I had adapted myself to the level of my classmates.

Later during the war, some of our younger teachers, who were wounded on the front, came back to teach again. They not only had our attention, but also our admiration. One of them taught English, using a magazine about the German air force as his prime reading and translation text, which we found more interesting than Herr Mozer's *Homer*.

Another one of the young war veterans was Herr Rosenfelder, who later married my cousin.

Dance Lessons

Like all teenage boys, we had our eyes on girls and crushes from time to time, but I knew very few boys in our high school class who openly dated a girl. A formal procedure existed for our introduction into the dating game: dance lessons. Boys in the tenth grade, together with girls in the ninth grade, would organize a dance class with one of the local dance studios. For me, it was in the fall of 1942. One Wednesday evening we put on our best clothes and went to Herr and Frau Singer in their downtown studio. We sat down, boys in a row on one side and girls in a row on the other side of the room. The first thing us boys learned was how to walk across the room to a lady, and, with an appropriate bow, ask if she wanted to dance. The next thing we learned was how to deliver an appropriate, and noiseless, kiss on the hand. According to etiquette, this was to be used primarily with elderly women as a form of respect. Later, in the United States, it made me smile when the women to whom I occasionally applied this gesture responded with a "thank you."

Our dance lessons continued once a week for fourteen weeks. Every lesson, we were assigned a different girl to pick up before and take home after the lesson. One big question was how to assign the girls. We were eleven boys and eleven girls and there were fourteen evenings. Hence, us boys would have three girls as our partners twice. Everybody proposed a different scheme—alphabetical order, living close in town, etc.—whatever would get us our best choice of the double dates beyond week eleven. A solution was found somehow.

In our dance lessons, we learned the fox-trot, Viennese waltz, slow waltz, march, tango, and rumba. Dancing played an important role in social life during and after the war. You danced at parties; there were balls and practically everybody had learned ballroom dancing. Within our dancing class, we had two special events: an interim ball and a final ball. By the time of the final ball, some closer ties had developed and the assignment of who would go with whom to the ball was another big puzzle to solve. Little did I know that my regular school life would end less than three weeks after our official final ball on January 27, 1943. I, along with my fellow male students, was transferred to an antiaircraft battery.

Shortly after our dance class ended, one of my classmates was told that we'd made an omission: "We should have obtained permission from the Hitler Youth administration to hold the dance class." None of us had any idea that we should have done that. What does our dance class have to do with the Hitler Youth? We were amused about the comment and never heard about our misdeed again.

The dance class was a very enjoyable activity. I must confess, however, that since I was by far the smallest in our class, I was sufficiently plagued by insecurities when it came to the other sex. Nevertheless, ballroom dancing continued to play a significant role in my social life. It is probably fair to say that, without it, I would probably not be in the United States today. As it is in life—call it predetermination or chance—it was a series of events growing out of my love for dancing that led me to the United States. While a university student in Germany, I organized a student ball that made me known among the student officers. Someone suggested that I run for the student council, where I became vice president. Through this, I heard about a scholarship to study in the United States, and I enhanced my chances of winning it with my student council experience.

Air Raids

By 1942, the British began air raids against towns and industrial centers in northern and western Germany. Germany had declared war on the United States in November 1941. In January 1943, the United States joined Britain in the air raids, primarily in the form of strategic day attacks, while the British flew the night air raids directed toward the cities.

These attacks affected our daily lives more and more. Every house had to have an air raid shelter. Like practically all houses, our basement had a big room with a curved ceiling, which was called the cellar. It was used primarily for storage of food, from the daily milk and butter (if there was any butter) to potatoes, fruit, and canned food. Also stored there was firewood or coal for heating. The coal was delivered directly into the cellar from the street through a small window. The basement also had another room, similar to what we would call a hobby room, for activities like ironing. Then there was the washroom, and, at the basement entry door from the garden, a small storage room where we kept our bicycles, among other things.

The cellar was converted into an air raid shelter. A steel door replaced the original wooden door to the cellar, and the little window facing the street was replaced by a steel window, just big enough to escape through in an emergency. At some point later during the war, an emergency passage was made between our shelter and that of the Stahls on the other side of the wall. Given our poor relationship with our neighbors, we never utilized the passage, nor did we even try it out.

Throughout the city, signs were posted that led you to the nearest public air raid shelters. Most of the air raids occurred during the night. The sound of the air raid sirens had increasingly become part of our daily, or I should say nightly, lives. The sound still haunts me whenever I hear a fire siren. We had bunk beds installed in the shelter, since we had to spend so much time there. After all, we needed to sleep since we still had to go to school the next morning, though sometimes school started later after an air raid alert.

Because of the air raids, a general *Verdunkelung* (blackout) was enforced. Streetlights were turned off or set very dimly at night. Cars had covers over their headlights with slits in them. We had to place a similar cover over the lights of our bicycles— every bicycle had to have a light—with a half-inch high slit in the middle, just to let enough light through to see at least a little bit of what was in front of us.

The American and British air raids against German cities, which counted in the hundreds, were primarily directed against the civilian population. One reason for the raids might have been a hope on the part of the Allies that the German population would rise against Hitler.

During much of the air raid period, our hometown of Heilbronn was hit only by minor localized attacks. However that would later change—on December 4, 1944 to be exact.

The War Goes On

In the summer of 1941, my oldest brother Uli was drafted at the age of eighteen. After basic training and officers' school, he was sent to German-occupied northwest France. By 1943, he felt embarrassed to lead a fairly good life in France, while his schoolmates and former buddies fought the war in Russia. He applied to be sent to the Eastern Front. Of course, this came as a big shock to our family and we had difficulty understanding Uli's decision. In the summer of 1943, Uli was transferred to join the Russian campaign.

We had hoped that he would be deterred from such a step not only by the news about the bitter fighting and hardship on the Russian front, but also by the personal news that our family had received in August 1941 about our cousin Manfred. As I write this, I have a photographic copy of a postcard from Manfred in my hands—the first photographic copy I ever made with my father's glass-plate camera. Manfred wrote from a field hospital in Russia. He had been hit the day before, and had about forty shell splinters in his body. It was very painful, he wrote, but tolerable, due to the morphine injections, and it was not life threatening. Don't worry, he said

Manfred died the day after he wrote the postcard. A few weeks later, someone recognized him in the weekly news program in a movie theater. Because of his death, our family could receive copies of his picture from the movie agency. Unlike the situation for many other families, Manfred was the only relative from my extended family to die in combat during the war.

A few years ago I had a discussion with one of my wife's cousins, who was born after the war. She voiced her opinion about the war generation: "We all wanted to die." She added that if everybody in Germany at the time had refused to serve in the army, there could have been no war. I can't imagine how the latter could have been implemented in any country, be it dictatorial or democratic. Under Hitler, the first to speak up would be executed. Once you were drafted, the death penalty was declared for cowardice in the face of the enemy. Such a verdict would be implemented within hours or days. As for the alluded wish to die, nobody wanted to die. We looked at being drafted like any other person that is drafted in any country in the world. It was the duty and obligation to serve your country—you had no choice. The concept of a "conscientious objector" was unthinkable under Hitler.

Two years after Uli joined the army, my next oldest brother, Volker, was drafted. After his basic training, he wound up in the Partisan war in the Balkans, i.e., the war against the hidden partisan troops. In the German military, obedience was more important than intelligence; hence, Volker, whose technical abilities were close to nonexistent, was sent to join the communication troops, whereas I was later sent to the infantry. Volker was assigned, as a German communication specialist, to a division of Russian Cossacks who fought with Germany against Bolshevism. He later told many romantic stories about the Cossacks sitting around the fire at night and singing Russian songs, and about the exercises and attacks the Cossacks led on horseback with their sabers drawn. He also told the story of how he experienced the end of the war when he stormed Marshal Tito's palace only to find that Tito had escaped, and how he later became a British prisoner of war. The Cossacks later escaped with the German troops to Austria, but the Allies turned them over to the Russians knowing that they faced certain death. The Cossack officers were hung on butchers hooks.

After Germany's occupation of Poland, our father was transferred to Poland. Because of his age—he was over fifty at the time—he was not assigned to combat, but instead to a prisoner of war camp. Toward the end of the war, he was assigned to a prison camp for French and British officers in a town neighboring our hometown. As was typical for him, our father took groups of officers for leisurely walks in the woods, armed only with his pistol. He believed in the goodness of man and enjoyed conversing in French and English with these prisoners. Very late in the war, he was discharged from the army for age reasons, only to be called up again during the very last months to join the so-called Volkssturm, or "People's Storm Troopers," a form of militia that was considered an auxiliary of the Wehrmacht. The draft of all males between the ages of sixteen and sixty was a last desperate attempt to "defend the homeland."

As the war went on, the German military forces were scattered through many battlefields across Europe and North Africa. In Russia, the harsh winter hit the German army hard, both physically and militarily. The army was not prepared for the conditions in Russia. For example, the German army had a precision machine gun, designed in 1934, which was a technical masterpiece. The Russians had one that seemed to rattle when you shook it; however, in the bitter cold of Russia, the German machine gun froze and stopped firing, while the Russian gun kept working. It took some time until the German machine gun was replaced by a new design, strongly resembling the Russian machine gun.

The soldiers stayed on the war front for many years. There was no such thing as rotation of troops. The only chance of getting home was being wounded. The only other exception was for soldiers who'd lost several brothers in the war and were the only male survivors in their family; they had a chance of being assigned to a unit farther away from the front.

The turning point in the war came around January 31, 1943, with the Battle of Stalingrad. About one million Germans died in that phase of the war. The battle, combined with the air raids, brought about a significant change in the morale of the population. For the first time, the chances of winning the war were openly debated within the population.

The propaganda from Berlin spoke of *Wunderwaffen*, the miracle weapons Germany had in the works. There was much discussion in the population about whether there was any truth to this propaganda. V2 rockets verified that there was at least some truth to it. Berlin must have also had the development of a uranium bomb in mind, even though it was top secret and never mentioned in the propaganda. However, the German technology for the bomb was much less advanced than the rocket technology developed in Peenemünde under Wernher von

Braun. Nuclear research was also less centralized and not as well coordinated as the rocket development. Any information about nuclear research and development was kept absolutely secret. Even after the war, much of this knowledge was not made public because of the Cold War.

Slogans began to make the rounds in the population, like the rhyme "Räder müssen rollen für den Sieg, Hitler's Kopf muss rollen nach dem Krieg" (Wheels must roll for victory, Hitler's head must roll after the war). But how to end the war? And what would come afterward? Nobody could imagine what life would be like after the war, assuming that they survived. I remember the propaganda telling us that, according to the American "Jewish Morgenthau Plan" (Henry Morgenthau was the U.S. Treasury secretary at the time), not only would Germany cease to exist as a country, but all German men would be sterilized.

In reality, a proposal for the sterilization of all Germans—men and women—did not come from Morgenthau, but from the book *Germany Must Perish!* by Theodore Kaufman, chairman of a group that called itself the American Federation for Peace. Morgenthau's proposal only specified a breakup of Germany, the prevention of Germany's reappearance as an industrial power, the execution of the top Nazis, and the prosecution of all sympathizers. His and Kaufman's ideas were exploited by German propaganda to justify their messages about the "Jewish threat."

My family spent more and more nights in the air raid shelter. News about the destruction of German cities was increasing. At the same time, communication among people, other than through the government-controlled radio, diminished. Travel, other than military, was nonexistent. Joseph Goebbels, the minister of propaganda, declared "total war" on February 18, 1943, at a rally in Berlin, as a last attempt to win the war. Measures to recruit all people into the war effort included the announcement of the death penalty for refusal of service or public critique of the government's work.

Joining the Antiaircraft Auxiliary of the Luftwaffe

On February 15, 1943, three days before the declaration of "total war," all high school students in tenth grade, born in 1926 and 1927, assembled in the school auditorium. The school president and a representative from the air force informed us that we were to become part of the military effort. We were to serve as *Luftwaffenhelfer*, which translates literally as "air force helpers."

Following the draft orders sent to our parents, we reported for duty on February 18, dressed in our new uniforms. One day later, we were sworn in. Those born in 1926, like myself, were assigned to the heavy antiaircraft batteries on the outskirt of towns. The younger ones, born in 1927, stayed in town and staffed the twenty-millimeter antiaircraft guns on the rooftops of some tall buildings and factories. This later turned out to be the more dangerous assignment. The oldest students in our class had already been drafted or were close to be being drafted for regular service. In northern Germany, students were assigned to the navy as "Navy Helpers." Being assigned to the antiaircraft forces, we were also called *Flakhelfer*. FLAK, meaning *Flugabwehrkanone* or "antiaircraft cannon," was the acronym for the antiaircraft branch of the air force. Between February 1943 and the end of the war, about 200,000 students served in these air force and navy auxiliaries.

My youth had ended. I was not yet seventeen. I left home as a child, to return home five and half years later as an adult.

Eighteen students from my high school class moved to an 88-millimeter antiaircraft battery in Nordheim, a village about three miles from our town of Heilbronn. What was the purpose of having an antiaircraft battery so close to our town? It was not for the defense of Heilbronn; that was the objective of the younger students on the rooftops with their smaller twenty-millimeter guns. The Neckar River, which flows through Stuttgart and Heilbronn (and joins the Rhine fifty miles downstream near Heidelberg), makes a bend south of Heilbronn that is similar to its bend around Stuttgart. The idea was that the enemy would mistake our fairly open countryside for the city of Stuttgart and would drop its bombs there. Lights were used to simulate a city, whereas the real Stuttgart was darkened at night. But if you simulate a city, you need to simulate defense. And that was our task. Our four 88-millimeter antiaircraft guns were 1916 models and were only crudely guided by a radar station on our base. We were supposed to shoot only roughly in the direction of a plane, so the plane would think we were real. Did it help? It probably did for a few months. After that, I am sure the British and Americans used us for orientation to find the real Stuttgart, rather than being fooled.

Our new home was a set of small wooden barracks, containing bunk beds and a small table in the middle. We were proud of our uniforms, which were air force uniforms with a special patch attached to signal our status as Luftwaffenhelfer. A big disappointment came a few months later when the order came from Berlin that we also had to wear the red-and-white Hitler Youth armband with the black swastika. We thought, and were proud, that we had become soldiers and were no longer Hitler Youth.

In addition to these two functions, we were also still high school students. While the younger ones in the town went into their school building for their regular instruction, we were too far outside of town; the teachers came out to teach us on the base. The most pleasant part for me was that my father, whom I never had as a high school teacher before (except a few times as a substitute), became my official teacher for German and English.

My father made a point to wear his officer's uniform when he came out to our base.

Whether we learned a lot academically during our time as Luftwaffenhelfer is questionable. Instead, we went as far as pre-arranging with the antiaircraft soldiers on duty to call out the magic word *Edelweiss*, when our teachers threatened us with a quiz. Edelweiss was the code name for an air raid alert, and naturally, had priority over school.

In addition to our high school instruction, we had our share of military instruction. The training on radar was the most interesting part. During that phase of the war, radar technology was a cat-and-mouse game with the enemy. The Allies had just developed chaff—the metal foils that were dropped from planes to confuse the German radar. Within a few months, Germany developed the means to separate the chaff from the target, and a few months later, the Allies developed new tricks; and so the fascinating game went on.

In addition to radar training, we had a course in ballistics. Because of its mathematical content, our base commander, Captain Kreft, taught it himself. We enjoyed his attempts to explain to us the parabolic shape of the course of a missile, when we had been dealing with parabolas and their analytical treatment in differential calculus during the preceding school years. We thought we knew more than he did, at least on this topic.

One of the prime reasons for drafting high school students into military service was to free regular soldiers for duty on the front. The air force soldiers that served in the army at home, and formed the cadre around us, were an interesting mix of people, primarily older soldiers, not all of whom were the brightest.

Our battery had originated in northern Germany, in Westphalia. Not only was the northern soldiers' language quite different from our Swabian dialect, but their cuisine was not to our liking. Needless to say, there was not much that might be called "cuisine," considering our meals usually consisted of potatoes, carrots, and peas, and, occasionally, a bit of meat. Surprises came, for example, in the form of sweet pasta with dried fruit in milk sauce or sweet green salad. Regarding green salad, my father used to say, humorously, "North of the river Main, they use sugar in the salad, and south of the Main, for a wife to use sugar in the salad is a reason for divorce."

In addition to the Westphalian soldiers and us students, we also had Russian prisoners of war in our battery. They had to do heavier work like carrying the ammunition to the guns. We had been indoctrinated by the propaganda that Russians were another of the "inferior races on earth." Because of the complete language barrier, we had no communication with the POWs to either prove or disprove this. How often did I recall this form of brainwashing propaganda later in life when I met many Russian friends or admired Russian people on TV, like the beautiful and lovable Ekaterina Gordeeva at the Olympic Games in Sarajevo in 1984?

I was lucky. During the time I was at the antiaircraft base, we did not have any major attacks, though there were many alerts when planes flew overhead toward other cities. One night, together with another Luftwaffenhelfer, I was assigned to our twenty-millimeter gun (which we had in addition to our main cannons), when an enemy plane flew past our base at an altitude of only a few hundred yards, too low to be aimed at by our big guns. The plane had obviously been hit and was close to crashing. We tried to shoot, but the gun would not fire. Captain Kreft came running and yelled, "Why didn't you shoot? I would have nominated you for the Iron Cross." The Iron Cross was the German military decoration. He apparently thought he could claim we were the ones who shot down the plane with our twenty-millimeter gun.

Other than schooling and aircraft alerts, our life was pretty dull. When one of my schoolmates was asked about what he did in the evenings, he responded, "Watch how the others do nothing."

We were allowed to visit our families on many weekends. During one of these leaves, on June 26, 1943, it was time to harvest the cherry tree that we had in our small garden. For some reason, I did not feel like picking cherries. My mother got the ladder out anyway and we set it up. I told my mother I thought the ladder was not standing properly, but she told me I was just trying to find an excuse not to pick the cherries and that the ladder was standing well.

As I was some fifteen feet up the ladder, it began to sag into the ground. I could only save myself by jumping down over our fence into our neighbor's concrete backyard. The good news was that I had solid boots on, but the bad news was that I suffered a spiral fracture of the tibia. The doctor in the hospital I went to was renowned in town. He and his assistants were amazed by the fact that my ankle did not suffer from the impact. As we found out after six weeks in the cast, this was not correct. A fracture in the calcaneus, the heel bone, had been overlooked.

That fracture affected me for the rest of my life. The pain was particularly bothersome during military night exercises on uneven terrain and later during work in the forest as a prisoner of war. Without extra stress on my foot, I was fairly normal. When the pain increased again ten years after the accident, a physician suggested that I get a car modified with a manual control for the gas pedal, so I would not need my right foot for driving. Fortunately my foot got better and I never considered this again.

At one time, I had my foot examined to see if I could have the injury recognized as a wartime injury, but the doctors at the government facility said they could not see anything; however, my foot was swelling after every extended stress. When I was forty years old, I went to a local physician here in the States, by the interesting name of Dr. Stitch, to inquire about corrections that might be possible. After I explained to him that my ankle acts up especially after much walking or standing, after hours of dancing, and, especially, when skiing, he told me that, at my age, I would be giving up skiing soon, anyway. As I am writing this, I am almost twice as old as I was then and I am getting ready for my next ski trip, having learned to live with my foot problem.

It took some three months for my leg to heal sufficiently so that I could report back for antiaircraft duty. Meanwhile, our battery near Heilbronn was dissolved, since the simulation of the river bend of Stuttgart was no longer effective. My school group was transferred to a battery in Sillenbuch, a suburb of Stuttgart. Shortly before I resumed my duties as a Luftwaffenhelfer, this new battery was involved in some serious attacks and suffered some casualties. For our school education we were assigned to a high school in Stuttgart; we actually got to go into town.

Early in 1944, we were discharged to get ready for our next phase of pre-military service. Before turning in our uniforms and other assigned equipment, my classmates decided that we would all keep one blanket and wrap it up with our own belongings, saying that we all never received one. This put me in a big quandary. I could not abandon or indict my comrades, yet I also could not lie and commit what might possibly be conceived as a serious crime—theft of government property—which in the later war years, became punishable by death. Fortunately, the checkout was very superficial, and I came home with the blanket.

To get the high school diploma in Germany, an *Abitur*, which is the prerequisite for college, you have to pass a grueling examination lasting about six weeks and consisting of written and oral exams. In early 1944, my fellow Luftwaffenhelfers and I had not quite finished the twelfth grade, and the degree of scholastic learning during our final school years was more than questionable. Instead of having to pass this exam, we received a so-called *Not-Abitur*, which literally means "emergency high school diploma." This document later allowed our parents to enroll us, in advance, in college. Even though there was no chance of entering college at the time, this advance registration, called *Fern-Immatrikulation*, was useful if you were wounded and received a medical discharge from the military.

My oldest brother Uli enrolled in agriculture, with the dream of working after the victory, if there was one, in the newly opened eastern territories of "Great-Germany." Volker enrolled at the University of Tübingen for medicine and I enrolled at the Institute of Technology in Stuttgart in mechanical engineering. The acceptance card of my registration at the institute, which I received on July 10, 1944, was addressed to me with my new title as student of mechanical engineering: *Herr stud. mach.*

How I, or my parents, came to choose engineering is not fully clear to me. We had no engineers or scientists in our family and I was not really a tinkerer at home. However, I remember when, many years earlier, my father took me to an office in town where we met a civil engineer. My father explained to me that this engineer built bridges and that someday I would be an engineer, too. I think that an alternative just never came into the picture.

As I approached my draft into the army, I also registered to become a reserve officer applicant. Of course, we could not imagine when and how there would ever be a demand for an army reserve in Germany's future. But there was an advantage to the program: you would not be sent to the front immediately after basic training, but instead would be sent to receive additional instruction toward becoming an officer in what was called the sergeants' school. Similarly, you would later come back from the front to participate in officers' school, from which you would then be commissioned. The danger of being a reserve officer applicant, however, was that during your times at the front, you were placed in higher risk situations, both before and after becoming a lieutenant. The casualties among the young and inexperienced officer applicants and officers fresh from school were extremely high.

Joining the National Labor Service (RAD)

In July 1934, the national socialist government established the Reichsarbeitsdienst (RAD), meaning "Reich Labor Service." It had its origin in work camps that the German government set up in 1931 for young men, mostly unemployed, who volunteered for labor service. It was initially similar to Roosevelt's Civilian Conservation Corps (CCC). The primary purpose of the new service was to provide jobs for those who were out of work as a result of the depression. But just a year later, in 1935, service in the RAD became compulsory. Hitler saw the RAD as a valuable tool in building his new Germany. He envisioned manual labor as a way to break down social and class barriers and mold the character and political education of young people. He also wanted to revive interest in the dignity of manual labor. The RAD undertook the construction of Germany's new innovative autobahn system as well as the construction of other roads, and was involved in land reclamation, drainage projects, and soil conservation. It later also helped to construct military fortifications and installations.

For those registered as reserve officer applicants for the army, the normal six months of service in the RAD were reduced to three months. I expected, therefore, that after the final discharge from the RAD, I would be drafted into the regular army three months early. However, I was lucky: instead of my RAD service *ending* three months sooner than it did for the others who had not signed up to become reserve officers, it *started* three months later.

In February 1942 I had to report for duty. We were given our new brown RAD uniforms (the brown was meant to symbolize working the earth) and a shiny spade, the RAD symbol. The spade was used in exercises and parades, like soldiers use a rifle. We were then put on the train to Zychlin, Poland, west of Warsaw. On our long trip to Poland, whenever the train passed through a station at a reduced speed and a young woman was in sight, everyone would yell "Agathe." This was an unusual first name that someone must have started using for fun and everybody on the train followed.

I remember that right after our arrival in Poland, we had to write a short essay about the objectives of our service in the RAD. This was not a difficult task. We saw the pre-military training and fellowship as one of our prime objectives. But during the critique session, we were told that, while our essays were quite good, not a single one of us had mentioned one of the prime purposes of the RAD, namely national socialist education. We smiled because that was the last thing on our minds and appeared as a novel idea.

Life in Poland was all but enjoyable. We built roads around the camp, hammering and shoveling rocks. We actually felt like prisoners as far as the work was concerned. A few times we were allowed to go into town, but neither could we communicate with the population nor was there much to do or to see. The only fun we had during our time in the RAD was at the expense of some of our superiors. All of us new recruits had finished high school. Some of our superiors, on the other hand, came from remote rural areas of Germany, with little education or intellectual capacity. They volunteered to stay in the RAD, perhaps in the hope of postponing their draft into the army. Needless to say, we played many tricks on them that they were helpless to cope with.

A slightly scary, but in the end very pleasant, break came for me after some routine chest X-rays were taken in our camp.

A few days later, I was singled out with a few others to be sent to a sanatorium for lung diseases in Lodz, Poland, called Litzmannstadt at the time. The reason for being sent there was so they could take X-rays with a higher resolution than the quick thirty-five-millimeter X-rays that had been taken at our base. The three-day stay was paradise. The food was excellent and we always had a glass of wine. A beautiful park surrounded the sanatorium's buildings, and during a stroll in the park, you could hear classical music from the loudspeakers. It is one of the pleasurable memories of classical music I have that followed me later in life. Fortunately (or perhaps unfortunately), after three days, all but one of us were sent back to the base since the new X-rays did not show anything abnormal.

Several weeks later, in May of 1944, my three-month service was over and I was sent home to get ready for the draft into the army. It was near my eighteenth birthday.

While I was in Poland, my sister, Ursula, was also drafted into the female branch of the RAD. Fortunately, she wound up in the more beautiful surroundings of the Black Forest. For much of the time, she was assigned to help a multi-children family with the household chores.

Joining the Army

My original draft order was to join the infantry. Because of the continuing problem with my foot from my accident a year earlier, and my parents' connections to some influential people in town (including someone on the draft board), my mother succeeded in changing my order. Instead of joining the infantry, I was to become a *Panzergrenadier*, or "tank grenadier."

On June 30, 1944, I reported to my assigned garrison, Burgholzhof-Kaserne, in Stuttgart, and joined the Panzergrenadier E. and A. Battalion 119. A friend that I knew from high school, Werner Haag, also wound up in my group for basic training.

Almost twenty years later I would see him again in New Jersey, where he found a new home as a scientist.

Basic training in the army was anything but fun. It was essentially a boot camp. There was very little theoretical or technical training. The German army was based on discipline and obedience. One of the fundamental laws was that, if you were asked to perform any dehumanizing or otherwise immoral or possibly even criminal order, you had to execute it first *before* filing a complaint, if there even was such a possibility. If a soldier was asked in combat to kill a prisoner, this law would apply.

Such orders were more likely if you joined what was then considered the German military elite troop known as the Waffen SS, or literally "weapons SS," to distinguish it from the civilian SS, the former elite branch of storm troopers. It had never even crossed my mind to join the Waffen SS, and with my height of 5'6", I would not have been tall enough to meet their minimum height requirement of about 5'8". None of my schoolmates or friends joined the SS. However, I recently read an article in the *New Yorker* by Günter Grass, one of the most prominent German postwar writers, in which he described his involuntary assignment to join the SS.[1]

The Panzergrenadier units were essentially infantry troops trained to be carried by armored vehicle to a hot point of combat. In effect, we were just plain infantry. Only once or twice during our training did we use one of the armored vehicles to learn how to roll off it backward for combat on foot. The roll-over technique was similar to the way scuba divers roll into the water. In the later years of the war, not many of these armored vehicles were still in use, even on the Russian front. Because of the shortage of gasoline, our training vehicles were powered by wood burners, mounted on the side or top of the vehicle.

---

1. Günter Grass, "How I Spent the War," *New Yorker*, June 4, 2007.

Throughout the country, many if not most, commercial trucks used wood burners instead of gasoline.

As a soldier, if your response to a question from a superior began with "I thought…" you were told, "You're not supposed to think. Thinking should be left to the horses. They have the larger heads." This was somewhat descriptive of many of our superiors as well. Similar to our experience in the RAD, we found intelligent superiors in short supply. I found only one during basic training.

One thing that we disliked very much in basic training were the so-called mask balls, another game of boot camp chicanery. You were given a few minutes to change into different appearances, like a formal uniform, bathing suit, or combat attire with gas mask. We had already gotten a taste of this game in the antiaircraft battery and the RAD. This kind of dress change still follows me in my dreams as one of my less severe nightmares. In my dreams, I can never get to the point of completing the change of dress. It takes me forever and I start to dream of something else.

Another feared exercise was the gas mask drill. We had to enter a room filled with tear gas and then put on our masks once inside. Prior to leaving the room, we had to take the masks off, but our superiors made sure there was a minute or so left between taking them off and our exit to fresh air.

Of course, the food in the army was not exactly first-class cuisine, especially since the general population had nothing to eat and the country, isolated from the rest of the world, was in its fifth year of a war. Our main army fare was a soup of potatoes and peas with occasional traces of meat.

There was not much military leave or distraction in this phase of the war. We could only go out into the public after learning the proper behavior and etiquette as a soldier, in particular the perfect military salute. In late July, an order came from Berlin that the salutation for all branches of the military was to be replaced by the Hitler salute. Up to this time, the Hitler salute had only been used in the military by the Waffen SS.[2] Otherwise, the conventional military salute had been in use for decades, if not centuries, and we found the change unnecessary and upsetting. We did not mind being soldiers, but we greatly disliked this connection to the party.

I remember one time when we had leave and went into town to a cabaret. The big event of the show was a totally nude woman, but she was way in the back of the dark stage and hard to see. That was a first for me, as you normally would not see nude women in your day-to-day life, either in person or in newspapers or magazines.

My registration as a reserve officer applicant had one major advantage. Instead of being sent to the Russian front upon completion of four months of basic training, I was sent to sergeants' school, a precursor to officers' school. However, the basic training continued equally hard. I remember many exercises, especially the ones at night where my right foot acted up very painfully from walking on the uneven ground of the fields.

One of the few fringe benefits of our advanced training was that we learned to drive. For our military driving school, we used trucks that were fueled by wood burners; from time to time we had to stop to stir the charcoal. Admittedly, I was not a competent driver after finishing driving school. On my final exam, I got stuck in a narrow street of Stuttgart with the bus that I was driving. I did not dare to swing out sufficiently before entering the side street for fear of being yelled at. The teacher had to maneuver the bus to get out of the jam.

My driving training was a big advantage after the war, since I could convert my military license into a civilian license, after taking only a written test. Normally, you had to take many hours

---

2. The Waffen SS was formed from the original SS as an elite military branch under its own command, independent of the three conventional branches of the army. It grew from a few regiments to thirty-eight divisions.

of expensive driving lessons to earn a license. Even if you already knew how to drive, driving teachers—whom you needed to take you to the test since you could not bring your own car—would insist that you needed more driving experience.

It was during my basic training, in July 1944, that news reached my parents that my brother Uli was missing in action in Russia. This was all the more a terrible shock for us because we hadn't understood why he'd transferred there from France in the first place. At least he was not reported dead and there was some hope.

We all estimated that our chances of surviving the war, especially since the turn of the war with the battle of Stalingrad, were far from certain for all of us. I remember my mother making somber remarks on my very last visit home before the end of the war about us possibly never seeing each other again.

One assignment during basic training was particularly hard for me. An air raid had struck Stuttgart and we were assigned to help with the cleanup. The sweet smell in the city's streets was terrible. It came from the dead people in the houses and rubble. We had to pull the dead from the cellars of their homes, an almost unbearable task for me. It was the first time in my life that I had come into direct physical contact with a dead person.

The rubble from the Stuttgart air raids was later carried away to form an artificial mountain south of Stuttgart. The people nicknamed it *Monte Scherbelino*, which you might translate as "Mountain of Shards."

Heilbronn Air Raid

My second round of training as a future reserve officer at the sergeants' school, took place in Reutlingen, at the foot of the mountain range, Schwäbische Alb. It was almost as tough as basic training and was filled with many tough exercises. During one of the night exercises, the northern sky was somewhat bright and red. We had no time to pay special attention to it until the next day, when we heard that an air aid had taken place on my hometown of Heilbronn, forty-five miles away. Heilbronn and its suburbs had their share of industry, especially metal processing and machinery. As was typical during this phase of the war, these air raids at night were strictly directed toward the civilian population.

During the night air raids, a wave of planes would first mark the area to be destroyed with flares on small parachutes, nicknamed "Christmas trees." In Heilbronn, the marked area was the old downtown, comprising about one square mile. The marking planes would then be followed by a second wave of planes, which would drop their bombs—primarily incendiary bombs—into the marked area.

In Heilbronn, the firestorm was so intense that no person, creature, or even tree could survive. It was a holocaust in the original Greek linguistic sense of the word—"burned whole, or entirely." Only a few people near the border of the marked area, who immediately ran out of their shelters, survived. More than 6,500 people died during the twenty minutes of that raid on December 4, 1944. The only buildings left with walls standing higher than one story, though gutted, were some of the old medieval buildings, like the main church, the town hall, and a large castle-like complex dating back to the Crusades. The scenery was not unlike the pictures that we later came to see of Hiroshima after the atomic bomb.

My parents' house was only three blocks from the area of total destruction. It suffered some damage, which made my parents move temporarily to the countryside, but did not burn.

Today, the church bells are rung every year on December 4 at seven o'clock, the time of the air raid, and a memorial concert is usually given inside the main church. A memorial for the 3,435 soldiers killed during the course of the war, 7,137 civilians killed in the air raids, and 405 people who lost their lives during the war because of their religion, faith, or conviction, was established next to the restored city hall. A model of the downtown before and after the air raid is on display in the memorial.

My father was invited to write a four-line poem, to be engraved on the memorial wall. My mother helped him with it and primarily wrote the second verse. The following is the text:

In Brand und Sturz, im Schwinden und Werden,
Über Särge und Wiegen, wölbt hoch die Gnade ihr Zelt.

Aus der Toten Gedächtnis erwachse der Wille,
Das Gute zu wirken, dem Frieden der Erde zu dienen.

This can be translated as follows:

In fire and ruin, in ending and beginning,
Over tombs and cradles, grace spreads its tent high above.

From the memory of the dead may arise the will
To do what is right and to serve the peace on earth.

The Last Weeks of the War

As a consequence of the air raids, and the desperate state of the war, personal travel, as well as all forms of communication, practically came to a standstill. Even the official news became sparser because there wasn't much good news to report. Nobody had any idea what the future would bring, provided there was any future at all. Everybody struggled for his or her own survival.

While nobody expected any pleasant treatment from the three Western occupation powers at the end of the war, the worst fear was to be captured by the Russians; many thought it meant certain death. As the Russian troops advanced west, millions of people tried to flee to Germany. Some of the largest tragedies of the war took place during the advance of the Russian troops. A friend of ours here in the United States, Klaus Heck, described in his memoir how, being newly wounded, he successfully boarded a former German luxury liner, the *General Steuben*, on February 10, 1945, when only women and children and the most severely wounded were allowed to board.[3] Shortly thereafter, the ship was hit by a Russian torpedo and sank within seven minutes. About 3,600 of the 5,000 people on board drowned. Klaus was swept into the waters and later rescued. He subsequently flew to Berlin on the last air force plane that left the nearby airfield.

Another German refugee ship, the *Gustloff* was sunk eleven days earlier by the same Russian submarine, S-13, under the command of Alexander Marinesco. The *Gustloff* had about 8,000 to 10,000 passengers aboard, mainly women and children, plus some wounded soldiers. Only about 1,250 people could be saved from the waters. This loss is four to five times greater than the 1,595 people that perished on the *Titanic*. But it was war, not peace.

Combat and Retreat: My Triple Survival

In March 1945, our contingent of reserve officer applicants was transferred back to the barracks in Stuttgart. I wrote a few letters to my parents, which they received ten months later, expressing my concern and worry about the war and its end. The Americans had moved into the Neckar Valley, but then withdrew back to the Rhine. The letters, which I still have, spoke of my happiness of receiving a package from home and of a stop at a restaurant at the Stuttgart train station, eating spätzle, possibly with some eggs in them, which was my last luxury meal for quite some time.

---

3. Klaus Heck, *Before You Cast the Second Stone* (Dillsboro, NC: Western North Carolina Press, 1979), 100–115.

According to the official military career plan, we were supposed to be promoted to sergeants in 1945 and begin two months of front experience before going to officers' school. The casualty rate of the young officer applicants during that period in their military career had always been very high. Those soldiers were typically assigned to the most dangerous missions and did not have the experience of the soldiers who had spent years on the Russian front.

However, the front moved into Germany. Easter Sunday, April 1, was a beautiful sunny day. We were sunbathing on the lawn of the barracks when news came that the Americans were ninety miles away, approaching Heidelberg. That same afternoon, we received our marching orders. We were to be sent down the Neckar Valley to combat the enemy. Our promotion to sergeant was announced in the bulletin of the day, but there was no time to register it in our papers. (This would prove significant a few years later.)

We spent the night in Besigheim. For me, this was already halfway home from Stuttgart. The next three days we marched on, inching our way closer toward Heilbronn, arriving on April 4, in a little village called Klingenberg, about three miles southwest of the city. Suddenly, there was rumbling in the distance that sounded like approaching tanks. Our lieutenant gave five or six soldiers, including myself, orders to get in position behind some bushes in a ditch, get our *Panzerfaust* (bazooka) ready, and fire at the tanks, in case they were our enemy. The lieutenant assured us that they were German tanks—and disappeared.

I noticed that we had no way to escape the ditch in which we were ordered to take our positions, since it was on an incline. I chose the topmost point from which I could have a slight chance to disappear behind the crest with a few yards of running if necessary. It was not long until we heard the tanks coming closer, accompanied by voices—yelling in French. Infantry accompanied the tanks. Our sergeant ordered me to run after our lieutenant and ask him to come back to hear for himself that these were no German tanks. I ran toward the center of the village without finding the lieutenant. Then I heard shooting behind me; it came from our assigned position. There was no going back for me.

I never found out if anyone survived in those ditches. I joined other troops in retreat. We all wanted to get away from the French troops. Knowing the area, I suggested we go down the hill to cross the Neckar River to the eastern shore, where we assumed the Americans would be. Along with twelve other bridges, the bridge over the river had been destroyed, probably by German troops, in the hope of halting the enemy. However, the Volkssturm had built an emergency footbridge over the ruins of the bridge, which allowed us to cross to the other side of the Neckar.

Everyone left from our military unit gathered on the other side of the river. This was about two miles from my home, but I knew that my parents had not lived there since the air raid and I saw no sense in running away to a nearly destroyed city, not knowing where to go and what to expect.

I heard after the war that east of town, near the village where my parents temporarily lived, the SS caught a group of sixteen year olds who had been recruited for the Volkssturm for the "final defense of their home country," and had tried to run away and get home. All of them were hanged from trees as deserters. Like the top of the Nazi government in Berlin, the SS troops did not see a chance to survive a defeat, and their conclusion was to stay alive through day-to-day fighting for as long as possible.

Everybody knew that the war was over. In the chaos of those last days, many soldiers were successful in getting home. This had less to do with political conviction or conscientious desertion, and more with a personal strategy for survival, or simply an assessment of the best chance of getting home. As the newspapers recently reported, Joseph Ratzinger, now Pope Benedict XVI, was one of those who left the army in those last weeks of the war to find his way home.

For the next eight or nine days, we moved around in the area, marching through various villages outside Heilbronn. One of the first ones we went through was Ilsfeld; it was still in flames after an air raid attack. During those days, I came in contact with a few of the local people and even met a friend and fraternity brother of my father, who was a minister in one of the villages outside Heilbronn. Once, I was stationed within the city limits on the Sommerhöhe, on the southern slope of the town. I chatted with a farmer who asked me to wait while he went to retrieve something. A few minutes later he came back with a few raw eggs. It was the first time in my life that I ate raw eggs; they tasted heavenly and it became a memorable experience.

On April 13, we moved up on a mountain south of Heilbronn, the Haigern. The weather was beautiful. I was lying with another soldier behind a tree, looking down over the city and the beautiful Neckar Valley. It looked peaceful, but it turned out not to be. Suddenly there was an explosion. A phosphor grenade hit the trunk of the tree we were lying under. The tree trunk protected me from being hurt, but the soldier next to me was not shaded by the tree and was fully hit by the phosphorous. I went into the farmhouse, talked to the owners there, and had myself checked out to see if I needed any treatment since I noticed some smoking spots on my skin and in my hair. Luckily, I was affected very little by the phosphorous, and nothing needed to be done. I saw the other soldier a few hours later that night; even with his entire face bandaged, the phosphorous shone through. I do not know what happened to him later in life or whether he ever regained his eyesight.

Obviously, the strategy of the American troops was to trade ammunition and materials for American lives. They shelled every village in which they could spot German troops, using bombs or artillery, before advancing their military. This usually caused more casualties among the local population than among the German troops. Spotting us on the Haigern Mountain is what had led to the shelling with the phosphor grenade.

That same evening we moved on to Schozach, another village within five miles of my hometown. The next morning, we found ourselves lying on the forest floor, waiting for new orders. A wide-open meadow was in front of us. We were not sure who was in the forest on the other side, friend or foe. I was ordered to cross the meadow to make contact with the German troops on the other side, if there were any. What was I to do? Refuse the order—and perhaps be shot for cowardice in front of the enemy? I went on and found nobody on the other side.

It was probably for this exploration that I received the Iron Cross Second Class, the primary war decoration. I was surprised with the decoration a week later, on April 20, Hitler's birthday. Apparently it was customary to hand out such decorations on Hitler's birthday, but I did not make the connection at the time. No celebration was held—for Hitler's birthday or my decoration.

I was not a hero. I would define true heroism as the conscious and voluntary risking of one's own life to save the lives of others. Yet, very often, acclaimed war heroism results from having no other choice but to hide your fears or maybe even your cowardice. I don't think being a soldier makes you a hero.

After I came back from my "heroic" excursion, we settled in the forest. Suddenly there was a small explosion next to me. Something shook me. A lieutenant who was lying next to me on the forest floor was injured. We found that he had a deep cut, about five inches in length, in his buttocks. I was lucky not to have been hurt. I realized how lucky I was later in the evening when I discovered that a hand grenade in my backpack had a dent, and that two of my five pieces of ammunition had empty shells. I was thankful to be alive.

The continuation of our retreat from the American troops led us farther and farther away from Heilbronn. Needless to say we never saw any foreign troops. By April 20 we were about ten miles east of Stuttgart, near Haubersbronn. April 20 was a national holiday to commemorate Hitler's birthday. But that year, we had no idea where Hitler was and whether he was still alive, let alone what else was happening in the country. There was absolutely no possibility of getting any news from the rest of Germany.

The situation became more and more difficult. We crossed the Neckar Valley toward the mountains of the Schwäbische Alb. Near Kirchheim, we hooked up with other troops in a meadow surrounded by forest. I met Götz Giese, a former classmate. As we were resting and talking, low-flying planes suddenly attacked us. The Americans had spotted our troop assembly. We split up into small groups and moved farther into the mountains. I did not see Götz again until some thirty years later at a class reunion.

Talking to some of the farmers, we learned that the Americans had progressed to the point that we were in fact encircled. The local people told us that the "Ami," as the Americans were generally called, had arrived three days ago. The locals felt that if the Americans captured us at a much later time, they might treat us as partisans, rather than as captured soldiers, with unknown consequences. We were a group of about eight people and decided to surrender the next day, spending the last night in a hay storage hut.

6

Prisoner of War

Capture

The next morning, after spending the night in a little shepherd's hut near the town of Wiesensteig, we took our rifles and placed them neatly in a small creek. We then gathered some sticks to which we tied our more or less white handkerchiefs. Then the eight of us marched down the nearest road. We did not have to go far. After about 400 yards, we were met by American troops.

To my surprise, they were primarily black soldiers. I had not seen a black person since visiting a circus in my youth. Each of us was "attended to" by a GI. I soon heard my first English words spoken by someone other than a teacher: "Knives and watches." I resorted to my limited school English, whereupon my capturer loudly exclaimed to his buddies, "I have a guy who speaks English."

During our preparation in anticipation of being captured, I had tied my wristwatch to a string and let it dangle from a belt loop on the inside of my pants. The GI did not find it. But his big trophy was my new Iron Cross, of which I was only able to save the ribbon, which I still have. He also took my toiletry kit and my fountain pen. When he was about to take my nail clippers, I said in my school English: "May I remain this?" confusing the word "retain" with "remain." He told me that it was too dangerous a weapon, and when I asked him how to cut my nails, he suggested biting them off.

We spent the night in a barn with many other prisoners. The next day we were loaded onto a truck which took us to a small military airport in Göppingen. I expected one or both of two things to happen: our sterilization, which I believed was part of the Morgenthau Plan, or our transfer to the United States. Instead, on April 26, we were loaded onto a series of about six large open army trucks, one hundred prisoners squeezed onto each one. I had never seen trucks as large as those.

Our convoy moved north, in the direction of Heilbronn. I was close to the right edge of the truck. After a good hour, I realized we were passing through the little town of Löwenstein, where, according to what I knew, my parents lived. As we raced through the town, I saw that there was a great amount of destruction. As we were moving down the long road toward the valley, I saw two people retreating into the ditch next to the road to avoid the noise and dust of our trucks. They were my parents. I raised my arms and yelled, but I saw no response. My father later told me that when he realized it was I who yelled from the truck, he was totally shocked. By the time he responded and raised his hand, I had already passed him.

To my surprise, we entered Heilbronn. We came to a brief stop at the intersection that was one house from our own. Civilians stood at the corner, among them one of my neighbors.

When I had realized earlier that we might be going to Heilbronn, I had scribbled a note that said:

> Please go to the Solothurnerstrasse, to the Köhlers or another house in the neighborhood, and tell them, I, Corporal Dankwart Köhler, became an American prisoner on April 24 near Wiesensteig on the Alb and was transported via Göppingen to Heilbronn, passing my father near Löwenstein, who, however, did not recognize me. I don't know where we are going.

I handed the note to my neighbor on the street corner, with the hope she could pass it on to my parents, which she eventually was able to do some time later.

Our convoy went on and, to my surprise, headed for our town's sports fields. My hopes were high that we might stay in the area. (I heard later that the Americans had set up a large prison camp not far from there.) One of the American soldiers yelled at us in German, made us descend from our truck, and chased us onto another truck, all the while swinging a stick and hitting some of us.

Rhine Meadow Camps

The adventure and the uncertainty continued. Our trucks moved down the Neckar Valley and came to a stop near Ludwigshafen, northwest of Heidelberg. A huge meadow and agricultural area was subdivided into many sections, each almost equal in size to a football field. This was to be our new home for the next six weeks. Each of the sections held 1,000 prisoners. It was open air, with no roof, and no facilities. We could not see the end of the camp. There were 100,000 prisoners at this location, which was one of many such camps known today as the Rhine meadow camps. Most of the five million German prisoners captured by the American and British troops were stationed in these camps.

According to the initiative of General Eisenhower, the German prisoners were considered disarmed enemy forces, rather than prisoners of war, which allowed for treatment that was not necessarily within the bounds of the Geneva Convention of 1929. Of course, we did not know any of this. We had no knowledge of what was happening in Germany, or anywhere else in the world for that matter. Only in the form of a rumor did we hear that Germany had officially surrendered and that Hitler was dead, but it was of no concern to us at the time. We just hoped to survive and did not know what the future would bring. Throughout my years as a POW, politics were never discussed.

I owned a triangular piece of canvas—a quarter of what would be needed to build a tent. Together with three other prisoners, two of whom owned blankets, we assembled a little shelter against the cold and the rain, about eight by eight feet square. Our meals consisted of about a pint of water soup with some barely visible vegetables twice a day and one slice of bread per day. We were given empty food cans, about a quart in size, in which we received water to wash ourselves.

After a few days, I experienced some itching and discovered that I had lice, especially in my pubic hair. One of the other prisoners, with whom I had been together in the last days of combat, asked me if I had also taken and worn one of the black shirts that we had found in a pile along the road during our retreat. My answer was yes and he told me that the shirts were full of louse eggs. If not from this source, I most likely would have gotten lice from the others next to me. There was no escape. The daily routine was to strip every morning in the open field, wash yourself with the daily allocation of a quart of water, and crack the louse eggs that you found on your body with your fingernails.

The latrines were erected along the side of our field section. Three horizontal beams stretched over ditches, an arrangement that in German was called *Donnerbalken*, or "thunder beam." I had become familiar with that architecture in our Hitler Youth summer camps. Naturally, the Americans were very concerned about the danger of an outbreak of disease. The ditches were filled with white foam: chlorine. The chlorine smell was very intense. Once there was a commotion in the camp. A prisoner had apparently fainted on the latrine beam and had fallen into the ditch. I doubt that anybody did anything about it. The war had ended. Everybody was fending only for himself. When somebody addressed a fellow prisoner as "comrade," which only happened when somebody wanted something, the common answer was "There are no more comrades. The last one fell in the war."

Years later when I compared notes with my brother Uli, who had been a Russian prisoner of war, we concluded that living as a prisoner was an experimental study in human psychology. Seeing how people behaved when they were concerned about nothing but themselves and all the barriers were gone, I felt ashamed to be a German. This experience was intensified later when I met French people who treated us POWs as human beings. I realized that it does not matter whether you are German or French, Jewish or Protestant, but who you are as a person.

On some evenings, something remarkable happened from time to time. A group of prisoners would begin to sing old sentimental folk songs and the whole camp would join in. My brother later told me that the same thing happened in his Russian prison camps, and it happened especially when the morale was at its lowest.

A few lucky prisoners were called to work for the Americans. They were well treated and fed outside the camp, but they were only a few of the hundreds of thousands of prisoners in the camps. We had no close contact with the American troops; we only saw them on the other side of the barbed wire fence. Our only interaction occurred when prisoners begged for cigarette butts or when GIs offered cigarettes for watches or wedding bands. The exchange rate was five to twenty cigarettes for a wedding band or a watch. Each GI on the other side of the barbed wire had a whole line of watches on one or both arms. Strangely enough, to many prisoners, cigarettes were more important than food, even in times of hunger. Later in my captivity, I wrote to my parents, "I am glad I am a nonsmoker. I am always reminded of Father saying that smoking is a vice." Yet long-term health concerns were not an issue at that time in the prison camps. Once I successfully begged some GI for a few cigarette butts, which I exchanged for a slice of bread from a fellow prisoner.

One of my fellow prisoners, with whom I shared our "hole," once asked me if I would sell my triangular piece of tent canvas. I said, "Maybe at a later time." An hour later he came back and gave me a piece of bread. He had sold my canvas. I do not know what he really got for it and I was mad for a long time, having lost a large fraction of what were my worldly possessions at the time. From then on, we lived completely under the open sky, without any protection.

A few prisoners told us that some of the GIs had asked through the fence where the prisoners with the horns were. They had heard that the Nazis were devils with horns, but to their dismay, we could not show them what they wanted to see. It is amazing what propaganda can do.

I spent six weeks in the meadows, with no roof over my head, in sunshine and rain, with less than the bare minimum of food. My nineteenth birthday came and went. Many people around me got sick. Thousands died.

American Prisoner of War in France

On June 7, 1945, we left the Ludwigshafen meadow camp. We were loaded into freight trains, one hundred prisoners per boxcar. An empty twenty-gallon can was put in the corner to serve as a toilet. The doors were closed and chained, with a gap of about five inches for air. This type of transport must have been similar to what recently was described as the transport for the Eastern Europeans brought to Germany to work as slave laborers in the factories. At that time, Germany was temporarily victorious. Now, in 1945, the victors were on the other side. However, there was one substantial difference: our transport consisted of only male prisoners, whereas the German transports consisted of women and children.

Reading the signs at the train stations we passed, we soon realized that we were going to France. The final station was Épinal in the Alsace region. Upon our arrival, we marched to the American barracks on the top of a hill.

Once there, we had to open our clothes and were powdered with white stuff to kill the lice that we all still had. Was it DDT? It certainly proved effective. Obviously the Americans were afraid of the spread of diseases.

As part of our transfer into the camp, we were registered. I still have the document, dated June 7, 1945, that designated me as American prisoner of war number 1917859. In German, the paper said that it was my prisoner of war number, but in English, the number was called an internment serial number, reflecting our official status as disarmed enemy forces, not POWs. As such, we normally would not have to be registered with the Red Cross. However, on the day of our registration in the Épinal camp, we did fill out and sign a Red Cross form card. It contained my POW number and had a place to check indicating that I was well, unwounded, and in France. The card was sent to my parents who received it in December.

The French barracks consisted of various old stone buildings. Finally, we had a roof over our heads, but the concrete floor was our bed. Somehow I happened to find an old door on which to sleep. The food was slightly better there than it was during the previous six weeks in the Rhine meadow camps. After ten days in the camp, I was lucky to get a job in the office. This included the opportunity to get more food and some new clothing, but my stay in Épinal would only last seventeen days.

The End of the War in Germany

The last weeks of the war around Heilbronn were fierce. Even though many army units, like the one I belonged to, never engaged in actual fighting, the mere presence of German troops led to much bombing and shelling by the American troops. Many SS troops were in the area. It is only natural that the fiercest defense came from the people who expected that surrender would bring them nothing but certain death. This applied particularly to the members of the SS troops and the top party leaders.

The fighting around the city lasted throughout the first ten days of April. The mayor of the city called for surrender, but Kreisleiter Drauz, the county party boss, called for resistance until the "last drop of blood." He was the same person who had threatened my father ten years earlier for protecting a Jewish student in his class. Drauz personally executed four civilians because they had hung white flags on their houses in the southern part of the city. He was found three months later and sentenced by an American court to death by hanging, not for shooting the four people, but for having executed an American POW.

Under the command and supervision of SS troops, my father was called to organize a Volkssturm unit to defend the town of Löwenstein, where my parents had moved to after the destruction of Heilbronn. But before it came to senselessly defending the town against approaching troops, the mere presence of German soldiers triggered a severe bombardment of the little town on April 14, 1945. The center of the town went up in flames. My parents lost many valuables, including many of my father's treasured books, in the ensuing fire. After the attack, my parents moved again, this time to another small town nearby. Within a day or two of the attack—about three days after the fall of Heilbronn—Löwenstein and the entire area around it became occupied.

After the war, my father had to defend himself in the denazification court against the charge of being responsible for the destruction of Löwenstein. One of the witnesses in the chamber was our former maid who lived in the town. She had been assigned to us since my mother was officially classified as *kinderreich*, which literally means "children rich"—the designation for mothers with four or more children. The maid testified that my father was a Nazi, and when asked how this manifested itself, she said, "You know, when Herr Köhler talks about the weather, he does so national-socialistically."

The denazification courts, officially called *Sruchkammer* (judgment chamber), were set up in accordance with the law for Germany's liberation from national socialism and militarism. The American courts were generally stricter than the courts in the French and British zones of occupation. Every former member of the party, and many others suspected of having actively supported the system—in total about six million people—had to be judged by the courts and were classified into five categories, from "war criminal" to "disencumbered." The most common standard verdict was "cleared as Mitläufer," the fourth level down. *Mitläufer* literally means "co-runner," i.e., someone who passively sympathized and went along with the party. At the end of his proceedings, my father was acquitted and classified as a Mitläufer.

The general population of Germany did not look at the American troops as liberators, but as occupiers. I heard of only one case where the American troops were applauded. This was because the people expected the Russians to arrive and were happy to see the American troops instead. By and large, the population was scared as the troops approached. My sister braided her hair to make her as unattractive as possible. Two young daughters of friends of ours told us later that they played sick, going to bed with a lot of medicine bottles on the nightstand. In general the American troops did not threaten the population—unlike what we later heard about the Russian occupation. However, many families were forced to live in their basements while the Americans occupied their living quarters, especially in the cities. Afterward, in many cases, the rooms looked like they had been ransacked.

My parents were able to return to their home in Heilbronn by the end of 1945. My father's offer to resume his voluntary duties as a weather observer helped in the recuperation of their house. The weather authority was now in the hands of the American troops. However, it took over a year to fully re-establish the weather station. When my parents moved back into their house, their roof still showed damage. The house was in relatively good condition otherwise, except that some GIs had inscribed their names and initials in the lacquered doors to the individual rooms, apparently to establish their ownership. It took three weeks of cleaning to get the house in order. Due to the general destruction of houses and apartments and the large numbers of refugees, my parents had to take in another family. The house had been built as a one-family house, but they arranged a makeshift kitchen for the other family, who stayed for over two years. Fortunately, it happened to be a family whose children were friends of us children.

Everybody in town had to report to work for the removal of the rubble left from the air raid, including my father who had never performed physical labor.

French Prisoner of War

On July 24, 1945, a sad line of several thousand German prisoners—dirty, hungry, and in shabby clothes—marched out of the American Épinal barracks and headed south. Every fifty yards, there was a Frenchman with a rifle who yelled at prisoners that would not, or could not, march, or who tried to get to the side of the road to relieve themselves. The march went on for eleven miles, ending in an old factory building in the small town of Pouxeux, under the authority of the French military. I became French prisoner of war number 1084523.

According to the Geneva Conventions, prisoners are to be released as soon as possible after a peace treaty. However, there was no peace treaty with Germany, because a German government no longer existed. It was even questioned whether the Red Cross had any say with respect to German prisoners. The International Red Cross insisted that the Geneva Conventions still applied. The transfer of prisoners to another country, essentially for slave labor, also had no precedent.

The French had about one million prisoners of war, one quarter of which were captured by French troops, and the other three-quarters of which were transferred from U.S. custody. Many of my fellow prisoners came from American prison camps in Germany. About 25,000 were transferred from British custody. Rumor circulated in the prison camps that the Americans sold us to the French for coal from the Saarland. By 1946, the Americans called on the other three Allies to release their prisoners, claiming that they had no more German prisoners. Yet, many of the prisoners that were repatriated from prison camps in the United States were transferred to French prison camps while passing through France.

Pouxeux was one of twenty or thirty camps for German prisoners in France. German officers were kept in separate officers' camps, since, according to the Geneva Conventions, they were not allowed to work. The bulk of another group of prisoners in our camps, namely those at the rank of sergeant and higher, but below officers, were sent to coal mines.

Prisoners that belonged to the former SS branches of the military, identified by a blood-type tattoo under their arms, were kept in separate camps. Many of them were sent to work clearing mine fields. This was, naturally, the most dangerous assignment. The French civilian guards assigned to these camps were therefore well paid. Some of the prisoners, who came back from *déminage* (demining) into our camp, told us that during the later part of the assignment, the guards occasionally buried mines for prisoners to find, so they could report to Paris that their function and use of prisoners needed to continue. By that point, mine removal became one of the good assignments since there was no work to be done.

Upon our arrival in Pouxeux, the French guards took the ample supply of soap, as well as toilet paper, the Americans had given us in the prior camp.

In a letter to my parents on December 21, 1945, in which I described some of the events of my earlier captivity, I wrote:

> It is good that we had enough soap when we were with the Ami in Épinal. We did not even know what to do with all the soap—same with toilet paper. Practically all was taken from us in Pouxeux. I succeeded in smuggling a little supply of soap and still have some of it. The ones in whose custody we came after the Amis are poor devils themselves.

My French base camp, Dépôt de prisonniers de guerre 201, in Pouxeux, was everything but fun. We knew that the French had not much to eat themselves and therefore we could not expect them to feed their prisoners well, but it was worse than we thought. We were introduced to a new fare: soy soup. This soup was made of soybean pomace, the residue left after the extraction of soy oil, normally used as animal fodder. Despite our hunger, it initially took a great effort to swallow it, since it smelled and tasted bad. But it took only a week or so until we would stand in line to get more, whenever there was a chance.

Every morning, the French flag, the Tricolor, was hoisted in the middle of the courtyard. Every prisoner tried to disappear as quickly as he could from the courtyard, so as not to stand in attention during the ceremony. In honor of the soup, we prisoners referred to the French flag from then on as the *Soyalappen* (soy rag).

Since I was only nineteen years old, I had no experience judging the extent to which a human being could endure a prolonged period of malnutrition. Some of the older prisoners estimated that you could survive for about six weeks. Others predicted that we would suffer for the rest of our lives from the shrinking of our stomachs, a thought that has recently come back to mind, as I hear about people undergoing stomach-shrinking operations as a measure against obesity.

At the entrance to the main building of the camp, the French set up a series of posters displaying the photographs from the concentration camps that shocked the entire world when they became public after the war, including the images of piles of human corpses. We did not quite know how to take it. Was it true? How extensive were these killings? Were there not horrors in every war? Was it a message to us from the French to justify our own treatment? This was not yet the time to open our eyes to the crimes Germany had committed against the Jews.

At the other end of the spectrum, one of my fellow prisoners told us that he had been liberated from the Dachau concentration camp, where he had been imprisoned as a homosexual. He said he would rather go back to Dachau than stay in our French prison camp.

We received another luring message from the French. They set up posters and invitations for prisoners to sign up for the Légion étrangère, the French foreign legion. Those who did join were immediately separated from us and placed in better quarters with excellent food. A fellow prisoner, about as old as I, told us that he was considering signing up. He reasoned that he would only have to join for five years as a free man and it would be better than staying for several years in the prison camp and possibly dying of hunger. I remembered and relayed to him some of the horror stories my father had told us children about people who had been recruited, and even drugged, to join the Légion étrangère after World War I, and about life in the legion. My friend had never heard of the Légion étrangère before, and I was happy to be instrumental in his decision not to join.

A few days after our arrival in Pouxeux, prisoners were called up in small groups. French organizations, companies, and individuals could request prisoners to work for them. This was not for day work, but for long-term appointments. The slave trade had begun. The selection for these *Kommandos*,[1] as they were called, was largely based on the professional backgrounds and experiences of the chosen prisoners. The luckiest were the ones who claimed to be farmers. They were picked up by French farmers and often stayed with them for a few years, in many cases being treated as part of the family. At the other end of the spectrum were the students, like myself, who could not claim to have any useful experience.

First Kommando: Le Val d'Ajol (July 27, 1945– April 30, 1946)

It took only three days of waiting until it was my turn to be called up. Together with about thirty other prisoners, I boarded

---

1. *Kommando* was the German term used in the military and in prison camps for groups of soldiers put together for specific short-term or long-term duties or transfers.

a truck and was taken to a small town in the Vosges mountains, Le Val d'Ajol. The good news was that we had escaped the Pouxeux camp; the bad news was that we were to work for the government, and not for civilians or any civilian organizations which were likely to treat prisoners of war more humanely than the government.

Our new work: logging. Our organization: le Département des Eaux et Forêts (the French Ministry for Water and Forests). The excuse the government used to employ prisoners for forestry work was they needed to cut the trees damaged by war activity. Indeed, a few times we heard our saws ring as we hit a shell splinter, but it was a rare occasion. Our prime assignment was instead to work for the forester and optimize the health of the forest. The forester marked the trees that we were to fell and cut. Most of the cut wood was to be used by the local population for heating.

We moved into an empty former mill in town. Our sleeping quarters contained two rows of wooden bunks covered with about one inch of straw. The toilet rooms in the building were built like round towers, curving out from the otherwise square building. The facility inside each room consisted of the usual French hole in the floor. The reason for the unusual architecture was so that the holes were positioned right over the creek that once fed water to the mill. The creek had become a sewage canal. At night our room was locked and a twenty-gallon can was placed in the corner of the room as a toilet. In the morning we had to take turns emptying the can—over the creek, of course.

The food in Le Val d'Ajol was better than in the base camp—which does not say much. For the first time in my life, I heard of calories in relation to nutrition. The French wanted to prove to us that we got enough calories to do the hard work in the woods: 1,800 calories to be exact. In addition to the famous soy soup, we had potatoes and an equal amount of various forms of root beets, from rutabaga to mangel-wurzel, a large beet that is cultivated solely to feed cattle.

An occasional piece of sausage or meat was added to our meal on Sundays. The meat allocation was about one ounce per day, and the meat usually was horsemeat, an ingredient not uncommon in simple French cuisine. Today you may still find butcher shops specializing in horsemeat in France. Our bread allocation was one quarter of a loaf per day. The interesting part, dividing the loaf, was left to the prisoners. Each round loaf—the daily allocation at the time for four prisoners—was cut into four parts. A homemade scale was built, consisting of a horizontal stick with a string attached to its center, and on each end, two short strings with pegs for sticking into the bread. It was similar to a mobile. This scale was used to equalize the bread portions, two at a time. After the weighing was done, someone held the two portions of bread behind his back and the respective two people chose their side. Interestingly, my brother later told us that they used exactly the same routine in their prison camps in Russia.

The day after our arrival, we were to begin our work. The guards had placed a pile of tools in front of the mill: large two-man saws, little saws, axes, sledgehammers, and wedges. They asked that each of us take something to carry to the woods; the work would be assigned later. I had never held any of the tools before, except for the small saw. Upon arrival at our work location in the forest, we deposited the tools in a pile. Then, most of the other prisoners quickly grabbed one of the tools. By the time I picked up something from the disappearing pile, I found myself with a sledgehammer. The guards did not assign us to particular tasks, and I was left to split wood with the sledgehammer. By noon, I had blood blisters on my hands. One of the guards saw this and made me switch tools with one of the taller and stronger prisoners. As it turned out, half a year later, I learned to work with all the tools and did not mind doing wood splitting from time to time.

Two in our team were mechanics by profession. Even though they were among those in the best physical shape, they were assigned to sharpen the saws, work which required skill but the least physical effort. They were busy most of the time.

Prisoner Mail

On the evening of our third day in Le Val d'Ajol, on July 29, 1945, we were each given a pencil and paper to write our first letter home beyond the Red Cross postcard we had filled out six weeks earlier. The paper had twenty-four lines, which we had to number. For the benefit of the French censors, our letter had to be written in printed letters. Here is what I wrote as part of this first letter:

> I want to, and can, calm you regarding my situation, and hope that you don't worry, at least concerning me. I will fight my way through and the day will come when this captivity ends... With trepidation and yet joyful expectation, I am wishing and hoping for the first news from you...I will never lose courage or give up the hope of seeing you again.

I had started my letter with the name of the town and date, but the name of the town was later erased and smeared over by the censors.

To facilitate censorship, future letters always had to be written in pencil and, initially, in block letters. It became official policy that letters written in ink and letters containing a geographical designation would not be sent to Germany. A few months later, we could use handwriting, rather than printing. However, the handwriting that I had learned in school was the handwriting equivalent of Gothic printing, called *Sütterlin*. Since our

Alsatian censors could not read this form of handwriting well enough, we had to write in Latin letters. Over time, I developed my own handwriting style using a fast form of printed Latin letters, and I still use it today. Depending on how fast I want to write, without changing style, my handwriting can be anywhere between nice printing and near total illegibility. Throughout my later career, my secretaries in the United States always had difficulty reading my self-invented handwriting.

While in Le Val d'Ajol, I addressed my letters to the last address I had for my parents, which was in the countryside where they moved after the air raid, not knowing that they had moved back into our house in Heilbronn. I had doubts that my letters would ever reach them. I began to write to almost all of my relatives for whom I remembered the address, in the hope that some of them would contact my parents. All of them could. In all of my letters I wrote the same message, namely that I was still healthy, that I was holding out, and that life and hardship would be easier to bear if I had news from home. Letters took typically about four weeks or less if they went to the French zone of occupation. A few times I had the opportunity to give a letter to a French officer who would be traveling to the French zone where he was stationed.

I recently read most of the letters that I wrote and received during my captivity. Today, fifty-nine years later, they make me humble and grateful for my life and my well-being.

On the first Advent Sunday, December 2, 1945, after almost eight months of captivity, I received the first letter from my parents. My parents and twin sister were alive and back in our home. My oldest brother Uli was still missing in Russia and my other brother, Volker, was known to be in British captivity, yet there was no direct mail from him. I wrote home:

> I can say that today is the happiest day of my captivity and I am certainly the happiest among my thirty comrades. As I

came back from my voluntary Sunday work, everybody came to me with my two letters, the first news for which I have been waiting so desperately since our separation eight months ago. I must admit that it was the first time in my captivity that I almost became emotional in view of the joy.

The next day I had the opportunity to write another letter, which a French officer promised to take to the French occupation zone. In it, I was able to describe in more detail what had happened to me during the past eight months. I also said:

> I completely forgot to mention Christmas, even though this should have been my Christmas letter, but our thoughts are so little oriented toward it that we wish we could cancel Christmas for this year.

Other great news came some two months later from home. My parents received the first news from my brother Uli on February 9. He was alive and in Russian captivity.

A few weeks later, on March 23, I received my first package from home. I wrote in my return letter that the package contained everything a prisoner could wish for: goodies found in times of peace. In addition to Christmas cookies and quinces, the package contained necessities like pencils, a comb, and toothpowder. The next letter from home brought the fabulous news that my older brother Volker returned home on April 9 from British captivity. He was luckier than Uli and I. He had been assigned to take care of the horses of a British officer. As such, he was well fed and had a fair amount of freedom. On the day I received the news of his release, I also received a package from one of my cousins. I began my letter home on that day with the words "how happy one can be."

Exchanging news from home among the prisoners was an important source of information, and not always without humor. One prisoner received a letter from his wife who complained that he was still away, writing, "All the Nazi pigs are home, only you are still missing."

The wife of another prisoner reported that, right at the beginning of the occupation, the GIs put up a sign in town, which said, "We are not Amis, we are Americans." The letter reports that the next day there was a new sign "We are not Nazis, we are National Socialists." Even today, Germans still often refer to Americans as "Amis"—without implying that it has any connection with the French word ami, meaning "friend."

Young German women who associated with American GIs after the war ended were referred to as Ami-liebchen, which means "Ami sweethearts," but was used as a slightly derogatory term. Many young single women were attracted to foreign soldiers, and numerous enduring relationships were formed. These women also enjoyed certain material benefits in those days of hardship and were often impressed by hearing that their American friend owned a house back in the States.

Lumberjack in Le Val d'Ajol

Le Val d'Ajol is a nice little town in the beautiful surroundings of the Vosges mountains, but I did not recognize its beauty until I visited it fifty-five years later. While I was a prisoner, its little church, which I compared with the church of Heilbronn, inspired me to make a picture frame with a little wood carving of the two churches. Later, while still in Le Val d'Ajol, one of my fellow prisoners, who had an aunt in French Strasbourg who'd agreed to send mail to our families, offered to forward her a small package on my behalf. To safeguard my piece of art, I sent it to her, but it never made it home. I still have the sketch I made for my woodcarving.

I remember our daily tedious marches in the morning to go to work in the woods, starting our hard labor in inadequate physical condition. Today, I still have occasional dreams of trying to walk with my feet and knees too weak to hold me up; I am sure these dreams go back to those mornings as a lumberjack prisoner.

With time, I became more skilled in cutting trees and splitting logs with a sledgehammer and wedges. We had no motorized saws or wood splitters. All the work was done the old-fashioned way. To make work a little bit more interesting, I began to challenge myself to fell a tree in a very precise direction, whether the tree was nice and straight or crooked. By putting some logs at precisely the spot where I expected the tree to come down later, I could make the subsequent cutting up easier. I could not have imagined that exactly on the fifty-ninth anniversary of the day I had been taken prisoner, I would be in the United States, using my old skills to fell and cut up two large trees near my house together with my wife, using a manual two-person saw for the first cut to warrant precision. The rest of the work was, of course, done with a chain saw.

The shoes that I brought into captivity quickly disintegrated. What I got to replace them were sabots, wooden shoes similar to those you see today in Holland, usually as part of local costumes worn for tourists. It was quite difficult to work on the uneven ground in the forest with such shoes, not the least because of the problems I was still experiencing with my right foot. Our clothing was not in much better shape during the first six months of captivity. I had to begin adding patches over the holes in my pants. Not having any regular sewing needles at the time, I sewed on the first patches with a homemade approximation of a needle. I made it with a small sliver of sheet metal from a food can that I cut to shape and added a slit. When we received some replacement clothing at the end of the year, I counted the number of patches I had on my pants: forty-nine.

Our daily norm that we had to fulfill was one *stère* (cubic meter) of piled split wood (30 percent more than a cubic yard).

Depending on how easy it was to split the trees, this could be accomplished in a day, especially as we gained experience.

In France, as it is in many other European countries, the forests are usually government property. A forester, who is a government employee, is responsible for the upkeep of the forests, which includes optimizing their growth and appearance and eliminating unhealthy trees. Most of the forests in Western Europe therefore look like wooded parks. Even though our formal reason for being assigned forestry work as prisoners was to eliminate damaged trees from the war, we simply had to cut all the trees that the forester selected, of which very few showed war damage. The forester marked the base of those trees below the cut line with a hatchet that had an embossed seal on one side.

Sometimes when we were short of meeting our quota toward the end of the day and none of the guards were close by, we would pick a particularly nice tree that was easy to cut and mark it in a similar way as the forester, smearing dirt over it so as not to conceal that it had not been marked with the proper seal. Then we worked as fast as we could to take the tree down and complete our quota. We called it "Revenge for the Black Forest" in reference to what some of us heard from home—that many sections of the Black Forest, which had become part of the French zone of occupation, had been clear-cut.

After we fulfilled our quota, we sometimes had a chance to find and pick some blueberries. Sometimes we also took dandelions home, which made good salads.

Going home from work was, of course, the best time of the day. We would see people in the street on our walk back to camp. Our guards would talk to them, which was particularly interesting for me since I was eager to pick up as much French as I could. Much later I could still remember a French word or expression I'd heard for the first time in the streets of Le Val d'Ajol. Unfortunately I did not have a dictionary at the time.

As we marched back to our quarters, the sight that struck us the most were the local people riding home on their bicycles from the bakery, one or two baguettes clamped onto their bicycle luggage carrier. One end of the bread was usually broken off as a sampling. How we envied them!

Since we were a relatively small group with only about five guards, we got to know each other somewhat well, fellow prisoners and guards. The "everyone for himself" mentality among us prisoners was no longer dominant. We began to talk about our backgrounds. The guards called us by our first names, but we knew only their last names. When the guards were not listening, we used nicknames. The head guard was the "Slave Holder." Most of the guards had been POWs in Germany and knew a bit of German.

One of my better friends in the group was a young dental assistant apprentice. He told us a detailed description of how his boss's wife seduced him. Talking about sex was quite common among prisoners. Even in the mass POW camps during the prior year, sex was, on par with food, conversational topic number one—it is what you desire, but don't have. My brother later corroborated the popularity of sex as a topic from his experience in the Russian prison camp.

We were severely undernourished and overworked, yet we still enjoyed an occasional special treat, thanks to the local residents. Some of the civilians in the small town would sometimes ask for one or two prisoners to work for them at their home on Sundays. I believe that many of them did so primarily to get us out of our confinement for a day, with the work to be done viewed as a secondary advantage, or even excuse, for them. Out of gratitude, we worked as hard as we could, sometimes to the effect that our hosts ran out of work for us to do. They all rewarded us with a Sunday meal that was beyond the wildest dreams of a prisoner. On that day in December, when I received my first letter from home in the evening, I had just been given a five-course dinner.

While enjoying one of those Sunday dinners, I noticed something that was strange to me: the husband made the coffee. I never had seen my father doing anything related to food or kitchen work, including making coffee. How times have changed!

I remember in particular being invited with a fellow prisoner to the house of Sage-femme Bernard, the midwife of the town. Her husband had died. She introduced us as soldiers to her daughter (which of course made sense, but it made us feel human for the first time in awhile). Maybe in today's terms her meal—complete with soup, meat, vegetables, and dessert—was not unusual, but for us at the time, it felt like a wedding feast. Of course, wine was also part of the meal. We were surprised, however, when on this, as on similar occasions, the children were also given wine mixed with water. In France, the amount of wine gradually increased with age, beginning with just a taste, maybe one tenth, for the youngest children.

Some thirty years later I visited Le Val d'Ajol on a vacation and asked in town for Sage-femme Bernard, only to hear that she had died. I had been looking forward to seeing her again and regretted not having visited the town many years earlier.

After about seven months in Le Val d'Ajol, our guards came with news from above that they no longer wanted us to work on Sundays for local families since it would drain our energy, and take away from our regular work. We tried to convince them that we drew more mental and physical energy from these Sundays than we lost from the work there. Subsequently, our guards either condoned our Sunday work or did not let their superiors know.

One day I was cutting trees with a fellow prisoner. Our next task was to fell a tree that was half dead and not very tall. I was examining the direction I wanted to fell it, when we were called for our lunch break. During lunch I had occasion to talk with a Frenchman who came with his truck to pick up wood. He had been a prisoner of war in Germany. I thoroughly enjoyed the conversation with him. I don't remember if we agreed on all aspects of our discussion, but I found him to be a very likeable person.

After lunch we went back to our tree. I was beginning to position our large two-person saw in the direction I had in mind for felling the tree, when my partner pulled the saw about forty-five degrees to the left, in order to fell the tree straight down the slope. I looked up the tree from where I was and saw that it was not very tall—why not fell it in that direction? As the tree started to fall, I realized it was taller than we had envisioned. It headed straight for the Frenchman's truck, on which he stood talking to our guard. As it came down, some of its top branches barely brushed the truck. The Frenchman had to jump down from his truck. I could have crawled into a hole, but continued my work and did not look in his direction.

I was later told that the man thought that I had done this on purpose. He had reached for the guard's rifle, but the guard did not let him have it. I was shocked. It took me some time to realize how this misjudgment of the tree happened. In hindsight I think I should have walked down, explain the mistake, and apologized. As a prisoner, I felt I had no rights and any explanation would have only made things worse.

One of my fellow prisoners had another notable event. He once killed a dog and cooked it. From then on we called him Dog Butcher. The guards never heard about this. A few weeks later, as we were working in a different section of the forest, a dog appeared. Dog Butcher got a piece of tree branch and positioned himself behind a tree, ready for the kill. The dog approached him, but suddenly changed direction and moved toward one of our guards to greet him. It turned out that it was the dog of the guard who lived quite close to where we worked.

On another day we experienced a tragic event, which affected us deeply. One of our fellow prisoners was cutting a tree, when a branch, fairly high in the tree and about four inches thick, broke off and hit his skull. After about ten minutes he died. We all were in shock. We did not consider our work dangerous. The end of the war with its terror of death lay far behind us. We had survived and thought that it would only be a matter of months until we would be home again.

Our most pleasurable times, apart from our work for, and meals with, a family in town, were Sunday afternoons. We would gather on the front steps of the mill and enjoy the sun and the view of the town and the surrounding mountains. In a mix of broken French on the part of my fellow prisoners, and broken German on the part of our guards, we had time and opportunity to talk. The conversations often centered around the prediction that we would be sent home in just a few months—not knowing that it would take more than two years. As the Frenchmen were talking about their new fellowship organization of the *ancien combattants*, or "war veterans," they assured us that we would be similarly celebrated and would receive our medals when we returned home from captivity. Of course, there would be no such thing; everyone in Germany wanted to treat the past, including military service and especially political events, as if it had never existed.

The key political issues and concerns that our French guards talked to us about were the Communist threat and *la bombe atomique*, the new atomic bomb. Some of them explained their prediction to us: we prisoners would soon join the French soldiers in fighting the Russians together.

When France began to release its first prisoners in 1946, some of the German prisoners received priority because they could provide documents showing that their families had treated their French prisoners, who had worked for them during the war, particularly well. Our guards began talking about getting such documents from us, in case it might be useful in the next war. Why our guards had chosen to become civilian guards of German POWs never became very clear to us. Probably it was easy money.

New Kommando: Cornimont (April 30, 1946– August 2, 1946)

After nine months in our woodcutting Kommando in Le Val d'Ajol, we were transported some twenty-five miles away to a new Kommando in the small town of Cornimont. The work was to be the same, though this time in pine forests. The food was significantly worse, which we had not thought was possible. Despite my hunger, I could barely eat the food on the first day. It took me a few days to reach the point where I could even ask for an extra scoop, when available. Now it was almost nothing but fodder beets—and no noodles or sausage on Sundays.

We were a much larger group of prisoners than in Le Val d'Ajol, and slept on the floor of a former factory. In my first letter home I wrote:

> While I enjoyed receiving a package from home so much before, I am almost asking you now to send me something nourishing, provided you can spare it. Some spices would also be welcome to add some taste to our food. We also expect to re-encounter problems with lice.

We were worried about our survival. I also asked my family to send some medication to fight against the diarrhea that many of us were suffering from. Shortly after my parents responded that they would soon send me a few things, I wrote to them that I was embarrassed to have asked for those things and that I had hoped my letter would get lost, considering the dire situation they were in themselves at home.

In my first letter from the new assignment in Cornimont, I also let my parents know which town I was in, even though we were not allowed to disclose that information in our letters. When my oldest brother left home for the war, we agreed on a secret family code. The first characters of every sentence, beginning with the second paragraph, would spell a message. And as a signal that the letter contained such a coded message, a person named Michael would be mentioned somewhere in the letter. It was a name that did not occur within our family or among our friends. So using that code, I sent them the message "Cornimont."

Those of us who had come from the Kommando in Le Val d'Ajol wished we were still there. Everything was worse: the food, the sleeping quarters, our relationship with the guards, and the work in the woods. A few times we were able to work on Sundays for some local people, but only in the beginning. One of my packages from home contained writing paper and candles; they were confiscated. Normally, the packages I received during my captivity contained things like dried fruit, biscuits, oatmeal, bouillon cubes, jam, pudding powder, and raisins. My cousin Dorothee Jäger worked in a pharmacy and several times she sent me a package with vitamins, like Dextro Energen, and other welcome food supplements. I had one good friend with whom I shared some of the treasures we received from home. But otherwise, everybody was back to looking out only for himself.

Quite often a Frenchman would tell us about executions of civilians that the SS carried out in the nearby town of Gérardmer. We felt that the story, while true and describing a horrible crime, was again used to justify our treatment. Several weeks after our arrival, we were moved to a small farmhouse a mile east of the town. Things got worse. Some prisoners were hit occasionally, not in a brutal fashion, but nevertheless in violation of the Geneva Conventions.

From other prisoners in the base camp, we had heard that some prisoners had been sent home for health reasons. One prisoner was sent home for having an edema in his leg. In response, we all experimented with eating spoonfuls of salt, trying to generate our own edemas. Salt in such quantities is not only dangerous, but tastes awful.

Another trick we used was to pulverize aspirin and roll it into cigarette tobacco. It was supposed to generate symptoms of heart problems. I tried it once before going to a doctor, since my malnutrition had gotten so bad that my weight went down to 50 kilograms, or 110 pounds, which was not much for my five-feet-six-inch frame. The doctor signed papers saying that I was unable to work and I was supposed to be taken back to base camp. It did not happen.

One time, we were marching along the road to work when a huge American-made car passed us and then stopped. I had never seen one of these cars before, which Germans later nicknamed "street cruisers." The license plate said "Geneva, Red Cross." A well-dressed gentleman stepped out and asked if any of us spoke French. Since none of the other thirty prisoners responded initially, I said I could speak some French. I told the Red Cross representative about our situation, about the dismal food and hard work, about the occasional beatings, and about being declared sick and forced to work, instead of being sent back to base camp. Our guard received instructions from the Red Cross representative, which I did not really understand.

The same night I was transferred to another prisoner unit on top of the mountain. It was set up specifically for SS prisoners of war. Of course, their conditions were even worse than ours down in the valley. The next day a guard took me to the doctor. I had smoked an aspirin-laced cigarette before leaving for the doctor's office, and in the waiting room I held my breath several times as long as I could. By the time I saw the doctor, my heart was beating fast. Upon seeing my general condition, the doctor signed the papers saying that he declared me as unable to work and that I was to be sent back to the base camp. The guard indicated to me afterward that he had received instructions from his superiors to tell the doctor that he must declare me fit for work. His instructions, which he might not even have relayed to the doctor, were overruled.

And so I was taken back to Pouxeux the next day.

Back to Base Camp (August 2, 1946–around October 26, 1946)

It was good to be back in base camp. The situation there had gotten a bit better since a year ago. On the one hand, I enjoyed not having to work. On the other, I was closer to the source of information and gossip and soon realized that my dream of being home before the end of the year would not come true.

One week after my arrival in Pouxeux, our march from Épinal to Pouxeux, which had brought us into French captivity a year earlier, was repeated in the reverse direction. Unfortunately, this time we did not move back into American custody. The Americans had given the Épinal barracks back to the French. On our return trip, the little bit of baggage that we had accumulated was carried for us. We moved back into the same barracks.

I met many friends. One of them was Dagobert Wissmann, who was from my high school class and dance course. Like many other prisoners, he had been an American POW in the United States, received his discharge papers, and, during his transit through France, was transferred to the French.

Another prisoner, a barber from our hometown, told me that he had been in Russia with my brother Uli, whose hair he once cut. When their battalion was encircled, my brother organized ten people to try to cut through the Russian lines. The barber was one of three who succeeded. He told me he never heard about the others. It was a few days later that Uli was taken prisoner. Realizing that he would be captured, Uli tried to shoot himself. His gun would not fire and a Russian solder said to him in broken German "Du jung, du verrückt," which means "You young, you crazy."

Within a month of returning to Épinal, I had recovered noticeably from my malnutrition. A medical examination revealed no specific health problems; my chances of being liberated as "unable to work" had dissipated.

During one of my earlier assignments, a fellow prisoner gave me a valuable present: an old, beaten-up French dictionary. Whenever I heard a new French word during the day, I would try to remember it and look it up in the dictionary in the evening. This dictionary became my most valuable possession and was my key to learning French. It was not only responsible for significantly improving my French in captivity, but it continues to serve me well up to this day. Encouraged that my French was getting better, I signed up to be available as an interpreter. That meant that I would not be sent to an outside Kommando, but would possibly be used inside the camp whenever knowledge of French was needed. Several prisoners that had been assigned to work in the administration of the camp were sent home for health reasons, which made their positions available.

I was assigned to work occasionally in the accounting office and later as an assistant to the principal camp interpreter. We were located in the guardroom at the entrance to the barracks, where I later even slept. Along with the job, I received better food, just like all of the prisoners who belonged to the staff, or cadre.

A few other little perks came along with my position. Once, I was allowed to go into town with a guard and I bought myself a watch in a watch store. While I was inside, the guard, a Moroccan soldier, stayed outside. He told me afterward that I was more respected and accepted in the store as a prisoner than he was as a black Moroccan soldier in the French army. Whether this was true or just a perception, I could not tell.

Unfortunately, my "dream job" would not last for very long. Word came from Paris that sergeants and higher ranks could no longer be sent to outside work. Hence, they were utilized in the staff functions, and prisoners of lower rank had to make room for them.

Kommando: Raon L'Étape (around October 26, 1946–May 17, 1947)

After only six weeks at my new staff job, I was sent on my next outside Kommando. I had wished to at least receive an assignment with a family or a small private company, which, among other advantages, would have helped improve my French. In October 1946, I arrived, together with other prisoners, in the little town of Raon L'Étape. Our employer was the township. Our unit consisted of only twenty prisoners, but we were housed together with several other units in an old factory, which had been used before as a dance hall. It looked more like the former than the latter. After six weeks of various tasks, primarily splitting wood, I was back in the forest, playing lumberjack. It was winter again. Fortunately, our clothing situation had improved, and so had the food.

By now, my knowledge of French had improved somewhat beyond my original high-school level. My new dictionary was an invaluable asset. I, and a few others who knew some French, had great fun hearing one of our fellow prisoners, who was considered the official interpreter by our guards, conversing with them. His French sounded fluent, but his grammar left much to be desired. Knowing that the words *de, le,* and *la* had a high occurrence in the French language, he more or less randomly sprinkled them into his sentences. He'd say something like

"Vous cherchez lettres de la de poste la?" instead of something like "Est-ce que vous avez cherché nos lettres à la poste?" when asking the guards if they'd gotten our letters from the post office. As we walked to work, our guards also took advantage of his knowledge of French by intensively questioning him about his sexual practices at home, which was a true eye-opener, or rather "ear-opener," for me and the other young prisoners.

In reading through the letters that I wrote to my parents now, it appears that half of the space in my letters was dedicated to responding to the mail I had received, including the many packages my parents sent me. I wrote relatively little about our work and about myself. A big joy came in the form of a photo that my brother sent home from Russia. He looked quite well in it. I began to tell my parents to stop sending packages since we had enough to eat, at least quantitatively. The news about the condition back home in Germany was anything but good. The situation was even worse than it was during the war. The shortage of food was extreme. I still don't know how my parents got all the goodies together that they sent me in captivity. Clothing and coal for heating was as scarce as food, and money was of less value than bartered goods.

On March 28 I wrote to my parents:

> I became rich all of a sudden. I received your huge package, which reached perhaps the limits of earthly things. Further-more, I received a colis américain (an American package) from Aunt Junia with fantastic canned meat, cocoa, chocolate cookies, real honey, a shirt (almost too good for a POW), and a package of Chesterfield cigarettes, for which many people are approaching me.

Aunt Junia was a former friend of my mother from the teachers' seminary, who emigrated from Germany to the United States and lived in Springfield, New Jersey. I used the cigarettes, which I did not smoke, wisely. Cigarettes were the best currency, both in the prison camps and at home. For one cigarette, I got an extra form that we needed to write our letters on. On Easter, I bartered two cigarettes for an Easter egg. Later, I got two more packages from her. One came just in time for Christmas; it was the best Christmas present I could think of.

My parents asked if I had an opportunity to learn or somehow advance my education while in the camp. I said that I did not get to learn actively, but rather passively, by reading newspapers when I had a chance or translating for others. It was not like sitting down with pencil and paper to study formally, since there was no time for that. I was too tired in the evening to study, since every other night it was my turn to do kitchen duty.

By April, many rumors had started about a program to release the prisoners from France, but nothing actually happened. In one of my letters, I asked my parents, through our family letter code, whether they thought it was a good idea for me to attempt to flee. They were upset and answered back that I should erase any thoughts along those lines.

In fact, many prisoners tried to escape, but the chances for success were very small; perhaps one in twenty or fifty made it. Crossing the Rhine River was one of the main problems. Many drowned in the attempt and some were shot. The French government established a reward of 1,500 francs for catching an escaping German prisoner. Many young Frenchmen found themselves in a new well-paying occupation by getting a rifle and patrolling the banks of the Rhine, hoping to catch prisoners. The caught prisoners were sent back to their base camp where they received the standard punishment of having their heads shaved and spending thirty days in the prison camp's jail.

My parents told me in one of their letters that a family friend, who owned a retail and repair shop for electrical household goods, received a radio to repair from the city's American commander. Inside the radio, he found a sticker with my father's name on it. It was obvious that this was our radio, which had been confiscated from our home at the beginning of the occupation. The repair shop contacted the commander, and to the great surprise of my parents, the commander returned the radio a few months later.

Another problem had developed for me while in the prison camp: a toothache. I applied to the dépôt, my base camp, to use the money that had accumulated in my prisoner account from the daily allocations to have my teeth fixed. A couple of weeks later, the approval came. I could go to the dentist. By the time I saw him, it was too late for one of my two troubling teeth; it had to be pulled. The other one needed a root canal. My Saturday visits to the dentist became a highlight of my stay in Raon L'Étape. The dentist treated me like a human being and the receptionist was, in my eyes, the most beautiful creature I had seen in many years. My fear of going to the dentist, that I had in prior years, was more than gone. I looked forward to going back to have a crown fit on the tooth and was sorry when the treatment was finished. The bill was 1,000 francs, which I paid for using my account—nine months of work for a pulled tooth and a root canal. The treatment was finished just in time before the assignment in Raon L'Étape came to an end.

In my last letter from the Kommando, I reported home that my weight had gone up to 65 kilograms (145 pounds) from the earlier 50 kilograms (110 pounds). I forbade my parents to send me any more packages, especially when they needed everything badly at home for themselves; whereupon my mother wrote back and told me I could not forbid them to do something like that.

While in Raon L'Étape, I briefly established written contact with the former mayor and the deputy mayor of Heilbronn, who were in a nearby officers' prison camp. According to the

Geneva Conventions, officers could not be forced to work. As a result, they were worse off than we were in 1947. They still had not given up the old camp mentality from the early months of captivity; many officers walked around all day with pot and spoon, in the hope of getting something to eat somewhere. This was quite different for my brother Uli in Russia, who, as a former officer, went on work assignments. In general, the Russians treated officer prisoners significantly better than non-officer prisoners; allowing them to work was a benefit rather than a disadvantage.

However, the German officers in French officers' camps—and those in Russian camps, as my brother later reported—had one advantage over us. Their large and well-educated group represented a significant resource for intelligence and knowledge. They were given the time and facility to organize series of lectures, courses in many fields (some of which approached the level of university courses), as well as other cultural stimulation.

Épinal (May 17, 1947)

On May 17, two days before my twenty-first birthday, I was back in the base camp at Épinal. Again, I was glad to see some old friends and hoped that my next Kommando would be a good one. The topic of being liberated was at the top of everybody's mind and at the tip of their tongues. During this time, every prisoner received a form from the French, offering a contract as a *travailleur libre*, "a civilian worker" in France, for the duration of one year. It certainly was better than the offer we had received two years earlier to join the French foreign legion for five years. A fair number of prisoners signed up for the new program. Their motivation was probably not so much the hope of coming home sooner—even though that would have been true in the end for young unmarried prisoners like myself—but the thought that life in Germany after liberation would be more miserable than working in France as a civilian. Some planned on supporting their families from France.

Most of us interpreted the French offer as a sign that the prisoner release might be happening soon. And indeed, the French set up the first ten categories for liberation. Category 1 was for those persecuted by the Nazi regime. This was followed by categories for the elderly and for prisoners with many children. Five additional categories were established a year later, with young bachelors like myself in the last category, category 15.

One day, one of our fellow prisoners told us that he was liberated in 1945 from the Dachau concentration camp, to return to his home in the French zone of occupation. Shortly thereafter, he was picked up, and, being young and healthy, sent to France as a prisoner of war. When the liberation categories were announced, he asked for an audience with the French discipline officer in our camp, and requested to be assigned to category 1. The French officer asked him why he was in Dachau and he said that it was for homosexuality. The officer told him that homosexuality was also punishable in France, and sent him out the door.

I was barely a week in the camp when I had a new job. I became a waiter in the cafeteria for our French guard troops. My customers were those with the rank of sergeant, most of whom were Tunisian or Moroccan. I found that the most difficult part of my job was remembering who wanted what at any given moment, since each person came on his own time. For years to come, this experience gave me an appreciation for the job of a waiter.

While waiting tables, I noticed with amusement that the plates of the Tunisian and Moroccan soldiers were usually black with pepper before I even brought them their meal; hence, the pepper shaker needed constant refilling. Some of the Tunisian soldiers, who on average were lighter skinned than the Moroccans, were well educated. I had some very interesting conversations with some of them—about their status in France, about war and peace, and about our prison camp. Both the Moroccans and the Tunisians said they felt like second-class citizens.

As a waiter, my bedroom was in the cafeteria building, which was outside the inner barbed wire that surrounded the regular prisoners, but within the outer walls of the barracks.

While there, I also met a civilian who worked in the camp and told me I should always let him know if I needed anything. He had been a German POW in southern Germany. Throughout my years in France, I found that many Frenchmen who had been German prisoners of war showed a strong empathy toward us and treated us particularly well. They could understand our situation and had learned to distinguish between a regime, or system, and an individual human being.

The French were very accommodating for their troops, including the Moroccan and Tunisian soldiers. They established a bordello, and the ladies of the night—and day—lived within the barrack compound.

The release of prisoners according to the new categories had a very slow beginning. The United States had told the world that they had no more prisoners and asked the British, the French, and the Russians to release their prisoners too. The fact that we were originally American POWs was forgotten.

I sent an apology home to my mother for having forgotten to send a Mother's Day greeting in my prior letter, but followed it with the words that, for a prisoner, every day is Mother's Day. Apart from the freedom I still lacked, I was finally well fed and got some more clothing; most of it was American. I was happy to write home the good news.

We played Ping-Pong on a makeshift table; however our games were cancelled after a few weeks since they gave the impression that we were leading too good a life as POWs.

After five weeks in the waiter business, I lost my job. The two head cooks were fired because the salad was not up to par. They were downgraded to waiters and had priority over me since I was not officially part of the prison camp staff. When some French officers heard about this a few days later, they told me they would get me back and intervened on my behalf.

In the mean time, I was fortunate enough to get an assignment in *la comptabilité* (the financial office). Together with three other POWs and two Frenchmen, I worked on the prisoners' accounts, administrating the five francs that the prisoners' employers had to pay those working for them as a daily salary. The French government paid another five francs to each prisoner every day. As a comparison, a domestic postage stamp at the time was about eighteen francs and the exchange rate with U.S. currency was about one cent per franc. A lot of work was to be done in the accounting office, especially since many prisoners were to be released after having signed up as free workers. I was happy with my new job and no longer pushed for getting back into the mess hall.

One day, as I was walking through the camp, a French sergeant, who knew me from my time as a waiter, asked me to come to his room. There, he had a quarter loaf of bread on his table and said to me, "Si tu marches, je te donne ce bout de pain" (If you play along, I will give you this piece of bread). I was no longer starved and thus had no idea why he offered me bread. He would not say much to enlighten me, but repeated his offer several times. It took me probably five minutes until I realized it was a sexual offer. So I said to him "C'est une saloperie" (That is a dirty thing), whereupon he let me go. I did not know whether there was anything I should have done about it. I felt that, as a prisoner, I had no rights and I did not think of telling anybody about it, let alone denouncing the Frenchman to his superiors. It would have been his word against mine.

A few days later, I happened to be at the front entry gate to the barracks, where I'd had a job during my prior stay in Épinal. The discipline officer of the camp brought two German prisoners to my former boss, who had a key position in the camp, and said in somewhat broken German, "Diese Mann sind wie keine Mann, diese Mann sind wie eine Frau," which translates literally as, "These man are like no man, these man are like a woman," to which the officer added, "Heads shaved, thirty days jail." He indicated that he had found the two prisoners with the same sergeant that had approached me, and then turned around and left. I told my ex-boss that I had received a similar offer from the sergeant a few days before. He said I should have told him about it. I never found out what the punishment for the Frenchman was.

Three days later I was notified that I would be transferred. I assumed this to be a consequence of the happenings with the French sergeant, and that the discipline officer who was informed by my ex-boss did not believe my innocence and wanted to punish me; therefore, I asked to see the French commander of the camp. I told him that I could not understand why I would be punished for something that I did not do. Without going into details, he told me to see the discipline officer. I did not go since I assumed that it was the discipline officer who wanted my transfer in the first place. Very likely, however, my transfer was not even related to that event. I had applied earlier for a very desirable Kommando and was now offered a transfer to a different prison camp instead, further north in France, in Lorraine. The function of that camp was to assemble the various transports of prisoners who were being sent home according to their respective categories.

Sarralbe (July 31, 1947)

In the last days of July 1947, I was one of forty prisoners sent from various camps throughout France to join the staff of Dépôt de prisonniers de guerre 2101 in Sarralbe, located in the Lorraine region. Six of us came from Épinal.

Together with Alsace, Lorraine had a mixed history. Beginning in the ninth century, they had been part of the German empire. In the seventeenth century, they were occupied by the French. From 1871 to 1918 they were German again, and, through the Treaty of Versailles, they became French again in 1919. When Hitler occupied France, he considered Alsace and Lorraine part of Germany, but at the end of WWII, they returned back to France. Throughout history, the people there have spoken a German dialect. But like the Swiss, the locals would not call their dialect German but rather Alsatian, Lorraine, or Swiss German, respectively. Using a little bit of exaggeration, I keep telling people that if you address an Alsatian in German, he or she will answer in French, to show you that he or she are not German. If you address them in French, their answer will be in their German dialect to show their fellow Frenchmen they are special. Today, the use of the German dialect is diminishing; it is primarily spoken by the older generation. My view of the cultures of Alsace and Lorraine is that they combine the best of both countries: German neatness and diligence with French *savoir vivre*. Politically, both the Alsatians and the people from Lorraine clearly consider themselves French today.

In Sarralbe, we were to replace the prisoners who had been liberated or who were about to be liberated. A need existed in the camp for people who knew French. My French was not what you could call fluent, let alone perfect, but very few prisoners had a reasonable knowledge of the language. Throughout my captivity, I had always been surrounded by fellow prisoners and never lived in a French-speaking environment. But, at least, I tried to learn as much as possible, even if it was only from listening to the guards talking to each other. Except for our French boss, even in the new environment in Sarralbe, I was still surrounded by German-speaking prisoners. All the paperwork that had to be done in my new assignment was in French, which provided a new challenge and intellectual stimulation. For the first two days I was in the filing office, but was then assigned to the head financial office. Our boss, Émile Paine, a French warrant officer, was a friendly and gentle man. You could not have wanted a nicer boss; we never heard a harsh word from him. His own office was right next to ours.

On the prisoner side, the financial office consisted of about twenty men. The German head of the finance department, Albert Schambach, and I had oversight responsibilities and a series of additional tasks. These included managing cash flow, conversions between prisoner money and the official French currency, prisoner head counts, military head counts, military and sanitary personnel salaries, the finances of the prisoner shop (including payment of bills), and the administration of soap and tobacco. The bulk of the work of the people reporting to us concerned the files of the prisoners that came through our camp, especially the administration of their personal accounts that grew out of the ten francs they earned per day. A French civilian later joined our French boss. One of his main duties was to sign the many papers required by the paper bureaucracy, which we as prisoners could not sign. We were not as lucky as our fellow prisoners in the personnel department, who had a beautiful, young French secretary working with them in their office, which was a new sight for all of us.

One benefit for us in the head financial office was that we were the place where prisoner money (small bills denominated in French francs) could be exchanged for commercial francs, and vice versa, since both forms of money were needed in the management of the camp. You could often see us on the floor counting millions of francs in prisoner money or in regular French money. The regular French money was needed especially by the German kitchen heads and the prisoner store for outside purchases. Prisoners in general were only allowed to possess prisoner money. With our access to French money, we could also help many friends acquire things on the outside that were not available in the prisoner store, usually by asking the head of the store to purchase the items.

Another very useful duty for us in the financial office was the distribution of cigarettes. Every prisoner now received eighty cigarettes a month, instead of the previously allotted twenty. The cigarette was a military cigarette, called La Troupe. We jokingly described it ironically as "La Troupe, la meilleure des cigarettes" (The Troupe, the best of all cigarettes). Paris set up a system for all prison camps in France wherein each camp could base the order of their monthly tobacco allocation on one day of their choosing between the twentieth and the twenty-sixth of each month. For a normal camp, the fluctuation between those days was minimal. Since our camp was a transit camp for prisoners who stayed for only a few days before leaving for home, we had a few thousand prisoners one day and possibly only a hundred a few days later. We always found a high occupancy day within Paris's span of dates to order our allocation. As a result, we always had plenty of cigarettes in the closet of our office. Our boss, Messieur Paine, relinquished the administration of the cigarettes to us in order to avoid any conflicts of conscience that might arise if he took prisoner cigarettes for himself. He knew that he could always get enough for his personal use by asking us. Even the commander of the prison camp regularly came to one of the two of us and asked if we had cigarettes left for him, which of course we always did. As for myself, I rarely ever smoked. Whenever I had a chance to get cigarettes before, during my captivity, I would trade them for something that I felt was more important.

In contrast to my early years of captivity, an excellent camaraderie existed among the people on the staff. Albert Schambach, with whom I shared our sleeping quarters, was a very nice and modest man. Before being drafted, he worked in the social offices of the city of Trier and had reached a fairly high level in the Hitler Youth. He was fourteen years my senior and still a bachelor. Schwemm, as we called him, often asked me if I thought he was too old to marry. He once told me a story about a woman whom he took for a walk in the woods, which resembled the joke in which a woman on a bicycle says to a man, "Now you can have anything you want from me," and the man takes her bike. At one point, Schwemm's female companion told him he could have anything he wanted from her. Probably scared by his lack of experience with women, he said, "Let's go home" (meaning, in those days, you to your home, and I to mine.) They parted ways and he regretted it ever since. I had the impression that this encounter was not followed by many other similar "opportunities" before the war took over his life.

Schwemm and I had living quarters very close to our office. Later on, we set up our room in the office itself, separating it from the working section with a curtain. As time progressed, we decorated it like a little studio. We had a number of craftspeople on the camp staff, many of whom, like the carpenters, plumbers, or tailors, were not only doing upkeep work in the camp, but were also doing small favors for the French staff. As we supplied these staff prisoners with cigarettes, or helped them obtain real money to buy needed things on the outside, some opportunities opened up for us, too. The carpenters, for example, built some simple, but nice, furniture for our studio room.

As far as food was concerned, I had no reason to complain. I wrote home that we had meat with almost every meal, even though it was frequently horsemeat. After years of malnourishment, I began to look almost unhealthily healthy, with puffy cheeks. This, however, was a symptom of the sudden transition from malnourishment to eating well. In addition to the food in the camp, our French boss and the other Frenchmen on staff occasionally invited us to their homes for a pleasant Sunday for *un repas de première classe* (a first-class meal). I described one such dinner in a letter home: "It was like a wedding dinner."

We also enjoyed being treated by the French people around us as human beings, which usually included being addressed with the formal "vous," instead of the informal "tu" or "toi" which signify familiarity and closeness, but can also imply superiority or disrespect. Occasionally, we were allowed to leave the camp for a walk or swim in the Saar River, first with a guard and later, on certain occasions, with just a special pass. The locals called the military beach, which had been built by the Americans, the "Hollywood Beach." I am certain that by today's health standards, swimming in the Saar in 1947 would not only be unadvisable, but would be outright forbidden, due to the severe contamination and pollution of the river at the time.

Our work kept us extremely busy, especially in the middle and at the end of the month, with the financial reports. Our work hours amounted to about seventy-five to eighty hours per week. It was our own decision to work so much, since the necessary work just had to be done—and it made our time in the camp fly faster.

The Sarralbe camp also offered some opportunities for entertainment. We could play Ping-Pong, buying the balls in the prisoner store with our prisoner money. The camp also showed a fair number of movies, and occasionally presented a theatre piece or concert.

Through our fellow prisoner, who was responsible for the prisoner store, we on the camp staff could occasionally get our hands on alcoholic beverages. One day, our craftspeople had a birthday celebration and asked me if I could provide some cigarettes. When I brought them a carton of La Troupe, they offered me Pernod—a strong anise-based aperitif and successor to absinthe,

the dangerous beverage outlawed in France in 1915—in a drinking glass. Obviously I drank too much. In the evening, a movie was shown in the camp. The film was *Dial M for Murder* with Grace Kelly. I woke up the next morning and said that I had really wanted to go and see that movie. My friends told me that I was indeed at the movie, but had slept peacefully through it. Not only did I sleep through the film, but I also was sick for twenty-four hours. It took me not just years, but decades, to try another sip of Pernod.

Being housed next to our office had other advantages. I could use the typewriter to write my letters home. I took the opportunity to learn ten-finger typing, a skill that comes in handy in today's computer age. I also started learning Russian; however, given the difficulty of learning a language strictly from a book, and since admittedly my interest in Russian was not particularly strong, I did not progress much beyond learning the Cyrillic alphabet.

Like the other prison camps I'd stayed at, the Sarralbe camp had an inner camp for the regular prisoners, separated by a barbed-wire fence from the outer section where the French soldiers lived and the offices were located. Another barbed-wire fence sealed the entire compound from the outside world. Sand fleas infested a few of the innermost buildings. In some instances, artificial puddles of water were created to keep them away from the sleeping quarters, with varying degrees of success.

In April of 1948, Schwemm reached his turn to be liberated on account of his age. I succeeded him as *chef de comptabilité*, German head of the financial office. This implied a fair amount of responsibility, especially due to the freedom our French head financial officer gave us. Now, the French commander had to come to me, a twenty-two-year-old prisoner, to ask for cigarettes.

One of the major benefits of being part of the administration was meeting many prisoners that were on their way home to my hometown. Whenever new people arrived, I looked through the list to find those who were to go to Heilbronn. During the three or four days they were in the camp, I looked after them. I would give them two cartons of cigarettes, one for themselves and one to be taken to my family back home, sometimes with other necessities like soap, detergent, or razor blades. Many of the latter items we could buy in the prisoner store. In Germany, money was considered of no value, until the currency reform of June 1948; hence, cigarettes represented the best substitute currency. Volker was the one to engage in the respective trades back in Heilbronn, using the goods I sent.

Having the returnees take letters to my family allowed me to write more frequently and more freely, even though the censorship of our regular letters was now significantly reduced, compared with the early days of captivity. Later, I even got our camp tailor to make me a suit from army fabrics, which I sent home through another prisoner, in preparation for my days of freedom.

Some of us prisoners in the financial administration established a very good and friendly relationship with a local Catholic priest, Franz Goldschmitt, who took on the pastoral care of the Catholic prisoner community. From December 1942 until the end of May 1945, he was imprisoned in the Dachau concentration camp. He had been arrested because he was too outspoken and rebellious against the German occupation while he was the representative of the bishop. Father Goldschmitt had written a book in German about his experiences in Dachau, entitled *Zeugen des Abendlandes* (Witnesses of the Western World).[2] He gave me a signed copy. My own summary of his book can be found in Appendix B.

We found a compassionate friend in Father Goldschmitt. I had the chance to visit him once at his home in the nearby town of Sarre-Union. He had asked me to take some pictures of his

---

2. Franz Goldschmitt, *Zeugen des Abendlandes* (Saarlouis, German: Felten Verlag, 1947).

sanctuary and make photographic reproductions of some paintings that he owned. He then lent me his camera so I could take pictures around our camp. He developed the films for me.

On my twenty-second birthday, to my big surprise, I was congratulated over the camp loudspeaker. The announcer said that they were trying to establish contact with my family through Radio Stuttgart in Germany. They then played the *Poet and Peasant* Overture by Franz von Suppé in my honor. This was followed by an audiotape in which my sister, Ursula, expressed her birthday wishes and reminisced about our youth. She had sent me the tape for my birthday. I was reluctant to let my friends borrow it, not knowing what they would do with it. I guess I was both pleased and embarrassed, especially since my sister spoke with an unmistakable Swabian accent. For the evening, my friends organized a special meal for me with pasta, meat, bread, and sardines, accompanied by wine and homemade egg liqueur.

News from Home

The transports of prisoners that were released from our camp to the Russian zone of occupation, which later became East Germany, were accompanied up to the border by one of our camp physicians. He arranged to bring back letters from our families that they had sent to a certain address in the border town; however, this arrangement ended in September 1948, when the doctor took advantage of his privileges and did not return. No successor was assigned. Fortunately, the possibility of sending uncensored letters home through liberated prisoners continued.

My parents told me in their letters about the progressing cleanup of my destroyed hometown, Heilbronn, and about the first signs of reconstruction. Starting with the end of the war, every citizen in the town had to do what was called an "honorary service for the reconstruction of the city," originally for several months. The citizen's regular employer was responsible for providing a leave with pay.

This work was very hard for my father, who was not used to physical labor. Following this reconstruction service, my father did various types of more or less strenuous work. Later, he was assigned to work in an office. Getting back into his teaching profession was a lengthy procedure. Practically all of the schools had been destroyed, and it took some time for the town to set up temporary schools. To be reinstalled as a teacher, my father also had to wait for his clearance from the denazification court. My parents received a card in the mail, addressed to me, to report for two weeks of reconstruction service in September 1947. It said to wear work clothes and to bring a mess kit with a spoon, since a warm meal was offered. After I returned home a year later, I was excused from the service due to my long captivity.

Some three years after the war, the food, heating, and clothing situation in Germany was still very dismal and not much better than it was during the later war years. In addition to this, coal and wood were extremely scarce and people huddled in one or two rooms during the cold winters. Only many years later could my parents switch over to gas heating and install a needed new heating system. Rationing of food and clothing continued after the war, as it had during. For example, a person could buy a new pair of shoes only every three to four years. There was even a wine allocation of one 0.75-liter bottle per year.

I was very surprised when my parents wrote me that they had begun to raise chickens. Not only was our house near the center of a city with only a small garden of less than a twentieth of an acre around it, but I could not imagine my parents, especially my father, raising chickens. Times had changed. My father gave each of the chickens a name and if one of them was ready for the dinner table, it was quite old.

My father was happy that he could resume his voluntary duties as a weather observer after his return to Heilbronn. For him it was both a duty and a hobby. In connection with it, my parents again became the proud owners of a telephone.

One of my fellow prisoners, who was also part of the prison camp staff and worked in the kitchen, was unusually overweight. Obviously, he must have had some good previous camp assignments. When he was released, he had a friend make him a backpack to hold some one hundred army ration cans of horsemeat in beef gravy. This was a favorite item to buy in the prisoner store. He wanted to make sure he would not starve when he got home. A few months later, he wrote to us to find out if it would be possible for us to help him find a position as a free worker in France, since he found the situation in Germany intolerable. He was living as a refugee in Germany and thus considered to be a second-class citizen in the eyes of many. He did not mention what role the food situation played in his plight.

My brother Volker and my sister Ursula tried to normalize their lives in Heilbronn and find enjoyment when and where they could. They started dating and dancing. I corresponded with them about the new radio music, which I could hear frequently over our camp speakers. I wrote to them, "We are hearing much good music in the camp, but we don't hear as much of the new 'negro music,' which has not much to do with the pop music that we liked as teenagers." I mentioned boogie-woogie as an example of the bad dance music (not knowing that I would later love to dance the boogie-woogie, or jitterbug, and even win first place in a dance contest forty-five years later while dancing with my youngest daughter on a vacation).

Money was not a desirable commodity; merchants were not interested in selling their goods for money. Food and cigarettes were more appreciated as a substitute currency. The packages and cigarettes I sent home to my family through liberated prisoners were a substantial aid to them, since the stores were empty and nobody was willing to sell goods. All of that changed on Sunday, June 20, 1948, the day of the *Währungsreform* (the currency reform). The new money, the DM, or deutsche mark, which replaced the RM, or reichsmark, had been in the printing presses in the United States since the end of 1947. Every person initially received forty deutsche marks as starting money—enough to buy food for one or two weeks at the time. Salaries and pensions were to be translated one for one, from reichsmark into deutsche mark. Savings and investments were reduced ten to one, except for Jewish people, for whom it was one to one, as a gesture of recognition for their past suffering. All forms of rationing were suspended. From one day to the next, the stores were full of merchandise, but money became a rare commodity. People still ask today where all the goods had been hidden. The *Wirtschaftswunder*, or "economic miracle," took place. The black market disappeared, and confidence in money was restored.

Efforts to Advance My Release

Toward the end of 1946, the French authorities decided that prisoners with a rank of sergeant or higher, should not be sent to work in Kommandos anymore. I am not sure if this was related to the Geneva Conventions or not. While I had been promoted to sergeant in those last days of the war as part of my normal progression toward reserve officer, it was not recorded in my papers. When I wrote this home, my father started writing letters and tried to find my former army superiors and fellow soldiers in order to obtain proof of my promotion. This became a very complicated process, especially in the chaos of the postwar period. However, everybody in Germany tried to help, particularly because the French became skeptical about declarations people gave "to the best of their knowledge."

Becoming classified as a sergeant became even more significant when the French began the release of their prisoners according to the fifteen categories. One category, category 4, was specifically assigned to those with the rank of sergeant or higher, who were involved in heavy work up until that point. Category 8 was for the rest of the prisoners with the rank of sergeant who had done lighter work. If my promotion to sergeant had been previously recognized, my last Kommando in Raon L'Étape would still not have been accepted for category 4 since it was a community Kommando. Yet most of my time there, I worked as a lumberjack, just like in prior Kommandos.

When my parents heard that recognition of my promotion would now have concrete consequences, they stepped up their efforts to obtain the necessary documentation. I told them I considered this effort to be hopeless, and assessed my chances of soon being liberated, as close to nil. They continued nevertheless and succeeded in obtaining a set of documents from some officers and former comrades. I submitted them to my camp commander in November 1947, but he considered them insufficient.

My parents only intensified their efforts and finally found the commander of my former military battalion. They obtained a set of more meaningful documents. I submitted them again to the respective officer in my camp. It turned out that he was not interested in personnel changes within his German staff, as my release would have implied. In August, he declined to consider the matter further. The camp was looking for people in the staff who would volunteer to stay until the final closing at the end of the year.

Meanwhile, my parents submitted a set of papers to the French administration responsible for all prison camps, which was in Metz. I heard from a prisoner, who was a minister in that camp, that no more applications for priority release would be considered, but my father still did not give up and sent a petition to the war ministry of France. On October 10, an order came from Metz that I was to be released with the next transport to the American zone on October 25, 1948. The official reason was not my classification as a sergeant, but that I was considered a "Cas douloureux, ayant un frère en captivité Russe" (Hardship case, having a brother in Russian captivity).

On the Way to Freedom

My freedom became a reality, and I joined the transport to the prison camp of Tuttlingen, in the French zone of occupation. The Tuttlingen camp served as the exit camp for French prisoners to the American zone of occupation. There I stayed for two nights and finally, on October 27, 1948, three and half years after the war had ended, I received my papers and a cash sum of fifty deutsche marks to start my new life.

I had left home as a child and returned as a man, twenty-two years old.

A year before my release, my father had sent me a series of poems, one of which had a special meaning for my brother Uli and me. In 1961, my father published some of his lyrical poems in a small book, entitled *Durch's Augenglas der Liebe*, which means "through the looking glass of love."[3] I regretted that he did not include the one that I treasured especially, written two years after the end of the war. It beautifully reflects the beauty of his poetry and of his personal struggle to get his life back from the horrors of war.

The poem, which follows, is in German. My attempt to translate it into English is included.

---

3. August Köhler, *Durch's Augenglas der Liebe* (Bad Cannstatt, Germany: Cantz, 1961).

Fruehgang (1947)

Heut' nahm ich mein altes Reich in Besitz:
die sonnige Frühlingsau,
den braunen Hang, den grünenden Wald
und der Ferne schimmerndes Blau.

Weit hinter mir ließ ich Verfolgung und Not
und Sorge und Enge und Trug
und sah, wie das Leben der Erde entquoll,
die der Winter so grausam schlug.

Des Sohnes dacht' ich im fremden Land,
um den sich die Steppe dehnt,
und des jüngsten, der auf welschem Grund
seine liebsten Menschen ersehnt.

Nach Osten hob ich den einen Arm,
den andern ins westliche Land,
und als ich nach meinen Söhnen griff,
da reichte mir Gott die Hand

Morning Walk (1947)

I took possession of my old world,
the sunny spring meadows,
the brown hill, the green forest
and the blue glow afar.

Far behind me I left prosecution and misery
and sorrow and constriction and deception
and saw how life sprung up from the earth,
which winter had cruelly beaten.

I thought of my son in a foreign land,
surrounded by the steppe,
and of my youngest on western soil,
who longs for his loved ones at home

I raised one hand to the east
the other to the western land,
and as I reached for my sons
God offered me his hand.

PART II

7

Beginning a Second Life

Coming Home

On the morning of October 27, 1948, three years, six months, and six days after my capture by American troops, and thus close to three and a half years after the end of the war, I emerged from the gates of the Tuttlingen camp in the French zone of occupation. A free man, I went to the train station and boarded the train for Heilbronn, which was in the American zone, armed with the fifty deutsche marks I had received to start my new life.

As we pulled into the train station in Heilbronn, I was happy to see my brother Volker waiting for me. Even though we could have walked home with my small bundle of prisoner luggage, he got a taxi for us. A taxi was a horse-drawn carriage in those days. My brother kept telling me afterward that he was very embarrassed the horses were nothing but old farm horses. They could not compare with the elegant riding horses he tended for the British officers during his British captivity in Austria.

We arrived in the Solothurnerstrasse at the house that had been my home from the age of four. Our mother stood waiting in the door, and a few moments later our father came out to greet me. This was the next to last step in reuniting our family after the war. My brother Uli, however, was still a prisoner of war in Russia.

Since it was close to midday when I arrived home, it was time for lunch, which was, and in most families still is today, the main meal in Germany and many other European countries. The meal was quite simple: potatoes and vegetables. I concluded that, given such a meal on such a special day, it was apparently true that Germans were still struggling economically. My mother later said that she could not forgive herself for not cooking something better and more special, but she was so excited about my coming home, that all thoughts about preparing a special meal did not even cross her mind.

The next days were filled with seeing relatives and old friends. Then came the task of becoming registered as a citizen. As is customary in Germany and other European countries, I needed to be registered as a resident with my town to receive my dispensation from the air raid rubble clean-up, and my clearance from the denazification court.

There was no hero's welcome, no notice in the newspaper, when I came home. No psychiatrists were assigned to a returning prisoner to cope with the horrors and experiences of his personal past. Nobody talked about post-traumatic stress disorder or even thought of something like that. After all, there were tens of millions of Europeans who all had horrifying war experiences of one kind or another. There also was no recognition of our service to the country, no membership in a national veteran organization, and no decorations. The fact that I had received the Iron Cross during my military service became totally irrelevant—nonexistent—and still is, even to this day. People wanted to forget their past as much and as quickly as possible. All I experienced was occasional pity for myself about the fact that it took so long for me to come home.

Germany as a nation could not deny its past and its responsibility for it. It had to be careful to implement changes when rebuilding the nation. A case in point was the new military, which was, and still is, a compulsory service. It defined the new role of the soldier as a "citizen in uniform," in contrast to the absolute and unquestionable obedience of the old soldier under Hitler and the kaisers before. The national anthem, the *Deutschlandlied,* was changed from the first verse to the third verse of a hymn by Hoffmann von Fallersleben. The first verse begins with the words "Deutschland, Deutschland über alles, über alles in der Welt," which literally means "Germany above everything in the world." This is occasionally misinterpreted as the desire for Germany to dominate all countries in the world; however, one needs to understand that in 1841, Fallersleben wanted to call on all Germans to overcome the fighting by local warlords, to unite as a country, and thus to put Germany above their differences. The subsequent words in the first verse of the anthem "Von der Maas bis an die Memel" (From the Maas river to the Memel river), refer to borders which had belonged to Germany at the time the song was written, but became parts of other countries at the ends of either WWI or WWII.

To ensure that Germany was prevented from regaining its technological power, the occupying powers ruled that no electronic equipment could be built that would operate at higher frequencies than the frequencies of sound, i.e., twenty or thirty kilohertz. That meant that no sophisticated equipment could be built. Fortunately this unrealistic restriction softened fairly quickly and later disappeared.

There was also a trend in the new Germany to ban all military toys, like toy guns. Coming home from the war, we all said to each other that we would not allow our children to play with such toys, let alone with real weapons. We were indeed "demilitarized." The collective, and my personal, belief was that war should never be a tool to solve a political problem. I think a vivid example of this thought, or rather of its violation, was the British invasion of the Falkland Islands in 1982. Politically, the desire to avoid military conflict more recently was reflected in Germany's and France's oppositions to the war in Iraq. This opposition was heavily criticized by the United States, especially by President Bush, who called Germany and France the "old Europe," in contrast to other more supportive European nations. But this opposition needs to be understood in the context of the people of two nations who still have the horrors of World War II in their recent past, and desire nothing more than peace—I was one of them.

Like practically everyone in Germany, I was ashamed of the country's past and felt a sense of guilt, even though I thought my captivity was sufficient punishment for following Hitler. Germany did not deny its past. But in the population at large, the past was shrouded in silence. Teachers in school would not speak of the past. My nephews told me that their history lessons in high school, which traditionally used to go from the Middle Ages or earlier, to the present, stopped around World War I. As I mentioned in the introduction, all teachers, very few of whom were strongly opposed to the Third Reich, were afraid to say anything that might be interpreted as supportive of the Nazi government. In a sense, I can sympathize with that position. I believe a number of readers will take my attempts to explain why and how the citizens of a country, myself and my parents included, sympathized with Hitler, not as a historical explanation, but as a continued support. As I said in my introduction, it is the power of seduction that makes a criminal dictator dangerous.

I become enraged when I see images of American neo-Nazis on TV. I can understand why someone would have strong nationalistic feelings, but to invoke Nazism to express these beliefs today is beyond any comprehension. The only small consolation is seeing what kinds of people participate in these movements; they look like the scum of society.

Discussions about our political past were, if not taboo, generally avoided in personal conversations in Germany, be it with friends, coworkers, or strangers. People wanted to leave the war behind them and often were still struggling with their own experiences. After returning home from the war, I talked very little about my experiences in combat and in captivity. Even later in the United States, I spoke very rarely about my past, opening up only a little more in recent years. Of course, it was, and still is, especially difficult to talk with my Jewish friends about my views and experiences under Hitler. Because of the sensitive nature of the topic, I can only discuss it in rare instances—when a conversation is deep and intense and when I sense my partner is interested and open-minded.

Professional Decisions

The next step after settling down as a new citizen was to ponder my professional future. My experiences as a POW taught me that people who learned a trade had advantages over academically trained people. My parents were acquainted with some owners of large businesses and factories in our town. When looking for a career for my brother Volker, a couple of years earlier, these owners told my parents that it was more useful for them to hire men who had learned their business from the bottom up, instead of coming from college. We were friends with a family who owned a silverware factory in town. Both of their sons were sent to college, one for a business, the other for a technical education. The businessman was Herr Doktor now, and let everybody in the factory know who he was and how he had to be addressed. This was in stark contrast to his grandfather who knew every worker and shook hands with every one as he walked through his factory.

Another aspect of my professional decision process was our financial situation, which spoke against going to college. My father had still not resumed his duties as a high school teacher when I returned; therefore, foremost in my mind was the idea I had nurtured while still a prisoner of war, namely, to become an electrician. I had mentioned this in one of my letters sent to my parents from captivity. I thought this trade might use my technical and mathematical abilities more than most. There was also the fact that the Not-Abitur, or "high school equivalency diploma," that was given to us when we were drafted into the army, was no longer valid.

On one of my first weekends home, Walter Dietrich, a former member of the antiaircraft auxiliary and a schoolmate, came to visit me. He was studying physics in Stuttgart. Walter strongly advised my parents and me to visit the electrical engineering department at the Technische Hochschule, the Institute of Technology, in Stuttgart. He suggested I give it a try and see what Professor Feldtkeller, the head of the EE department, had to say about my chances of studying there. Walter explained that I could also take the necessary make-up courses for my missing high school diploma at the same institute, prior to beginning my academic studies.

When I visited Professor Feldtkeller, he strongly encouraged me to take the equivalency course and follow the study of electrical engineering. When I told him that I had never played with radios or other electronics like other electrical engineering students I knew, he emphasized that he preferred students like myself, who came with an open mind and an interest in theory, over the tinkerers who thought they knew everything already.

Many of my professors later stressed similar sentiments: students with a lack of interest in theory should not attend an academic engineering college, but should instead attend one of the specialized engineering schools, called *Fachhochschulen*, that offer a nonacademic curriculum with an emphasis on the practical aspects of engineering. Those schools do not require a German high school diploma. Instead, many students undergo and finish their training in some trade prior to attending a Fachhochschule. The degree from these schools might be considered similar to an American bachelor's degree. The option to attend one of these schools is one of the reasons why German academic colleges and universities did not offer a degree similar to a bachelor's degree after only four years of college. (However, German colleges have begun to adopt some aspects of the American degree structure.)

Professor Feldtkeller also said it should be possible to take care of the financial aspect of university attendance, one way or the other. It is worth noting that tuition and fees in Germany at the time, and largely still today, amount to a fraction of the high costs of studying at a college in the United States. All German universities are public, and apart from occasional emphases in some fields, the academic levels, and thus the value of a degree, does not differ much from one university to the other. However, this is gradually beginning to change today.

Catching up with Life

Like it was for most returning prisoners, one of my biggest desires was to catch up with life, in particular with all the social life I had missed. After all, I had barely had occasion to speak with a young woman for the previous four or five years. A week or two after my arrival home, my brother introduced me to some of his female friends. One of them was Doris, who was very good looking. I was not sure whether I knew her from earlier years. Volker told me later that my eyes fell out of their sockets when I saw her for the first time. She later became Volker's fiancée, but, in the end, not his wife. We remarked jokingly at the time that some engagements end happily and others in marriage.

The music we liked at the time was primarily dance music. Many of our favorite songs were American, German, or French hits of the forties and fifties. Dances were the highlight of our social life. Volker and Ursula had participated in a second dance course with their friends after the war. Our "dance fever" after the war was quite intense. Volker, together with some friends, organized several balls, and I was only too happy to participate in their preparation. We would find an appropriately large location, hire a band, prepare a little program, conceive a title theme for the event, and send out invitations to the many friends of my brother and sister. One of our balls was called "Ç'est si bon," after a French song that was popular at the time.

As part of our social life of partying, dating, and dancing, almost all of us began to smoke, myself included. Four to six cigarettes a day, and only in the evening, was my maximum. Given my relatively minor addiction, it was not too difficult for me—and my wife—to break the habit a few years later. Dick Robrock, a later friend of mine at work, had a great technique to stop smoking. He told all his friends and acquaintances that two months from then, on a specific date, he would stop smoking. This allowed him to continue to enjoy his habit for a while, but he would have been too embarrassed not to stop on the given date. He succeeded in quitting smoking, using this technique. I still use the technique on other less critical occasions, for example when I am eating something dangerously good, like chocolate. I take a few pieces out and put the rest away immediately, while still enjoying what is in front of me. I call it "the Robrock effect." We drank wine at our parties, usually a glass or two. Its purpose was to enhance the festivity and our enjoyment; I can't recall anybody ever getting drunk.

Despite the tight economic situation, happiness returned to our family. Everybody worked together. I remember helping out in the kitchen by drying dishes and complaining that my brother Volker, while standing next to me, was not sharing in the kitchen chores. My mother and Ursula assured me that they were so happy to be entertained by Volker, that they would readily forgo his manual contributions; he was the better talker.

High School Diploma Course in Stuttgart

The decision was made: I was to study electrical engineering at the Technische Hochschule in Stuttgart, but first I had to take the high school equivalency course and its corresponding examination. The fall semester had already started. I had to decide which courses to take; twelve credit hours were to be filled. I was interested in math and physics, as well as modern languages. To this day, I am still not very interested in history.

Eventually, I selected eleven credit hours of courses, and was left with an interesting decision. I could either take Latin or life drawing for the required twelfth credit hour. The life drawing course was primarily set up as an option for students of architecture. While I was always fairly good in high school drawing, my strength was more in technical drawing than in drawing people; I decided to sign up for the class. I still have some of the drawings that I did that semester, and I feel that I can look at them without embarrassment. The fact that I had a good professor certainly helped.

I was intrigued by the study of architecture, and in hindsight, might even have preferred that to engineering. But I had two second cousins who were about to finish their study of architecture in Stuttgart and I thought I had to be as good as they were if I wanted to study architecture. They were among the top students in their class and began accumulating prizes while they were still students, which continued later in their careers. I probably set my bar too high by comparing myself with them. Much later in life, I cautiously suggested to our youngest daughter Kirsten, who was artistically as well as logically and mathematically talented, that she might want to become an architect—and she did.

As the high school equivalency course came to an end, it was time to get ready for the diploma exam. It was by far not as comprehensive as the regular Abitur, "the high school exam," which typically lasts for six weeks and consists of oral and written examinations for each subject. Nevertheless, an examination is rarely fun.

One of my friends told me that he had heard of someone who, on account of the courses he had taken in regular high school before being drafted into the army and because of the good grades he received, did get his preliminary high school diploma accepted as a full diploma by the ministry of education. I decided to try doing this as well. I went to the ministry, which was also in the state capital of Stuttgart, paid five deutsche marks, and received possession of a full-fledged high school diploma. I did not regret having taken the twelve credit hours of courses up to the exam—including the one in life drawing. But I was definitely happy that I did not have to join my fellow students in struggling through the examinations.

Uli Comes Home from Russia

In the last days of March 1949, my parents received word that my brother Uli was on his way home from Russian captivity. His release was quite sudden. My father and my sister took the train to Ulm to meet him at a transit point and bring him home. Then the big day arrived. On April 1, 1949, four years after the end of the war, our family was again complete and safe.

When Uli was a teenager, he occasionally kept a turtle as a pet. His last turtle was the model for the very first photographs

I made using my father's glass-plate camera in July 1940. Three or four years later, during the war, we were sad to notice that Uli's turtle had disappeared. Was it a miracle or a coincidence that on the morning Uli came home from captivity, the turtle reappeared in our garden?

Uli's adventures in Russian captivity could fill a book, and I wish he had written one. As I already mentioned, from a strictly physical viewpoint, he was better off than I was during my first two years of captivity.

Until the French defined the release categories for POWs, which allowed us to make more realistic estimates of when we'd go home, we always thought that we would be released in a few months. In contrast, the German prisoners in Russia were never sure whether they would ever make it home. The release of prisoners appeared to be totally random and unpredictable.

The Russians applied a tactic on the prisoners that seems to have been used quite extensively in the Communist world: mutual spying. Every German prisoner was asked to gather information about one or more fellow prisoners—in particular where they fought and in what unit. If someone belonged to a military unit by which the Russians claimed that war crimes were committed—such as the killing of a Russian prisoner—he would be sentenced to twenty-five years in Siberia for just having belonged to the unit. Such mutual reporting was also widely used in Communist East Germany, where the system engaged people to report the political standing and attitude of their fellow students or coworkers.[1] The difference, however, was that in East Germany, the spying was done by people who believed in their system, whereas the German prisoners in Russia had no choice. My brother and all of his fellow prisoners had to make a report, but they indicated the purpose of their interview to the interviewee, who then could choose what answer to give to the

---

1. More recently, Saddam Hussein in Iraq included spying on family members as part of his dictatorial control.

Russians. I am sure that such spying also existed in the Third Reich, even though I have not heard of any instances, perhaps because, at least in the population at large, the majority was on the side of the government.

One of the more positive elements for Uli in his Russian prison camp was that the community of officers, similar to the German officers in the French camps, represented a great cultural and knowledgeable resource. The camps offered a great variety of lectures and courses. Of course, the Russians added their share of compulsory instruction in the form of Russian propaganda. The prisoners learned, for example, that there was almost nothing important in the world that the Russians had not invented.

My brother was also assigned to work, even though the Geneva Conventions did not allow that for officers. But since most of his work assignments were tolerable, it turned out to be more advantageous than idling in a large camp. Uli was involved in a fair amount of work as a lumberman; we compared our experiences after the war. Uli had also learned to speak Russian fairly well. We also found that, for both of us, our practical language education started with the curses that we picked up from our respective guards. Of these, the Russian curses were by far more intense than the French ones.

Before leaving Russia to return home, prisoners were duly prepared and told that they would be coming home to one of the terrible Western zones of occupation instead of the paradise of Russian-occupied, or I should probably say Russian-liberated, East Germany.

Engineering Intern

Even though Professor Feldtkeller told me at my initial visit to the Stuttgart Institute of Technology that he preferred students interested in science and theory, rather than in tinkering, the curriculum did include a specific requirement for engineering students to obtain practical experience. Every student of electrical engineering had to undergo fifty-two weeks of practical work experience as a *Praktikant*, "a trainee." The first twenty-six weeks consisted of work in various mechanics shops or factories, to be concluded prior to the first semester. The other half of required experience consisted of similar practical training, but related specifically to electricity. Typically, the segments for this latter training were scheduled during the vacation terms between semesters and had to be completed as a requirement for beginning the fifth semester.

The training requirements were fairly well-defined, especially for the first six months, with specific assignments like five weeks on a vise, four weeks on a lathe, two weeks in a foundry, four weeks of welding, and so on. A nine-page booklet described these requirements. The selection of work experiences, and their associated documentation, was submitted for approval.

With the help of my parents and their connections in town, we found a few factories and shops in which I could obtain my training. Even though it was suggested that the training be carried out in the apprentice shops that practically all factories had, it turned out that, in several instances, I was involved in production work. I considered this to be slightly unfair since my pay in all these instances was zero. My father happened to tutor the son of the owner of one of the factories where I worked for free. My father increased the tutoring fee to make up, to some degree, for what his student's father should have paid me.

The second part of my training in electrical work used up of all my vacations between semesters; in other words, there was no vacation. In only one or two cases did I get paid—my pay amounted to some pocket money. Nevertheless, I found this practical education in both mechanical and electrical work quite useful, not only professionally, but also for my later work around the house.

The scariest moment during those weeks of practical factory training happened in a foundry where I had to exchange a switch. In order not to disrupt production, the switch—"hot" with 220 volts—could not be defused. I was standing on a pile of huge steel plates and working on the switch on the wall. Even though I tried to be extremely careful, my hand slipped once, and I touched a hot wire and got a hefty jolt. Fortunately, I did not have a firm grip on the wire and walked away with only a scare.

On the other hand, I remember a more pleasant event during an assignment in which I worked at a company called Mix and Genest. During the morning break with some of my bosses, including the director, one of them posed a mathematical puzzle. The task was to make a stack of bricks, always putting one brick on top of the one below. If you had only two bricks the one on top could theoretically overhang the one at the bottom by half a brick. In reality, you would need to back off a bit before it fell, but this practical consideration was to be disregarded. The question was, by how many brick lengths could the top block theoretically overhang the one at the bottom, if you had an unlimited supply of bricks? By lunchtime, I came back with the answer, which greatly impressed my bosses. The answer was an infinite length. I quickly discovered that you had to solve the problem from the top down, and not from the bottom up, which allowed me to develop the mathematical series, for which the answer is an infinitely large overhang.

Student in Stuttgart: The First Years

My friend, Walter Dietrich, who introduced me to the possibility of studying at the Institute of Technology in Stuttgart, also recommended that during the semester in which I took the high school diploma preparation courses, I should sit in on some of the essential university courses for first-semester students, without actually registering, just to get a feel for them. Attending these lectures proved to be an interesting experience and also gave me some psychological insight into the learning process. According to the old European tradition, a university course is strictly a presentation by a professor, called a *Vorlesung* (lecture). The number of students in the *Hörsaal* (lecture room) for the main courses that Walter had recommended—mathematics and mechanics—was typically 200 to 400. The only communication between the students and professor consisted of either knocking on your table with your knuckles or stamping your feet as a greeting or for approval, or scratching your feet for disapproval, say if the professor made a mistake. During the years that I studied in Stuttgart, no quizzes were given during the semester and examinations were only held between semesters. Homework was occasionally given in some courses, but it was not to be turned in and it was up to the student to complete it and to compare their result with the correct answer provided by an assistant to the professor.

I found it difficult to fully understand the course I sat in on. I did not completely feel I belonged there, nor did I attempt to do the suggested homework. Occasionally, a student next to me would ask to compare the solution to a problem, and I was always embarrassed that I could not do that. Some doubts rose in my mind about whether I would be able to complete these courses successfully the next year when I was a regular student.

In that subsequent year, I knew that I had to study hard and I did. The situation was completely different after I enrolled as a university student. The fact that I had audited some lectures before, while taking my high school diploma courses, helped me significantly. I could anticipate what the professor was about to present. I even felt that I had an advantage over many students around me in following the lectures. From this experience, I learned a lesson for life, namely that the attitude with which you approach a difficult task is essential in determining success or failure. If you think you might fail, you most likely will, and if you are convinced that you have no choice but to succeed, you most likely will. The same might be true when it comes to other aspects of life, like marriage.

Education in German universities is characterized by academic freedom. You are not required to attend lectures and you can even sit in on a class without registering (which was the reason I could attend classes while I was still completing my high school diploma). According to tradition, there was no roll call, and, as I said above, no quizzes or tests during the lecture months. Some of these old traditions have changed slightly since the time I studied. Nowadays, some pre-exams are occasionally held during a semester, but not during an actual class. This academic freedom makes the transition from high school to college much harder in Germany, than it is in the United States, where students have more freedom in high school to define their course of study and their schedule, but are more strongly guided in college, since their individual college curricula usually require approval, and advisors are assigned to students.

The German education system has advantages and disadvantages. The advantage is that it leaves a student with a high degree of freedom and teaches a student to take charge of his or her education. The disadvantage is that a student receives no personal guidance from the institution on what courses to take, other than a list of graduation requirements. Guidance and recommendations can only come from friends, or perhaps a professor. Every student must build his or her own curriculum and schedule. This is particularly bewildering when a student begins the first semester. Another disadvantage with the German university system is that, without strong motivation, the student in Germany will learn less than with the continued pressure of quizzes. Active learning is often postponed until preparation for examinations, which might be a year or two after a course is taken, usually between semesters. The student must learn how to learn.

At the time I studied, we had a few foreign students—many of whom came from well-to-do families—who took advantage of the academic freedom and enjoyed themselves, instead of going to lectures. I remember one student from Iran who had been enrolled for thirteen semesters without having completed the *Vordiplom* (pre-diploma), which requires passing examinations for all of the lectures of the first four semesters, before beginning the fifth semester. His father owned a bank in Iran and had sent his son to Germany to study, and also apparently to enjoy himself.

During the semester in which I took the high school equivalency courses, and the three semesters that followed, I lived with my parents. Each day I took the train from Heilbronn to Stuttgart, which took somewhat less than an hour, each way. After my first college year, in the fall of 1950, I became an official Stuttgart resident. Armed with a permit from the city's residence administration, I rented a room in a widow's apartment in an old sandstone house. Instead of a sink with running water, I had a washstand with a large porcelain bowl and a pitcher with water in it. From time to time, I could ask to take a bath, but that was for special occasions only and required an extra charge. Money was an issue in our family, especially since my father still had not resumed his job as a high school teacher, but my rental situation was not at all unusual for the times.

My accommodations were certainly different from what German students expect their parents to offer them today: their own apartment where they are free to come and go as they please. When I rented the room in Stuttgart, I was told at the beginning that I could not bring female guests to my room. Many other students heard the same explanation: the landlady would of course have no objection personally, but if the neighbors saw it and reported it to the police, she might be accused of the procuration of women. How times have changed since then!

My room was about two miles from the school. Most of the time, I commuted by bicycle. Since the Institute of Technology was very close to the heart of town, my bicycle path took me straight through the center of Stuttgart, along the Königsstrasse, and past the castle. Today, this is one of the busiest places in southern Germany and riding a bike would be close to suicide. Riding a bicycle through Stuttgart was only possible because bicycles are considered regular vehicles in Germany, and not toys to be ridden on sidewalks, as I sometimes have the impression here in the States.

My studies proceeded pretty well, as I benefited from having gotten a preexposure to some of the courses, especially mathematics and mechanics In mathematics, it was expected that you had already learned subjects like differential calculus in high school; hence, the first semester started off with determinants, vectors, a brief review of differential calculus, and integral calculus. It was, and probably still is, not customary in Germany to have a textbook. Normally, a German student has to find his own resources in the library. However, in many of my courses, such as mathematics and mechanics, the professor developed the subject precisely on the blackboard. If you carefully copied what the professor wrote, you had the equivalent of a textbook for the respective course. Of course, we were encouraged to study the literature, especially in preparation for the examinations, but I found most of my notes to be quite comprehensive, especially since I rarely missed a class. For some of our final written examinations, we were allowed to bring a crib sheet of, say, four pages. Generating these notes was in itself an excellent method to prepare for the examination, since it required a good understanding of the subject, and during the examination, there was usually no time to really study the prepared pages.

During the first four semesters, I had only one course that related directly to my major, electrical engineering. But, as our professors kept telling us during our studies, the purpose of our education was to learn how to think, and in our case, to learn how to think as a scientist and engineer. The two-year course on mechanics by Professor Grammel was a perfect example. It covered a huge field, from kinetics to thermodynamics to the static design of bridges. A few years later, when I had the opportunity to participate in faculty meetings as representative of the student council, the argument was made that the fields of mechanical engineering and electrical engineering had expanded so much that a four-semester exposure to mechanics by electrical engineering students was no longer warranted. Yet it was decided to keep this course compulsory until Professor Grammel retired, because it was one of the best courses in which to teach students to think as an engineer.

Apart from learning to think, we were also encouraged to reach outside of our own field of studies in what was called *Studium Generale* (general studies). Two classes stand out for me. One was a course in philosophy that I took with a well-known philosophy professor, Max Bense. I found the course somewhat difficult, but it was interesting to gain insight into a world of thinking that was so totally different from my own engineering world. The other class was a one-time event, a tour of an exhibition of abstract paintings. It was led by an art professor. Up to that time, I was inclined to look at abstract painting as more or less random paint on a canvas. (In the Third Reich, it fell under the category of so-called degenerate art.) But now I saw the differences among abstract paintings. I realized that in contrast to meaningless abstract paintings, good abstract paintings evoke emotions, feelings, and sometimes visions of some form of reality. They are not a random sprinkling of lines, forms, and color, as I used to think.

In a sense, the course of study leading to the engineering diploma consisted of three phases. The first four semesters were somewhat general and were completed with the Vordiplom. They were followed with four more semesters of specialized courses, and, finally, work on the diploma thesis.

As I said earlier, titles used to be important in Germany, and were featured on an individual's business card; this even applied to students. After I was enrolled in the Institute of Technology, I was entitled to call myself *stud.el* (student of electrical engineering), and, after I completed the Vordiplom, this changed to *cand.el.* (candidate for the diploma degree in electrical engineering).

The formality at the time I went to college was also characterized by the fact that we not only addressed the professors as "Herr Professor," but we also addressed our fellow students using "Herr." Using the word *Herr* goes hand in hand with using *Sie*, the formal version in German for "you," instead of the informal version, *du*. I can count the number of students with whom I used the informal form of address on one hand. Even students I was teamed with during laboratories in the upper semesters were addressed as "Herr." Some decades later, it became customary in student life in Germany to use the informal form of address and first names among all students. It is possible that the American custom of using first names played a role in this; many young people looked up to the United States and often copied American habits and customs.

Lectures in German, Swiss, Austrian, and some Scandinavian universities usually begin fifteen minutes after the announced time. The delay is called the "academic quarter." The original reason for it was that lectures would always be scheduled for a full hour, and fifteen minutes was the time needed for students and professors to get from one lecture room to the next.

This old tradition was no longer applied consistently by the time I went to college. To avoid confusion, the time in academic announcements was usually followed by the letters "c.t."(the Latin *cum tempore*, which means "with time") for when the lecture or event was to start fifteen minutes later, or "s.t." (*sine tempore*, meaning "without time") when it started on the indicated time. This academic quarter even carries over into the private sphere. When you were invited over by friends, it was, and still is, customary in Germany to come about ten to fifteen minutes after the indicated time, but not later. This allows the hosts an opportunity to catch their breath before the first guests arrive.

Student in Stuttgart: The Next Two Years

After I finished the Vordiplom, I was ready to start my fifth semester. Now the focus was on specific electrical subjects. The lectures were no longer held in the large auditoriums with 200 or more students—they were in smaller classrooms—yet they still lacked verbal communication between the students and professors. The lectures were supplemented with laboratory work, led by assistants—usually graduate students of the respective professor. The lectures were intended to teach you the basics and scientific foundations of a field, rather than to get you ready to start working in it productively on the future first day of your job.

My studies proceeded as planned—I did not have any major problems. In about the eighth semester I was interviewed by a professor, and in the spring of 1953 I was selected to become a scholarship recipient of the Studienstiftung des Deutschen Volkes (German National Merit Foundation). This organization—which might be compared with the National Science Foundation in the United States—selects about 1 percent of all students in Germany as stipendiaries. The objective of the financial assistance is to enable a student to concentrate completely on his or her studies without being compelled to work on the side for financial support. The amount of financial support is individually determined according to need, in particular the financial situation of the parents, and can range from a full scholarship to no financial aid. In either case, the student is given the distinction of belonging to this prestigious group of students. He or she also receives invitations to scientific events. I still receive occasionally literature from the organization today.

Once, the students in our class organized a ball.[2] With my love for ballroom dancing and some experience in organizing balls with my siblings, I volunteered to participate in the organization of the event. Thus, I came to the attention of the circle of students involved in the student administration. And so, one day, I was asked to participate in the student council, known as the ASTA, short for Allgemeiner Studentenausschuss. That was in January 1952.

Six month later, I wound up vice president of the student council. This brought with it several duties, some pleasurable, others not so much. I vividly remember a very unpleasant one. I had to represent the student body at a funeral for a student at the school and say a few words at the service. My problem was not so much the fact that I did not know the student and that it was a funeral, but that I was horrified to speak in public. Whereas children in the United States are exposed to speaking in front of others—even in kindergarten with show-and-tell—this skill was totally lacking in my education and that of most Germans at the time.

The most interesting of my student council duties was my participation in many faculty meetings, to which the ASTA president and vice president were invited as student representatives. On a very hot summer day, the first president of the

---

2. As I am using the word "class," I should add that I mean the students in the same semester. The American concept of a class, i.e. the year in which you expect to graduate, is unknown since the completion of the degree, the engineering diploma, varies from student to student and could be anywhere between five and seven years after beginning college.

Federal Republic of Germany, Bundespräsident Theodor Heuss, visited the Institute of Technology. He had been a professor of economics at the college before becoming president. A formal dinner was held in the student dining hall, the Mensa, which had no air conditioning. The president of the institute, who, according to academic customs, was addressed as "Magnifizenz," introduced President Heuss.

Heuss was known as not having lost his Swabian accent while being a politician in Bonn. As he gave his dinner speech, he said at one point, in good Swabian dialect: "His Magnifizenz said earlier that the president should always set an example. Well, I take off my jacket," and so he did. His Magnifizenz had no choice but to do likewise, but then stood there in suspenders, with the golden chain of his position around the neck.

I also had a chance to participate in an interesting discussion, relating to fraternities. During the Third Reich, the fraternities were dissolved, but naturally, they came back after the war. It was a tradition in many of the century-old fraternities that the students wore "colors," i.e., a cap and a sash with the colors of the fraternity. Before the war, fraternity students wore them at all times. Now, in the post-Hitler era, they wanted to wear them again, at least on special occasions.

Some fraternities also wanted to reintroduce the custom of fencing. Fencing was not only part of their fraternity training, but, at some point, each fraternity brother had to undergo at least one Mensur fencing match to prove his courage and dedication to the fraternity. These special matches were fought with sharp weapons and without a face mask; fencers only wore special glasses to protect their eyes. The matches were not considered duels and had very strict rules. The goal was to inflict a scar on the other person's face, and if you were hit yourself, to take it without wincing. After the event, the wounded students would often smear dirt into the wound so it would heal with a visible scar and demonstrate their courage for the rest of their lives. For most of us other students, as well as for the faculty, this demonstration of so-called courage was absolutely ridiculous, particularly after having just lived through a five-year war. But in those fraternities, the pressure came primarily from the alumni who used their financial leverage to have the students resume the old tradition. It seems that one of the alumni's prime motivations for restoring the practice was to maintain a justification for their own scars from their student days. The faculty meeting came to the following conclusion in Stuttgart: in order to be recognized as a fraternity of the school, the fraternity had to sign an agreement with the school which said that they would not wear colors in public, except at special occasions like funerals, and that they would not engage in Mensur fencing. However, Mensur fencing was reintroduced a few years later at other universities, accompanied by much political and public debate. I don't know whether Stuttgart followed suit.

Another memorable event related to my student council office was my participation in a student conference in Berlin in 1952. The interesting part was not so much the conference itself, but my experience of Communist East Germany and East Berlin. Analogous to Germany's division into four zones of occupation, Berlin was within the Russian zone, but was itself divided into four zones. Our conference was in non-Communist West Berlin. To get there from West Germany, our bus had to pass through Communist East Germany. Just as we were entering East Germany on the autobahn, our tour leader announced that we might get in trouble if, at the formal checkpoint for entering West Berlin, Western newspapers or magazines were found in our possession.

When we stopped at the checkpoint, all the female students had to leave the bus—and did not come back for a long time. It turned out that one of them had some magazines with her, and, upon hearing the warning, threw them out the bus window in order not to get caught. A motorcyclist who was behind our bus had observed this and obviously reported it. Now the border police were trying to find out which of the female students committed the crime of "distributing Western propaganda material in East Germany." After two hours, all of the students were released; none had made a confession and none were arrested. Jail would certainly have been the penalty.

While in West Berlin, we heard on the radio that the East Germans welcomed the conference attendees in West Berlin and invited us to pay a visit to East Berlin. This was some nine years before the Berlin Wall went up. The next day we took the train into the Russian sector. There we realized that it was the day of the May 1 parade. The streets were almost completely empty. As we came near the area of the parade, we suddenly saw police coming toward us. This scared us. We confessed that we were visitors from the West, attending a student conference. To our surprise, the police welcomed us to East Berlin. We carefully approached the parade and later made our way back to the Western sector. We later heard that some other students from our conference were forced to join the throngs of marchers. The police simply forced everybody from the side streets and sidewalks to become part of the parade. The East German radio proudly mentioned that even students from a conference in West Berlin participated in the great demonstration for democracy and socialism.

One of the faculty meetings in Stuttgart centered on a discussion of honoring an American, Max Kade. Kade was a German immigrant from Schwäbisch Hall in southern Germany, who made a fortune manufacturing a cough medicine, Pertussin, in his factory on Manhattan's West Street.[3] He gave one million deutsche marks to build the new student dining hall

---

3. Max Kade German-American Research Institute, "Who was Max Kade?" Pennsylvania State University, http://www.maxkade.psu.edu/kadeinfo.html.

at the Technische Hochschule. He subsequently donated money for the first student dormitory, which came to bear his name, "Max Kade Heim." He said that colleges in the United States had dormitories and therefore Stuttgart needed one too. This was unusual since the concept of a college campus was unknown in Germany in those days. Most, if not all, colleges and universities in Germany were located in the center of cities. Only in later years did they begin to build centers farther outside the cities, but even these clusters of buildings could still not be equated to an American campus.

The Institute of Technology wanted to honor Kade for his generosity. A long discussion ensued. In the United States, one would have bestowed an honorary doctorate degree. However, because of the protected role of this degree in German society, the faculty reached the conclusion that an honorary doctorate degree could only be conferred upon someone with a college education, or for a special academic achievement, which was not the case with Kade. It was concluded that he was to be made an Honorary Senator of the Technische Hochschule in Stuttgart.

Some years later, Kade was awarded honorary doctorate degrees from several German universities, including the Institute of Technology in Stuttgart, which must have had a change of heart. Through the Max Kade Foundation, which he formed with his wife, Kade also made donations to countless other universities in Germany. About seventeen Max Kade houses exist throughout Germany today. Many universities have Max Kade institutes or Max Kade professorships. The Max Kade Foundation is still in existence today, long after his death in 1967.

Being involved in student government exposed me to notices and news that I might not have heard of otherwise. The one announcement that was to change my life was the offering of a scholarship at the Georgia Institute of Technology in Atlanta. Even though it was an annual offering, I had not heard about it before. I applied and became the selected scholarship winner for the academic year of 1953/54. The scholarship was financed by the Georgia Tech World Student Fund, which, in turn, was administered by the Georgia Tech YMCA. A Fulbright travel grant for the voyage to and from the United States was part of the scholarship.[4]

4. Fulbright Commission, "The First Class of Fulbrighters" (Berlin: German-American Fulbright Commission, November 2003), http://www.fulbright.de/fileadmin/files/commission/program/downloads/first_class_fulbrighters.pdf.

8

Exchange Student
in America

Getting There Is Half the Fun

A few weeks before my scheduled departure to the United States, I was invited to participate in a three-day orientation seminar for Fulbright exchange students in the picturesque town of Weikersheim in southern Germany. The purpose of the event was to prepare us for our upcoming experience, both from a personal and an academic point of view. We were told that we would experience many things that might appear strange to us. I always remembered two of the messages from the conference, in particular. The first was that if we found something unusual or strange, we should ask the question, "Why?" We would often find a historical explanation for how things came to be different in the States than what we were used to in Europe. The other message was that we should say, "I don't know," if we didn't know the answer to something, rather than try to hide any ignorance.

Attending the conference also provided me with the opportunity to meet other students who were also getting ready for their first visit to the United States. I met some of them again later, on the boat, crossing the Atlantic.

We were reminded that one of the main purposes of our stay in the United States was to become acquainted with the American way of life, with American customs, and with American history. The program wanted us to spread the word afterward, back home, about what life in the United States is all about. This is why they would not allow us to stay in the United States after our academic year, even if we wanted to. Our social learning was as important, or even more important, than our academic learning, we were told. Hence, we were not expected to, and were even discouraged from, studying for a degree as an exchange student.

The time finally came to depart for America. Back in 1953, travel by plane was still significantly more expensive than travel by ship; hence, my Fulbright travel grant provided me with passage by ship from Genoa, Italy, to New York. My train ride to Genoa, at the end of September 1953, led me through Switzerland and Italy; I had obtained the necessary visas for both countries. The amount of currency I was allowed to carry on my passage was limited in those days and was marked in the visas; it amounted to less than forty dollars for each country.

On the SS *Constitution* of the American Export Lines, I quickly made friends with the other exchange students. One student, Wolfgang Walther, also came from Stuttgart and was heading for Georgia Tech. The boat had three classes. We were, of course, in tourist class, but we soon made acquaintances with people, i.e., young women, in cabin class. This allowed us to visit them and go dancing upstairs in the evenings, since there was no dancing in tourist class.

Sailing in the Mediterranean was quite pleasurable. A special event was our passage through the Strait of Gibraltar. While the ship was anchored at Gibraltar, many small local boats surrounded us to sell tourist souvenirs, like bracelets, scarves, and postcards, which did not interest me, personally. The objects for sale were pulled up onto the ship in baskets and the money was sent down subsequently. In order to keep the boats from getting too close to the ship and to keep the whole operation somewhat under control, the ship's fire stations sprayed water near the small boats, occasionally giving a boat a little shower.

Another beautiful view offered itself to us during our voyage, as we had our first look at the Azores in perfect weather. The Azores are the highest mountains on the globe if one measures their height from the bottom of the ocean. Here again, local vendors greeted us in their little boats with new merchandise.

Another interesting moment was when we passed our sister ship, the *Independence*, at night. Not only was it like seeing our own boat, but the *Independence* was also the ship on which I was to return to Europe ten months later.

After we moved away from the continent, the sea was no longer calm. On several days we experienced a fairly rough voyage. An image that is still stuck in my mind is that of many tourist-class passengers, in particular Italian women, stretched out half lifeless in the salon or on deck chairs, trying to overcome their seasickness and longing to arrive in New York. A few times I also suffered somewhat from a lack of appetite. I think that seasickness is a bit contagious, though, and is enhanced by seeing other people affected.

Still under the influence of the war that had ended only eight years earlier, I was amazed by the variety and quality of the food served on the ship. One of my first cultural shocks on my American adventure was seeing the amount of food taken back to the kitchen. In particular, I could not understand why the waiters would just stack the little plates of untouched butter on top of each other, ready for the dishwasher. This was totally against the culture in which I was brought up, even going back to before the war. It went without saying that I always finished the food on my plate. This experience of wasted food on the ship was later augmented by my experiences in the American South. My friends explained to me that if you finished your plate while a guest in someone's home, it could be interpreted as the host not offering enough; thus it might be considered impolite to do so. I always thought I could judge beforehand, when being served, how much I could eat, and I could never bring myself to leave much on my plate—perhaps just a little, to abide by this rule.

Finally came the day on our journey when we approached American soil. As I arrived on deck, it was early morning and still fairly dark. I was not a minute too soon though, because we were passing the Statue of Liberty just at that moment, and I enjoyed our first view of Manhattan. The cameras started clicking, mine included. Here I was, in America, the country that used to be our enemy, but was also the country that liberated us from Nazism and was key in restoring us as a free and increasingly prosperous nation; I really knew little about the United States. I thought to myself, *What will this new adventure bring me?* The thought that this new country might become my home in later years did not even cross my mind.

Disembarkation went slowly since there was some sort of strike in the harbor. After getting my two little suitcases, I left the pier to carry out a pleasant official duty. As arranged by the institute in Stuttgart, I was to meet Max Kade and hand him the document declaring his nomination as Honorary Senator, along with a plaque from the school. Wolfgang Walther was to accompany me.

When I called Max Kade, he did not sound particularly friendly at first. As I heard later from his secretary, he was called out from a meeting to answer my call and did not care much for honors, anyway. He advised me on the phone to call a cab at the pier, which he would pay for, and come meet him at his West Street factory. As Wolfgang and I looked around, trying to find out how to get a cab, a person at the pier asked me if I needed a ride. Upon my affirmation, he whistled, and a cab appeared. As we were getting into the cab, the man stretched out his hand to me. Only later did I realize that he was expecting a tip for his brokerage services.

The meeting with Max Kade was very pleasant. He took us out to lunch and afterward went with us to Pennsylvania Station, since he had to catch a train himself. He gave each of us twenty dollars, which was a lot of money for us. Wolfgang and I left our luggage in a locker at the train station, something you still could do in those days, and then took a long walk to see and absorb the sites of Manhattan. When we arrived back at the station, we realized that we had only ten minutes left until the departure of our train to Atlanta.

Arrival and Introduction to Georgia Tech

As we arrived in Atlanta and were contemplating how to get a taxi to Georgia Tech, two students approached us. They were sent by the school's YMCA to pick us up. Every year, about six exchange students were sponsored by the school—one or two who came from Stuttgart, one from Zurich, and the rest from colleges around the world. Conversely, some Tech students received scholarships to go abroad. Most of the money for the program was collected at halftime during a football game.

The first item of business in my introduction to the United States was the pronunciation of my name. My classmates stumbled over saying "Dankwart." "The name of the prior exchange student from Germany was Wolfgang and we called him Wolf, hence we will call you Dank," one of them said. I did not like this idea, and never liked it for decades to come, but what could

I say? I was only a foreign student who was a guest in the country. I had no knowledge of people's linguistic abilities, which, on average, were lower in the United States than in Europe.

After arriving at the Georgia Tech campus, we stopped at the college's YMCA office to meet its head, who, in a sense, was our boss. As I left the office, the two students who had picked us up at the train station said to me, "We'll see you pretty soon." I pondered what they said for a while. *Pretty* means "beautiful," so what does it have to do with *soon*? In school, the English we learned was more academic than practical, and this use of the word *pretty* had never come up in class.

My introduction to my room, in Smith Dormitory, came next. There I met Melvin Sires, my roommate. Melvin was a junior from Macon, Georgia. Everything in the dorm was new for me, including the lack of doors for the toilet stalls and the students running around naked to and from the shower. It was for reasons related to the latter observation, that females, including mothers, were never allowed beyond the downstairs lobby. Times were different then than they are today, when an increasing number of colleges are introducing coed housing in dormitories.

Having an assigned roommate proved to be very useful for me in becoming acquainted with my new life in America, which was so different from what I had experienced before. One thing that struck me as interesting was the informal and colorful dress of the students on campus. I was used to wearing a tie, even as a student, back home. A half a century later, this difference between American and German students has pretty much disappeared.

A few days after my arrival, my academic life began. I first met Dr. Dasher, the head of the electrical engineering department. He went over my academic background with me. I did not have a bachelor's degree, which did not exist in Germany. I had finished four years of college, but without having yet taken the required examinations for all of my courses.

Some people claim, and I have heard similar statements from German consulates, that the German high school diploma is equivalent to two years of college in the United States. I agree only to some degree. Most freshmen in the United States have to take very basic courses, including English and sports, in their first year. This is not the case in Germany. In fact, sports are totally absent from German college curricula. Furthermore, the level in math and science required for a German high school diploma is very high. I would therefore assume that a German high school diploma is equivalent to one year at a U.S. college, but not two, and definitely not in engineering. On the other hand, due to the enforced, more intense study I experienced in the United States, I believe that an American student catches up, and when earning a master's degree, is as well-equipped as the German student with his or her diploma.

Dr. Dasher felt that despite my lack of a bachelor's degree, I should start in graduate school and pursue a master's degree. This was in contrast to what I had heard back home when we were discouraged from pursuing a degree program in the States, and instead were encouraged to concentrate on social interactions and learning about American life. But the EE school looked only at the academic side of my year at Georgia Tech.

My enrollment in a master's program was acceptable to the EE school, but the administration stumbled over my lack of a bachelor's degree. I sent a telegram to Stuttgart asking for school records, but it took too long to receive an answer. Meanwhile, I got permission to start graduate school with an informal registration. The goal set for me was to complete a master's degree within the nine months I had available.

The first class I attended was about electrical power systems and was taught by Professor Nottingham. I expected a strictly technical lecture with electrical equations written on the blackboard; instead, he rambled on, telling both technical and non-technical stories. I understood close to nothing. One reason for this was that he had a very strong Southern drawl; I was only familiar with British English. American "Yankee English" was difficult enough for me. The prior warnings went through my head that the exchange program reserved the right to send a student home when his or her knowledge of English was found to be inadequate. I realized the two and a half years of English I had in high school were indeed not adequate.

Some relief came with my second lecture, given by Professor Dasher. The subject was determinants and matrices. He wrote everything on the blackboard and, most importantly, he was a Yankee from north of the Mason-Dixon Line. I understood practically everything he said and got the feeling that I might be saved.

From then on, things went fairly well for me. I found that the American system of having a roll call—making class attendance mandatory—and being exposed to a constant series of quizzes and examinations, forced me to study more intensely than back home. In comparing American and German colleges, I came to the conclusion that in later years, American colleges make up for the fact that much of a student's freshman year is either related to general education or is similar to what Europeans learn in their last high school grade.

As I applied to register for the winter quarter, my second quarter at Georgia Tech, I was notified that I was officially accepted for graduate study toward an MS with "special graduate standing," and that if my work continued at a sufficiently high level, my standing would be reconsidered.

Extracurricular Life

My scholarship included free tuition, pocket money of fifty dollars a month, housing in the dormitory, and fraternity guest status for meals. On my second day at Georgia Tech, I was introduced to my fraternity house, Kappa Alpha, a very Southern fraternity that prided itself on having been founded by Robert E. Lee. On weekdays, I had breakfast, lunch, and dinner at the fraternity house, which was very close to the EE school. I was also invited to take part in their social life, which included many dances, but I always felt a little bit like an outsider. I needed time to get used to the less formal American life and I also had the misconception that American girls—which is what young women used to be called in those days—would not be interested in someone who would be leaving at the end of the school year. It seemed to me that they wanted to get married as quickly as possible.

Dances held on Saturdays had to end at midnight, since dancing was not allowed on Sunday. Regardless of whether the dance was on a Saturday or another day of the week, whenever it was midnight at the fraternity, the activity stopped in order to sing, what I call the national anthem of the South, "I Wish I Was in Dixie."

At least once a week, the exchange students received invitations to parties or dances outside the fraternity through the YMCA. Getting my own date for these affairs was a bit of a problem, not only because of my above-mentioned perceived handicap, or shyness, but especially for financial reasons. You needed to either own or rent a car for a date, and inviting a young lady to dinner or a movie was a big strain on my fifty-dollars-a-month budget.

Melvin, my roommate, set me up on a few blind dates. Naturally, I liked some better than others. On one of these blind dates, Melvin informed me that he had told the date that I could not really speak English. He had told her that one of the few words I did know was "oatmeal." I have no idea why he picked that word; he probably thought it was funny. He begged me to say the word when he introduced me to her, and, trying to be a good sport, I did. She went into shock and did not recover for the rest of the evening. Melvin explained later to me that she once had an aunt from Europe, who stayed with her family and did not speak English at all. This experience had shocked her as a child, Melvin said. Not speaking English must have been tantamount to not being able to speak at all for the little country girl. But I still have trouble fully believing the story. Maybe the date was more shocked about us playing this trick on her than about my faked language deficiency.

While at Tech, I had a full class schedule, and, on top of that, a fair amount of homework. In one of my early letters home, I wrote that much of the homework was boring. Part of this perhaps had to do with the fact that some of the class material repeated what I had studied in Germany. But with time, my homework increased in difficulty and quantity. What I liked the least were the reading assignments, since I still felt a significant language handicap.

Furthermore, my social life tended to collide with my busy academic schedule. First there were the dances on campus. Then, a large number of invitations followed. Some of the invitations from off campus were from families for dinner or for a weekend with them. Other invitations came from organizations that invited foreign students to their meetings and dinners. These organizations included churches, often a Baptist church, women's organizations, nursery schools, the YWCA, and the local Lion's club. One of these clubs, the Cotillion Club, invited a few of us for their Presidents' Week celebration. We were amused when, in honor of George Washington's birthday, the ladies sang "Happy Birthday, Dear Georgie."

At many of these invitations, we had to give a talk about Germany or comparing our two countries. Once I was invited to speak to a group of "girls," but found, much to my disappointment, that they were between seven and ten years old. However, I did also get invitations from women's colleges, which I liked especially if a dance was part of it.

As much as my fifty-dollars-a-month budget allowed, I occasionally attended a concert with some of the other exchange students. I remember in particular a beautiful Christmas concert at one of the predominantly black colleges in Atlanta. My roommate later expressed surprise that I went to see "the niggers," as he worded it.

"How Do You Like it Over Here?"

Starting from the very first day of our trip, the standard question that everybody kept asking us exchange students was, "How do you like it over here?" Another question on the most frequently asked list was "How do you like grits?"—an essential ingredient of breakfast in the South. Of course, you would not dare saying something negative or go into any deep analysis of your experiences; that was not what the questioner wanted to hear. But giving the expected compliments whenever such questions came up or whenever I was introduced to something new, was not what I was used to doing at home.

At the same time, I was surprised to find how easy it was to make new friends. Usually, though, these friendships were less deep than the friendships I had back home, where relationships grew more gradually. The Southern expression "Come back and see us" is a farewell and not an invitation; though if you did actually return someplace, you would most likely be welcome. I became good friends with several fraternity students. I renewed acquaintances and friendships with some of them when my wife and I moved to Atlanta, six years later.

Many things that I saw and experienced were strange to me. On the one hand, there were the great American achievements in daily life: five-minute car washes, drive-through restaurants (such as the Georgia Tech Varsity which claimed to be the world's largest), drive-in movies, and self-service restaurants. On the other, there were things I found strange: people driving five minutes to find a parking spot to avoid walking a few yards, lack of good public transportation, "dry" counties, and many over-weight people. But I always remembered the advice from the introductory meeting for exchange students in Germany: always ask "Why?" This questioning often led to an explanation for the strangeness that I felt and observed. It takes time to get used to something. While now reading some of the letters that I wrote home and my mother saved, I notice that, with time, I usually turned from expressing surprise to expressing acceptance, and sometimes praise.

In the years after my return to Germany, I found that people who had stayed or visited the United States typically fell into two categories: people who enthusiastically praised the United States, and people who emphatically offered examples of what they considered bad about the country. I think that they were both right; the striking characteristic of the United States is that you cannot characterize it. Every country has good and bad aspects, and your reaction depends on what you want to see and what you pick out. It is almost like reflecting on whether you are an optimist or a pessimist, whether you see the glass half full or half empty. I recently heard it said that an engineer would answer, "The glass is too large."

One of the first instances of culture shock I experienced was in a lecture, when one of my professors explained that there were only two groups of students that he felt should be specifically fostered and supported by the school: the outstand-ing students and the football players. Of course, I agreed with the former, but I had difficulty accepting the latter. To me, and I guess most students in countries other than the United

States, the prime purpose of a college is to teach academics. Yet I later realized that Georgia Tech's football team played a big role in enhancing the school's reputation and attracting new students. The team was among the top three in the South at the time. In a sense, I had no reason to complain since my stay at Georgia Tech was sponsored by money collected at a football game.

I was glad that I was not a first-year student—a freshman—at Tech. The "rats," as they were called, had to wear a special orange cap with the word "rat" on it. The rats also had to follow other rules, such as not using the main entrance steps to the administration building and not entering the campus post office at certain times. Violating these rules led to a punishment in the form of getting a "T-cut," which meant having the head shaven clean, except for a *T*, which stood for "Tech."

Another thing I observed was that Tech students were allowed to smoke in class. In those days, you could practically smoke anywhere, including cinemas, but smoking in class was still new for me.

Not long after my arrival, I experienced another interesting and eventful day at Georgia Tech: homecoming day. The day had two highlights: the football game and the Ramblin' Wreck Parade. The parade's name alludes to the nickname of a student as a "Ramblin' Wreck from Georgia Tech," as described in the school's fight song. The homecoming event included a parade and a competition of old car wrecks transformed into magical vehicles. Some of the cars barely resembled an automobile; others stumbled on four legs instead of four wheels. Most of the cars were entered in the parade by the fraternities. The students spent countless days collecting and disassembling old automobiles and transforming them into their wreck, with the hope of—if not winning the contest—having their wreck at least make it all the way to the finish line of the parade.

Student Vacations

My roommate Melvin's mother declared that she now had a second son when referring to me. Indeed it was very pleasant to have a sort of a second home, and, at the same time, to obtain a more personal insight into American family life. I spent several weekends with them in their house in Macon, Georgia. Melvin also took me to visit his grandparents. He said that they were rich, explaining, "They have a Cadillac, which cost four thousand dollars."

On one of my visits, Melvin and his friends took me quail hunting, which was a first for me since I had never been on any hunt. I had not carried a rifle since the war, nor had I ever heard of quail hunting. The hunt occurred at night and they gave me a black bag to use to catch a quail. I was instructed to stand at a certain spot, hold the bag open, and wait for a quail, which I did. What I did not know was that this was a joke at my expense. After a little while, Melvin and his friends came back and revealed their secret.

It was particularly nice for me that Melvin's mother invited me to join their family for Christmas. I was curious to observe Christmas in the United States and compare it with Christmas back home. One of the first differences I noted was that the tree was lit long before Christmas Eve and that it was lit with electric lights rather than real candles. Most homes also had Christmas decorations on the outside. What was also new to me was that the main celebration of Christmas was on the morning of the twenty-fifth, and not on Christmas Eve, with the highlight being the opening of an abundance of presents. This was quite different from our festive celebration in Germany, and the pause for reflection we took when we first entered the Christmas room at home on Christmas Eve and saw the tree for the first time.

I told Melvin's mother that, back home, a glass of wine was part of the Christmas dinner and was sometimes even served during the celebration on Christmas Eve. Rarely did we ever drink more than a glass, but it added to the festivity, I said. On Christmas Eve, Melvin's mother took me aside and told me that she had put a bottle of booze in a brown bag in my closet for me to drink. I was instructed not to tell Melvin about it. Needless to say, I never touched the bottle of whiskey in that brown bag. What a misinterpretation of what I said!

Right after Christmas, I headed back to Atlanta to meet up with some friends for a trip to Florida. This turned into a marvelous experience with many new impressions: the vastness of the country, drive-through restaurants, never-ending orange orchards, beautiful beaches, the Everglades, and the Florida Keys, to mention a few.

Three months later, we had our spring break. This time, a fellow student from Wisconsin invited me to come home with him for the break. The trip became another interesting experience for me as it included a tour of Milwaukee and a visit to the Pabst Brewery, which, twenty years earlier, had primarily German-speaking employees, so I was told. The brewery still had German tradition written all over it. The old Gothic script lettering in the company's logo, the brewery's architecture, and the posters made it almost look like being in Germany. My friend's family wanted to make me feel at home by taking me there, but I found it more amusing and definitely interesting. From Wisconsin, I took a bus to visit Chicago, another exciting destination. Naturally, I took a fair amount of photographs during my various travels in the United States.

Political and Social Issues

When I think of social and political issues that struck me during my student stay at Georgia Tech, I find three that stand out: women, Communism, and racial segregation.

During the fall semester of the year I was there, Georgia Tech admitted the first seven female students in its history. Other than as secretaries and administrative staff, women had not been present on the campus, neither as students nor as professors. It seemed that the arrival of female students was generally accepted and the male students did not get overly excited, but rather enjoyed the novelty. The students I knew had been meeting "girls" through their fraternities or clubs. The Student Trial Board, which was part of the student government, however, needed to invent new rules for the female students, to deal with such issues as the possible violation of freshman regulations. It was decided that instead of the shaved head, with which the male freshmen were punished, female students would be required to wear their hair in nothing but pigtails.

A very hot issue in the South at the time was Communism. The fear of Communism reached its climax during the McCarthy era. Joseph McCarthy, an otherwise not very successful senator from Wisconsin, decided to put the fight against Communism at the top of his agenda. Communist subversives had infiltrated the democratic administration, he told the Senate. He branded his critics as being part of the Communist conspiracy and silenced them, until 1954, when other voices, critical of him, became too strong. The U.S. Senate later censured him for his conduct.

As part of my course curriculum, I took a course titled "Comparative Economic Systems." The lecture covered the various political systems, such as democracy, monarchy, Fascism, Nazism, and Communism. The professor compared the advantages and disadvantages, the strengths and weaknesses, of all of these systems. Since his comparison included both negative and positive aspects, some students took issue with his teaching, especially his coverage of Communism. To prove that he was not a Communist, the professor posted his obligatory clearance document from the McCarthy commission on his office door. That seemed to resolve the situation.

One evening I attended a beautiful performance by a Cossack chorus in Atlanta. When I told my roommate where I was going, he said that I should take a rifle and shoot them. This was probably a typical reaction in the days of McCarthy. But I told Melvin about my brother's experiences in World War II, when he was assigned to a Cossack division that fought against Bolshevism and Communism on the German side. Many Cossacks joined the German side to escape Stalin's oppression, also known as decossackization, with the hope of eventually creating their own independent homeland.

Especially interesting for me was my experience of segregation in the South. At the time, segregation was still a given fact of life, some fifteen years before the assassination of Martin Luther King, Jr. I still have the photographs I took of "White Only" and "Colored Only" signs hanging in waiting rooms at bus and train stations, and of the signs in Atlanta city parks stating the park's hours for "colored people." The buses still separated their riders: white passengers in the front and black passengers in the rear. African-Americans had to wait three more years until the resolution of the Montgomery Bus Boycott.

At Georgia Tech, segregation was not discussed much, since there were no black students admitted. Like Melvin, many of my fraternity friends still referred to black people as "niggers." Jazz music and spirituals, which were not yet very popular, were referred to as "nigger music."

Final Two Quarters at Georgia Tech

And so my studies went on after spring break, accompanied by invitations, parties, and other diversions. By the beginning of the spring quarter, the students of Kappa Alpha were all growing sideburns. This was in preparation for the fraternity's biggest annual event, the Old South Ball. The boys rented Southern gentlemen's uniforms and their dates wore Old South dresses. The fraternity students told me that they had hired Count Basie with his band. The name was new to me, at the time, but not so in later years, when I lived ten miles from Count Basie's birthplace, Red Bank, New Jersey. Since everybody said he was famous, I took a few pictures of the band at the ball. My photos wound up being printed in the student newspaper, though, I never got back the negatives I had submitted. Perhaps some student editor appreciated their importance too much to return them to me.

The ball was a festive occasion, at least initially. Because it was such a big event, alcohol was, while not allowed, at least condoned for this night. The result was that by midnight, most of the boys were pretty drunk, while the women stood around in their beautiful dresses and talked only to each other. For me, this was quite different from our parties and balls back home, where we usually drank a glass or two of wine, and rarely got really drunk. This is not to say that it did and does not happen. Efforts are under way in Germany today to increase the legal drinking age from sixteen to eighteen. Laws against drinking and driving are quite strict in Europe today—usually even stricter than in the United States. In Sweden, the tolerance for alcohol consumption before driving is zero; not a drop is permitted.

In Germany, we saw the lure of wine not as the means to get drunk, but as a way to enjoy company or to enhance a good meal. When I was invited into French homes as a POW, I was always surprised that wine was usually considered a natural part of the meal and given to children.

My final grade point average after my third, and last, quarter was 3.8. The head of the electrical engineering school was apologetic when he told me that, while I had fulfilled all the requirements for the Master of Science degree, I could not graduate since I did not have a bachelor's degree; thus, I could not participate in the graduation ceremonies on June 14. He made a deal with me though: once I returned to Germany and finished all the examinations that covered my first eight semesters at the Institute of Technology, Georgia Tech would recognize my passing of the examinations as the equivalent of a bachelor's degree and I could then apply for a master's degree, to be awarded to me at graduation one year later, which I was welcome to attend. Otherwise, I would receive the degree *in absentia*.

I was happy that I had completed a master's program in the nine months that I had available. I attended the June graduation ceremony as a spectator; it was a new and true spectacle for me. I watched it from the viewing stands of the football field. My good friend and fellow exchange student from Luxemburg, René Ney, insisted after the ceremony that I borrow his cap and gown and have my picture taken by him as a substitute for my expected absence in the ceremonies of the following year.

The Journey Home

My interesting days in Atlanta came to an end. Originally, I had planned to find some work for the remaining four weeks until my ship departed from New York, but I had only partial luck. For me to work as a foreigner, the companies to which I applied had to obtain "political clearance," which included a special clearance to prove that I was not "infected" by Communism. I found a temporary job for two weeks helping the Tech library move to a new building, but I decided to spend the remaining two weeks traveling with another exchange student. We found someone who was looking for students to drive a car from the East Coast to the West Coast. This gave us a unique opportunity to see the country before leaving, without having to rent a car, which would have been financially out of the question.

Our trip took us to Birmingham, Alabama; Memphis, Tennessee; and Little Rock, Arkansas, where we visited and stayed with other Georgia Tech students. In Memphis, our student friend, who had been an exchange student in Stuttgart, invited us on a powerboat trip with his father. He warned us beforehand that we should not offer to pay his father for the gasoline. We could never afford it, he said.

In Little Rock, the mother of our host worked at the local spa and invited us for a spa treatment, complete with bath and massage. This was the utmost in luxury, I thought, and another first for me.

As we continued along, we visited three national parks: the Carlsbad Caverns in New Mexico, and the Petrified Forest and incredible Grand Canyon in Arizona. Next on our agenda was Los Angeles. After visits to Sequoia National Park and Yosemite National Park, we reached our final destination, San Francisco. Shortly before turning in our car, my co-traveler managed to put a dent into it (and thus into our travel budget) while parking.

While in San Francisco, I paid a visit to Klaus Blech, a friend from back home, who studied political science at Berkeley and lived in the International House on campus. Klaus had visited me in Atlanta before Christmas, on a trip to Miami. It was not until almost thirty years later that I saw him again, in Tokyo.

Having turned in the car, the question for me became how to get to New York. My traveling companion planned to stay a bit longer in San Francisco, but I had to catch my ship about a week later. I decided to try hitchhiking, which in those days was still a fairly safe and not unusual undertaking. To get out of San Francisco and start my adventure, I took a bus to Sacramento. Then it was all hitchhiking—and I did it in five days. The key to my success was that I had a little metal suitcase, onto which I had pasted the Georgia Tech logo, with its big *T* and a yellow jacket. In addition, I made a cardboard sign that said

"German Exchange Student to New York." My intention was to give people an idea of who I was, which they could then verify hearing my accent. The logo and sign did the trick. Most of the time, people who were interested in meeting me would pick me up, as opposed to local drivers who were only going a few miles. It became a marvelous experience. Most of my rides were with families who were on a car trip, visiting the great sites of the country. Several times, I was invited to stay overnight with them in their motel.

One of my first stops was Salt Lake City. Before I resumed hitchhiking, I began to walk up the hills north of the city, to view the skyline and to enjoy the Utah scenery. I was more than surprised when a woman stopped her car to ask me if I needed a ride. Apparently, she wondered why anybody would walk around the middle of nowhere, unless he had car trouble or some other emergency. The little event seemed so American to me that it became one of the stories I later told people back in Germany.

I had a beautiful trip back East. With the help of my impromptu hosts, I had a chance to see two more national parks, Grand Teton and Yellowstone. As I drove through Pennsylvania, I was amazed how similar the landscape—with its rolling hills, forests, and fields—was to the one back home, especially after the unusual scenery that I had seen in the preceding days. On July 31, I arrived in Springfield, New Jersey, where I spent the last four days with Aunt Junia, a friend of my mother. She had sent me my first American care packages when I was a POW. She was part of a group of German-Americans who tried to help postwar Germany recover from the war, to which Max Kade also belonged. Aunt Junia introduced me to the life of Germans living in the United States. She took me to the German Club of Clark, New Jersey. Even though that club is less than an half-hour drive from where my family later lived for many years, I never made it back for another visit. My wife and I found that the German tradition, including the music that is cultivated and celebrated by German-American clubs in the United States, largely dates back to the Germany of half a century ago.

On August 4, 1954, I boarded the SS *Independence*, the sister ship of the SS *Constitution*, which had brought me to the United States ten months earlier. After a beautiful journey across the Atlantic and through the Mediterranean, followed by a train ride through northern Italy and Switzerland, I arrived home. I was enriched with a wealth of new personal, social, and political experiences, along with a significant addition to my academic education.

9

Back in Germany

Examinations and Graduate School

Shortly after my return home, I was back at the Institute of Technology in Stuttgart. Above all, I had to study for the exams covering the courses that I had taken in my third and fourth year of college. Since much time had passed since then, this required an extra amount of study. The examinations were always held in the vacation periods between semesters. Some were written and some were oral, some were easy and some were not. To my surprise, I got a perfect grade on the exams for a few courses in which I had zero interest when I took them. It was because of my reduced interest that I had studied especially hard for those examinations, which paid off.

The next step after I finished all those examinations was to begin a diploma thesis. It was a requirement for the engineering diploma and was a fairly extensive undertaking. The same professor who had advised me five years earlier to attend college rather than to become an electrician, became my thesis adviser. While discussing my thesis with him, we also laid plans for a doctoral dissertation.

The work for my diploma thesis consisted of developing and building the measuring systems that I would later need for my doctoral dissertation. The latter was entitled "Relaxation Effects of the Initial Permeability of Ferrites." What it is, in plain English, is the examination of the magnetic properties of ferrites. Ferrite is the material that makes up the magnets you use to hold your photographs and notes on your refrigerator. In the late 1950s, this was a totally new material, whose properties were yet to be explored scientifically. I made the measurements of its magnetic properties over a wide range of frequencies, from about 100 hertz (i.e., oscillations per second) to as high as 3.8 gigahertz (billion hertz) and over a temperature range from -196°C (-321°F) (the temperature at which air, or to be more precise, nitrogen, becomes liquid upon cooling) up to +100°C (+212°F).

The adviser for my diploma thesis, Professor Feldtkeller, was also my *Doktorvater* (doctor-father), as the adviser for a doctoral dissertation is commonly called in Germany. Despite this pleasant name, some PhD advisers are less a father to you than a god. In line with old traditions that may have only recently undergone occasional changes, professors are hierarchically organized. A full professor is at the top of the pyramid. Except for administrative aspects within the school, he or she reports only to the minister of education for the state and is appointed for life, becoming a professor emeritus when he or she retires. Associate professors, assistant professors, and lecturers and other assistants report to a specific full professor.

Professor Dr.h.c. Dr.rer.nat. Richard Feldtkeller, as his official name went, was highly respected in the field of electronics and academia. Before accepting the call as a professor, he had been head of wireless communication research at Siemens and had written several books, including some describing novel analytical techniques. One critical aspect for us, those students working under him, was that we did not dare ask him a question unless we had the query completely defined, as he expected us to do. The good news was that, in trying to identify precisely what you did not understand and what you wanted to ask him, you usually arrived at the answer yourself.

One of Professor Feldtkeller's idiosyncrasies was that when he was asked a question to which he did not know the answer, for example in a seminar, he would respond by saying, "Da bin ich überfragt," which, literally translated, means "Here I am over-asked." This statement was in accordance with his god-like status as a professor who is supposed to know everything and cannot admit that this is not always true.

While I was working on my diploma thesis, I also took a couple of courses out of curiosity. One of them concerned the newest technology that made the technical headlines: transistors, which were about to replace the old radio tubes.

Graduate Degrees

Needless to say, as soon as I finished the last exam for my first four years of study, I had the school forward the respective information to Georgia Tech, in accordance with the agreement that this would be considered the equivalent of a BS. By early spring, I was notified by Georgia Tech that I had indeed fulfilled the requirements for my Master of Science in electrical engineering. The actual graduation was not until May 1955. Naturally, I did not attend the ceremony. I had at least gotten my fake photograph the year before. I now belonged to the graduation class of 1955, to which I did not feel connected; I would not have known anybody had I gone to the graduation or to any of the later class reunions.

Four months after the Georgia Tech graduation, I finished my German diploma thesis and completed the requirements for my German diploma. There is no such thing as a graduation ceremony in Germany, but the printed engineering diploma that I received said that I was a *Diplom-Ingenieur*, abbreviated as *Dipl.-Ing*. This word is used both as a title and a professional designation.

Work on my doctoral dissertation proceeded on schedule. I was initially still sponsored by the above-mentioned Studienstiftung and could therefore devote my full time to dissertation work. Most of the other graduate students working on their doctorate were additionally engaged as assistants to a professor, which meant that it typically took them about five years to complete their dissertation. My Doktorvater said that he wanted to show the world that if you worked full-time, you could do a dissertation in about one and a half years. He also was of the opinion that if your printed dissertation was longer than seventy or eighty pages, you had failed to represent your essential results and just rambled on.

Other Activities

In addition to our work at the Institute of Communication Engineering, chaired by Professor Feldtkeller, we also had fun. My work, and that of some other graduate students, involved the use of frozen carbon dioxide (CO_2). I used it to obtain another special well-defined low temperature point, 99°F, between my two extreme temperatures. Carbon dioxide is liquid below that temperature (or at higher temperatures, including room temperature, under high pressure) and is therefore kept under pressure in a gas cylinder. As you open the valve and let the CO_2 escape slowly from the cylinder, you can capture it in the form of dry ice, before it evaporates as a gas. Our laboratory was located in the center of Stuttgart, on the third floor of the engineering building. On the other side of the street was a government building. A few times during lunchtime, when we saw a group of young women promenading on the sidewalk below us, we would make a dry ice snowball and drop it in front of them. We had fun watching their reactions as they saw a snowball in the middle of summer, which would disappear after a few seconds without leaving a trace.

I had applied to become a resident in the Max Kade Heim. I was accepted and enjoyed the luxury of a small room with convertible bed and a little corner kitchen—this was more than a step up from the rooms I had rented in Stuttgart in prior years. The dormitory was just two blocks from the electrical engineering building, where Professor Feldtkeller had his institute. It had fourteen floors, of which the thirteenth floor was for female students. It was administered by the Institute of Student Affairs, but otherwise had its own student self-government. After living in Max Kade Heim, I somehow became president of the dormitory. His Magnifizenz, who was elected president of the school for one year and was one of my electrical engineering professors, once said to me, "You always need a little position, don't you?"

Having this particular position proved not always to be easy for me. Professor Hecht, a young professor who was assigned to be our "liaison and confidence professor," moved into the first floor of the thirteen-story dormitory with his wife. The first floor housed a special family apartment for this purpose. At the time he moved in, we happened to be in talks with the administration about the curfew time at which female guests had to leave the dormitory in the evening. We were pleading for twelve o'clock and the administration for ten o'clock. We were highly disappointed when we heard that our confidence professor sided with the administration rather than representing us. Another point of contention was that there was a lot of piano playing in his first floor apartment, which disturbed the students on the next floor. It was not a pleasant task for me to be the intermediary in these issues.

However, the big issue was yet to come. The Institute of Student Affairs informed us that they needed to raise our rent, unless we could find other ways to reduce expenses within their budget for the dormitory. Some female students came to me and said they had been told that Professor Hecht would pay rent for living on the first floor, but that they had just heard that this was no longer the case. Even though I didn't like to get into fights over such touchy subjects, I had no choice but to look into the issues. I talked to the administration about Professor Hecht's rent and also mentioned the piano problem. Two days later, someone reported that the professor was mad at me for inquiring about such matters as personal as his rent. So I called him, and tried to make an appointment. As soon as I said who I was, I heard the words "I am sorry, I don't know you."

Since I had the full backing of the student community in the dorm, I wrote Professor Hecht a letter, expressing my shock about his reaction on the telephone and asking him to meet with me and some other students to discuss the events and to give me a chance to defend my actions. Then I wrote: "Should you not be willing to meet with me, I will call a student house meeting on Monday, where I will report on the recent events. I will, of course, do everything possible not to touch on any non-factual or sensitive issues, but I cannot guarantee that the other students will honor this promise. I shall ask for a vote of confidence and will resign if I do not obtain it." I invited him to the meeting.

A few of our female students obtained an audience with the professor and calmed the situation somewhat. Nevertheless, Professor Hecht took my letter to the president of the school and lobbied for my dismissal from the school for inquiring into the personal affairs of a professor and for threatening him. I took the letter to Professor Feldtkeller. He promised to defend me, but told me a life lesson that I never forgot and that I have heeded many times since then: "Just because you know you are right, you don't have to express yourself in a way that could be interpreted as a threat. Instead you should be as polite as possible." Fortunately, the affair quieted down gradually. Professor Hecht assumed a professorship at another school in another city, a move most likely initiated and suggested by the institute. Much later, I ran into his Magnifizenz, and he said to me, "That professor does not have ears. He has antennas."

As a former Georgia Tech exchange student, I was invited to participate in the committee that selected the student that would receive the scholarship for studying at Georgia Tech in the coming year. I remember two episodes from that meeting. First, was when one of the applicants appeared in what was considered very casual dress at the time—a colorful shirt and blue jeans—while everybody else wore a coat and tie. He apparently thought it would be useful to demonstrate that he was well Americanized. The American head of our committee said to us, "Even in the States, you don't dress like this for such an occasion."

The second moment that stands out was when an applicant answered the question of where Atlanta was situated with, "On the Chattahoochee." The homework he had done greatly impressed all the Americans on the committee, who probably did not know the connection between Atlanta and the Chattahoochee River. It was, however, no surprise to the Germans in the room, since the indication of the river on which a city lies is very customary in Europe. The designation of the river is often even part of the city's name, or at least used in addition to the city's name.

West and East Germany

As I mentioned in an earlier chapter, my family did not have relatives, or even close friends, in northern Germany. We also didn't know anybody in Communist East Germany, which was then officially called the German Democratic Republic. Even if we did have friends and relatives there, our ability to communicate with them would have been very limited. Mail was subject to censorship by the Communist regime.

Professor Feldtkeller was in close contact with two professors at the Institute of Technology in Dresden, who were famous in the field of electronics. He once visited them and upon his return, told us about his experiences. He said when his train crossed into East Germany, all conversations changed almost completely, both in volume, and in content. In East Germany, you did not dare express yourself openly. You did not know who in your vicinity was observing you, either accidentally or by higher order, and might even report you. Along the same lines, when Professor Feldtkeller visited his Dresden colleagues, they told him privately that, within the school, they could not trust most of the people around them. Very rarely would they know which of the students or assistants might be spying on them.

At the same time, the East German professors lived in a golden cage. Even though they were not blue-collar workers in the "state of farmers and laborers," they were considered the top of the "working intelligentsia." The government did everything to prevent them from fleeing to the West. Hence, they were kept as isolated from the population as possible. The professors shopped in special stores set up for members of the new upper class, like party functionaries and others the system needed to cater to. These selected few could buy luxury goods, like butter, which were nonexistent for the general population. Money was not a scarcity for the upper class. Even people in the population at large had more money than they could spend, given the scarcity of goods. It was much later that middle-class East Germans could apply to buy cars. Their waiting times were initially as long as six years, but later became at least six months.

Once, an organization within the Stuttgart Institute of Technology invited a group of students and a professor from Dresden for a discussion meeting in Stuttgart. These were not the kind of people my thesis advisor had met in Dresden. They were carefully selected and well prepared by the "system." They came with prepared questions and statements, such as:

- In the West, how do you save the worker from exploitation by the Capitalists?
- What freedom is there in the West, given the total lack of economic freedom?

(I don't recall or understand what they really meant by this question. Maybe they felt that our economy was controlled by the United States. They certainly had their own definition of freedom.)

- In the West, you force people to vote in secret ballots, whereas in the East, we give people the choice to vote openly.
- We would not be surprised if Western students behaved in an un-American and conciliatory way during our discussion here and later had to bear the consequences.

They repeatedly said that Germany was dominated by the United States. When we said, "In the West, we are free to criticize our government. In the East, the Party controls everything," the students from East Germany answered, "The people in the East stand 100 percent behind their government and the Party." They also remarked that we occasionally contradicted one another during the discussion, which demonstrated that the West was weak. Needless to say, the entire discussion did not lead anywhere and was not friendly. The president of our institution summed it up by saying, "It is incredible how people from the same country, after only a few years, could hear the same words so differently."

I came to the conclusion that it was impossible to have a fruitful discussion with Communists, because the underlying principles of belief, or axioms, are totally different in the two camps. I furthermore observed that the Communists were always extremely well prepared. They cited specific examples of events in the West that were indeed questionable and that we were barely, if at all, familiar with.

In the case of our student discussion with the East Germans, I would say that they more or less "won" the debate, at least from a dialectic aspect. In addition to their good preparation, the Communist representatives were specifically trained in the art of logic and reason. The main problem, though, was that their arguments appeared fairly logical, if and only if, you accepted some of their ridiculous basic principles. One of their principles was, "The State does not exist to serve you, but you exist to serve the State," an argument that I had heard in my youth under Hitler. For example, the East German students argued that if the state pays for all your high school and college tuition expenses and gives you free housing, the state has the right to tell you where you live and where you work.

Six years after our Stuttgart discussion, the Berlin Wall went up and the ideological iron curtain became a physical reality.

First Job at Telefunken

As the work on my dissertation approached its final phase, it was time for me to look for a job. In the last year of my dissertation work, my support from the Studienstiftung ran out, but Professor Feldtkeller obtained another scholarship for me, as he did for most of his other graduate students. He never told us where the money came from, but we were quite sure that it came from Siemens. It appeared that he did not want to make us feel obligated to work for Siemens after graduate school, even though this was what he most likely wished all of his graduate students would do.

I interviewed with the Telefunken Research Laboratory in Ulm and accepted a job to start work on June 1, 1957. The group that I joined was involved in the development of radiation measurement and monitoring equipment. Our group leader was Herr Professor Fränz. He had emigrated from Germany to Argentina after the war and became a professor there. I do not know whether he returned because of the improved economic situation in Germany or for other reasons. Due to his Argentinean title, he wanted to be addressed as "Herr Professor." We were a small group of less than ten people who worked together very closely.

My task was to develop an instrument to measure gamma-ray radiation with a Geiger counter. It was the first piece of radiation measuring equipment developed in our lab that used transistors instead of the bulky electronic glass tubes used up to that time (and which were still used by my colleagues in their development projects). I was glad I had at least audited a course on transistors while still at school, but I still needed to gain practical experience.

A good year later, I finished the instrument. One of my colleagues took the first model to a conference and trade show on nuclear radiation. He told me that he played tricks on the representative of one of our competitors, whom he knew personally and who tended his company's exhibit just across the aisle. When the competitor had a customer, my friend would point a collimated (i.e., a sharply focused) beam of radioactive radiation from a cesium source across the aisle to the competitor's booth. This radiation caused our competitor's radiation measuring equipment to go wild and set off an alarm indicating super-high radiation values. Today, my colleague would probably go to jail for shooting around such a potent radiation source.

Whenever someone had a birthday in our group, the person to be honored went across the street and got a few bottles of wine and some snacks. It was, and still is, a common practice in Germany for a person to invite people to his or her birthday, rather than the other way around. An hour before official closing time, we cleaned our lab benches off for the celebration. Of course, I never saw anybody drink too much at such occasions.

April 1 was another fun day. April Fool's Day is taken more seriously in Germany than in the United States. I remember that the newspapers had several fake front page stories on April 1, such as an announcement that an ocean liner had arrived on the river, which, of course, was impossible. At work, one of my colleagues, who had bragged about one of his publications being noted in Japan, received a formal-looking Japanese document on April 1. He showed it to everybody with pride until he found someone to translate it for him. The document said that he was entitled to wear red socks on Sundays. Another colleague had a firecracker go off when he opened his locker. Another mean trick was that people in one of our labs pushed a wired selenium rectifier under the wall into the neighboring lab and ran current until the rectifier overheated and burned out. The resulting smell of rotten eggs stayed for several hours.

Ulm is a beautiful city on the Danube and belongs to the state of Württemberg. In its center is the world's tallest cathedral. The cathedral was first dedicated as a church in 1405, although it was not completed at the time. On its roof sits the unofficial emblem of the city, the Ulmer Spatz. It is an iron sparrow with a straw in its beak, and it refers to an old story. When the church was built, some of the workers needed to bring large wooden beams into the city, and so they loaded them crosswise onto their cart. When they reached the city gate, the cart did not fit through. The workers did not know how to solve their problem, until one of them saw a sparrow that needed to get a long straw through a narrow passage to its nest. The sparrow turned its head so that the tip of the straw pointed forward. The bird inspired the workers and they reloaded the cart.

Ulm was also the birthplace of Albert Einstein and the home-town of Generalfeldmarschall Erwin Rommel, one of the most revered generals of the German army. Toward the end of the war, Rommel was given the choice of taking a cyanide pill and receiving military honors for his death, which was later declared the result of an earlier injury from an air attack on his car, or facing court-martial and certain execution for being involved in the July 20, 1944, assassination attempt on Hitler. He chose the former. It became known after the war that he knew about the plot, but was not a participant. It was also held against him that, after the Allied Normandy invasion, he considered the war hopeless and had proposed to Hitler a political end to the war.

My search for a place to live in Ulm was answered by a family who lived in a beautiful small house in a new residential section of Neu-Ulm, the sister city that lies on the other side of the Danube River in the state of Bavaria. The head of the family was director in a textile factory; I had to address him as Herr Direktor. His wife was twenty-one years younger than he was. They had a cute four-year-old daughter, Eveline, who managed to get from her parents whatever she wanted. She often wanted to play with me, which I sometimes did. I successfully taught her that, in contrast to her parents, when I said no, it meant no, and the decision could not be reversed by her insistence. For Christmas, the family set up a tree, even though they were Jewish, because they did not want Eveline to feel different from her friends.

I am still not sure why the family rented out a room; the house was not really set up for a tenant. But I received increas-ingly strong signals that the lady of the house wanted more than just someone to play with her daughter or pay rent. She involved a friend of hers to convey various messages to me. One was to let me know that I did not really need a car; I could use the Porsche if I engaged in a closer relationship with her. Unfortunately for her, I felt the necessary chemistry completely missing. Fortunately for me, however, an event came along at that moment that changed everything.

Thesis Defense and More

At the end of August 1957, I completed the write-up of my doctoral dissertation. My dissertation defense was held on February 8, 1958, in the auditorium of the electrical engineering department. It went pretty much as planned, except for one unexpected question. One of the physics professors asked me to explain the magnetic properties of ferrites in terms of the periodic table of elements, which hung in the room. With my general dislike of chemistry, I had no idea how to answer his question. I am quite sure that this cost me a graduation with honors. But after a short closed session, I was called back into the room and was told that I had passed the doctoral examination. According to German academic tradition, I could not yet call myself a "doctor of engineering." Instead, there was another title for my status, namely *Dr.des.*, or *Doctor designatus*, which means "designated."

Since my defense was on a Saturday, I did not go back to Ulm, but instead boarded a train for Heilbronn to visit my family. My mother apologized that they had committed themselves to go to the Singkranz's annual *Fasching*, or "Mardi Gras," dance party. Now called the Heilbronn Philharmonic Choir, the Singkranz was a local music organization whose primary function was to perform various choral concerts throughout the year. My oldest brother Uli belonged to the chorus and my parents were sponsoring members. My mother said to me that she assumed that I would be too tired to come along to the party, but I vigorously stated that I was ready to celebrate rather than to go to bed early. I did not have a date, but went with my brothers and some other male and female friends, in addition to my parents.

The dance was in a nice restaurant on the Wartberg, a mountain overlooking the city.

As part of the evening, the Singkranz organizers staged a show which poked fun at the latest fashion, which was dubbed "sack fashion," since women's dresses had no shapely distinction other than resembling a sack. One young woman in the show caught my eye. Shortly after the performance, I saw her in the hall, coming out of the ladies' room. She was eating a piece of bread, of which she offered a bite to a friend. I asked her jokingly "And who kisses me?" to which she replied, "The welfare."

I could not let that response stand. Not much later, I asked the young woman for a dance—and then another one and another one, and so on for the rest of the night. Some of my friends and relatives asked me if I had earned my doctorate in love, rather than in electronics. To make a long story short, the young woman's name was Christa Ischebeck. Today, we still dance together, but now as a married couple with three children.

Upon my return to work, a formal celebration of my doctorate was held at Telefunken. Unlike birthday parties, which were held among the individual groups, such an occasion called for a celebration by the entire research lab. The secretaries were called upon to serve champagne and offer cigars, and the director gave a speech.

My later graduation from the Technische Hochschule in Stuttgart was significantly less formal than this celebration at work. When my paperwork was completed and my diploma was printed, I was told that I could pick it up at the school. Upon arriving there, my thesis adviser's secretary asked me if she should give me the diploma or whether I would rather receive it from Professor Feldtkeller. I accepted the document from her. That was my graduation. My official title was now *Doktor-Ingenieur*, abbreviated to *Dr.-Ing*. It is the only doctoral degree in Germany that is written with a hyphen, followed by a capital letter, since it does not use a Latin designation, unlike, for example, *Dr.med.*, *Dr.phil.*, or *Dr.rer.nat.*

Ulm was about eighty miles from Heilbronn. My new VW allowed me to drive home for the weekends. Usually it was lunch with Christa's parents and dinner with my parents or vice versa, a game that continued many years later when we came back from the United States to visit Heilbronn.

Back in Ulm, the director's wife respected my new relationship; she stopped pressuring me. She even insisted that Christa sleep in my room when she visited me in Ulm for the first time, rather than staying at a hotel.

In the summer, Christa received permission from her father to go with me on vacation. Going on vacation with a girlfriend without being married was not as common then as it is today. Christa is twelve years younger than I am. My brother Uli also went on vacation with his future wife. He received an even more specific admonition from his future father-in-law, who used the beautiful words, "Don't cross the borders set by good manners, tradition, and religion."

Christa and I thoroughly enjoyed our trip to Switzerland and Italy. It was in Switzerland that I asked her to marry me. I did not go down on my knees—a custom which I had never heard about until I came to the United States—but regardless, she said yes. As was the custom at the time, upon our return home, I had to ask her father for permission to marry her. Things were no longer quite as formal as they used to be in the days of our grandparents—I did not need a top hat and gloves—but nevertheless, an official visit with my future father-in-law was to be made, where I asked for the hand of his daughter. I was lucky; the permission was granted. Our two families celebrated with an official engagement party.

Naturally, I spent practically all of my weekends in Heilbronn, with my time divided between Christa's home and that of my parents. Christa's father, who was the technical head manager for the railroad operation in our region (the northern section of our state), lived in an apartment in Heilbronn's former railroad station, which was still owned by the government. Christa grew up with four brothers. As a consequence of her having four brothers, she has always been a much faster eater than I. It was probably one of her survival skills, especially during the war years when she had to keep up with the boys.

On a Monday morning after a weekend in Heilbronn, as I drove back to Ulm in my new VW, I passed a wooded section of the autobahn near Stuttgart. The road appeared wet and shiny under the overhanging trees. I was wondering whether there was ice on the road, when my windshield was lightly sprayed with water. I passed a truck, and as I moved gradually back from the left into the right lane, my car started to slide and turn, and continued sliding for over 200 feet. As it reached the grassy shoulder, the car had rotated ninety degrees. The car overturned and finally landed on its roof. I managed to open the door and climb out. It did not take long for the police to arrive, since another car had a similar accident on the other side of the expressway. The road was a sheet of ice; it was almost impossible to walk on it. I deplored the fate of my new car, but was told by the police to be glad that I was not seriously hurt. They sent me to the hospital, and, indeed, I had suffered nothing but a few bruises.

I stayed with my parents for a short recovery time. My main activity was trying to sell the totaled car. I was told by a shop that, in contrast to the external sheet metal, the frame and engine were in good shape. We placed an ad in the local newspaper, and the phone started ringing. Most of the significant offers came from mechanics who worked in garages. For most people, cars were still unaffordable. But these mechanics would reconstruct a car in their spare time if the required work was primarily related to body damage. I had bought the car for close to 4,000 deutsche marks and sold it for almost half that amount. I am not sure why I did not have insurance to cover my loss. Fortunately, the 2,000 deutsche marks were just enough for me to buy a used VW.

Married

Our wedding took place on July 11, 1959. To be precise, we got married twice that day.[1] In the morning, we had our legal wedding performed by the city's registrar in our beautiful town hall, which was restored after the war to its original architecture from the Middle Ages. Afterward, we celebrated at Christa's parents' home with champagne. After two glasses on an empty stomach, I worried I might be slightly impaired during our subsequent church wedding. Fortunately, champagne on an empty stomach not only comes quickly, but also goes quickly. I was fine by the time of the ceremony.

At two o'clock, our church wedding took place in the restored cathedral of Heilbronn, the Kilianskirche. One of Christa's relatives performed the wedding. Another uncle provided the Mercedes for our transportation. Our reception took place in a hotel about ten miles outside the town. Christa's father hired a bus, operated by the railroad, so the guests could leave their cars at home. It was a very hot, but memorable, day.

Our honeymoon led us through the Moselle valley to France and Switzerland. On the way, we visited some family friends from the days when Christa's family lived in Metz, France. We also drove past some of the places where I had been as a prisoner of war, like the barracks in Épinal and Pouxeux and the old mill where I stayed during my first Kommando in Le Val d'Ajol. All

---

1. A church wedding is not recognized legally in Germany; only the town can legally marry a couple. The record stays with the town. This can be a useful feature for people who want to trace their ancestry. Except where records were destroyed by air raids, records might go back several centuries.

of the buildings were empty and looked run-down. It certainly was a strange feeling to be back there, a free man, looking at what seemed to be a distant and unreal past.

From there, we went to the famous Chapel of Notre Dame du Haut by Le Corbusier in Ronchamp. One of the highlights of our trip was probably breakfast at Château de Chillon on Lake Geneva, two miles from Montreux. Sitting in the morning sunshine on a castle terrace, overlooking a beautiful lake with my new wife, is hard to beat.

Following the honeymoon, we settled in Ulm, where I still worked at Telefunken, and looked for housing. We found a beautiful apartment on the thirteenth floor of one of the few high-rises in town, on a small mountain. Christa also found a job in a well-established women's clothing store in the city.

10

Atlanta, Georgia

Journey to the United States

Ever since my stay as an exchange student at Georgia Tech, I had been corresponding with one of my former professors. I had declined an earlier invitation from him to come to Georgia Tech to teach. His offer came up again after Christa and I were married, and we pondered the proposal. We thought it might be an interesting experience. After some serious deliberations, we decided to accept the offer, with the condition that it would only be for one academic year.

Our next step after finalizing the necessary agreements with Georgia Tech was to obtain American visas. We went to the American consulate in Munich. What they provided us with was not a visa, but the famous green card. Until 1965, the time when the United States changed their immigration laws, it was much easier for Europeans to immigrate to the United

States and obtain a green card, than it was for people from other continents.

And so, on March 15, 1960, my new wife and I traveled to Geneva to board the SS *Cristoforo Colombo* for America. The weather was not as rough as it was on my first student crossing, but Christa still did not fully enjoy the sea travel. My stomach held up much better than it had seven years earlier. When we arrived in New York, we waited in line on the pier for our luggage, which consisted of a large overseas trunk, two suitcases, and some hand luggage, to clear customs. As we watched the happenings, we felt sorry for the Italian man immediately ahead of us, who was caught by the customs agents with a trunk full of brand-new shoes. Obviously he had hoped to use his treasure to start a new life in America and was possibly a shoemaker. We never found out what his fine was. As far as we were concerned, we did not think there would have been anything worth smuggling into the United States.

We stayed one night in a simple hotel near Pennsylvania Station. The next morning, we began our train ride to Atlanta. As we watched the scenery go by, I felt somewhat bad for Christa, since much of the scenery consisted of rather unattractive backyards.

Upon our arrival in Atlanta, we headed for our apartment at the Howell House, next to the Georgia Tech campus. One of my former professors, Dr. Dan Fielder, now my colleague-to-be, had arranged the rent for us. It was a typical city apartment, without much charm or ambiance. As is typical for most big cities, we never got to know any of our neighbors. In view of the proverbial Southern hospitality, this was still unexpected for us.

Dr. Fielder was the one who had invited me to come to Georgia Tech and he was very helpful in getting us settled in Atlanta. He and his wife had a habit of driving around Atlanta at night, as a pastime. He invited us to accompany them, which we liked to do, except not late in the night (or, should I say, early in the morning?). We went with them a few times during the day and it was useful to see other parts of Atlanta that way. Dan showed us the newer sites of the city, such as the Lenox Square shopping center, to help Christa adjust to her new environment and overcome some of her culture shock. He introduced us to a delicatessen where we could get what we called "real bread," as opposed to the typical supermarket soft bread, which we called "sponge bread."

As time went on, I also got in touch with my former roommate, Melvin Sires, and some of the fraternity students I'd known, in particular Frank Hollberg and Randy Seckman. Christa and I also enjoyed meeting some of the former Georgia Tech exchange students who had studied in Stuttgart some years earlier.

We also became friends with some of the other faculty members. Many of them had learned some German as part of the language requirement for their doctoral studies. Occasionally, I was at a loss answering their questions about rules in the German language. I realized that I could never teach German, unless I really studied the technique of teaching German to a foreigner. You don't learn your own language by learning rules, but simply by practice.

My colleagues also tried to pronounce my last name correctly, i.e., according to the German pronunciation. Like most English-speaking people, they had great difficulties, even though they were introduced to the pronunciation of the vowel *ö*, or *oe*, in their German courses. One day one of them came to me and said he'd discovered how to pronounce "Koehler." "Just think of it as being written *curler*," he said. I agreed that, at least, it was fairly close.

Teaching at Georgia Tech

There was not much time between our arrival and the first class I had to teach. I had some general information about the courses assigned to me, but no specifics. Fortunately, there were textbooks. This time, the benefit of their existence was even greater to me as a professor than as a student. Before teaching, I had to learn the material myself. In all the courses that I was to teach, the material was fairly new to me. I could only get through about the first three lessons of each subject, before my first classes. In general, I tried, and succeeded, to stay at least three lessons ahead of the students.

I found that teaching is the best way of learning any new material. My mathematical formula for this is that, in order to teach, you need to know about three times as much as you will present; whereas, the student learns about one third of what is presented. That means that by teaching, you learn about an order of magnitude more than as a student.

I was the first professor at Georgia Tech to teach courses and hold laboratories on the physics and use of the new device that was replacing radio tubes and would revolutionize the world: transistors. My other courses related to electronic circuits and electromagnetic wave theory. It became clear to me that I had to work very hard and spend a lot of time preparing my lectures. I guess things only become easier for a professor when he or she teaches a course three or more times. I also found that one of the most difficult tasks was the generation of homework and, especially, of quizzes. Textbooks provide some help, but it is still difficult to create good problems, especially if you want to deviate somewhat from the book, if the material is fairly new, or if there is no textbook with relevant problems. You must invent many problems and then try to solve them yourself. In doing so, you need to create one that is not so easy that everybody in class can get it quickly, nor so difficult that no one can solve it (including yourself); above all, the problem should allow you to separate the good and the not-so-good students.

Grading papers was another task that I found to be quite tedious. There was an easy way to grade, which used to bother me when I was a student at the school. Some professors only graded according to whether an answer was right or wrong. To do justice to your students and to give a meaningful grade, you need to see where they made their mistakes and what the nature of each mistake was. It is true that in engineering, a numerical answer that is way off any rough estimate or intuition should be caught by a student and should be considered in grading. However, I think grading should focus primarily on judging a student's ability to understand the course material; that takes time.

When it came to final grades, there was one aspect to grading that I really took issue with. A student should have a right to see his or her professor to discuss his grade, but when a student comes to you saying that he wanted a different grade because his B grade upsets his perfect 4.0 GPA, I cannot see this as a reason to change a grade. I told some of these students that I thought a 3.9 sounded like a more realistic GPA than a 4.0, and that a B was still a top grade.

Toward the end of every academic quarter, the students had to fill out forms to evaluate their professors. Usually, I was content with the results. But I found it interesting that the evaluations sometimes covered the whole spectrum from very positive to very negative, and that the course difficulty ranged from too difficult to just right. There was a strong correlation between the two results. They largely reflected the spectrum of the students' abilities: good students who understood the material would give a better evaluation of the professor than the students who had problems.

In contrast to German institutions where a rigorous professorial hierarchy exists, from the teaching assistant up to the full professor, I found almost no difference in the United States between my duties as an assistant professor and those of the full professors. The difference was only in status and salary. Very often, younger professors taught the technically newer subjects, while full professors stuck to their habitual subjects. In addition to courses, the curriculum included laboratories, or "labs." Unlike at some of the major universities where graduate students run and grade these labs, the Georgia Tech labs were run by the professors, without any help from student assistants.

Six years earlier, I had found that the efficiency and content of many of my labs were quite poor. The professor usually handed out a sheet describing the experiment, complete with a circuit diagram and the measuring instruments to be used. The student simply had to follow this cookbook recipe; his most elaborate task was to write the report, which usually amounted to many pages. It had to be written very neatly and with colorful diagrams. All students complained that the time they spent on these reports was wasteful and took away from learning the material. When it was my turn to set up and run a lab, I decided to do it differently. Since it was the first circuits lab to use transistors instead of the bulky tubes, my first assignment to the students was to design their own circuit. Groups of four students would subsequently work together, building and testing their own circuits. They had to decide how to measure it and where to place the measurement instruments. A report had to be written, but it was not expected to be a work of beauty. A year after I left Georgia Tech, my successor, Demetrius Paris, carried the idea even further by giving each group a kit of components with which to work, instead of using a prepared component box.

Following a nomination by my colleagues, I was invited to join and became a member of the Sigma Xi, The Scientific Research Society, a national honor society.

With all the preparation for courses and labs and grading, I usually worked late into the evening, which was not very pleasant for Christa. Fortunately, there was one advantage to college life, which did not exist in industry: long vacations.

Extracurricular Life

It was not long after arriving in Atlanta that we needed a car. We decided on a used 1956 Studebaker, which looked appealing to us with its sleek styling. It was also not as big as the typical cars of that time, the ones Germans nicknamed "American street cruisers." Shortly after our purchase, Melvin, my former roommate, invited us for a visit with his family in Macon, Georgia. It was nice, particularly for Christa, to see and be included in a bit of family life. Our trip to Macon was our first excursion with the car. I was not yet very familiar with the car and trusted the dealer, as I was accustomed to doing, coming from Germany. He had assured us that the car was in good shape and up-to-date with its service. I did not check the oil level and did not pay attention to the engine temperature. On our way back to Atlanta, the car started overheating and, a minute later, the engine was completely stuck. We were stranded in a little town in the middle of nowhere: Cochran, Georgia. The car was towed to Atlanta the next day for a major repair.

The first major vacation was at the end of the academic fall quarter. We decided to go to Mexico for Christmas and the New Year. As part of our trip, we also wanted to visit a friend of Christa's family who lived in Mexico City and worked as an engineer. At Georgia Tech, we had met a few Latin American students who badly wanted to spend the holidays, if not at home, at least in a Spanish-speaking country. We decided to take them along.

We only encountered two minor problems on our trip. One was that, as we drove through northern Mexico, the air temperatures were quite chilly and our car did not have a built-in heater, since a heater was rarely needed in Atlanta. The other issue was the choice of hotels. Our students were on a tight budget, while our own budget was somewhat larger, but still not particularly generous. So we chose some smaller hotels and were somewhat surprised by their conditions. At least we were not bitten by any bedbugs or shocked by the exposed electric wires. The Christmas mood was dutifully triggered by the continuous exclamations and songs on our car radio, wishing us a *Feliz Navidad*.

In Mexico City, we dropped off our students with plans to pick them up a week later for the return trip. We stayed with Christa's friend, who showed us around the city, and took us to our first bullfight and the floating gardens of Xochimilco. While the gardens were quite picturesque, we referred to them as the "stinking gardens," since the standing water dissipated an unpleasant smell. From Mexico City, Christa and I went south to Taxco, where we bought a supply of rugs, some of which still adorn our house. The highlight of our trip was our stay in Acapulco where we celebrated the New Year. Again, our car developed a problem and needed repair; luckily, many friendly Mexicans helped fix it.

For Easter, Melvin again invited us to visit his family in Macon, Georgia. This time, our Studebaker behaved properly. The weather was beautiful, and the dogwoods, so typical for Georgia, and other spring trees and bushes were in full bloom. Christa experienced another introduction into Southern life when she was fitted by Melvin's family with the obligatory hat to wear to church for the Easter service.

Racial Issues

With respect to racial segregation, times had changed somewhat in the six years since I had been in Atlanta as an exchange student; yet we experienced a few events that were notable.

When I was a student at Georgia Tech, the big exciting change in the student population was the first admission of seven women as freshmen, or rather as "freshwomen." Now, while I was a professor, the anticipated (and largely dreaded) event was the possible admission of black students.

I attended a faculty meeting of the entire school where the issue was discussed. The question was what to do if a "Negro" applied for admission. The faculty was pretty much split in two. A slight majority suggested doing nothing and downplaying the unavoidable event, but the others were adamant that we should do everything in our power to prevent it from happening. In May 1961, the first three black students were admitted to Georgia Tech for the fall. The campus stayed quiet, and no demonstrations took place.

For me, personally, I felt it was a natural course of events to strive toward ending discrimination. I did not draw any direct parallels with what I experienced in my, by then, distant past—in particular, Germany's persecution of the Jews—but I think the ideas of fairness and justice were ingrained in my subconscious and values.

Christa and I experienced discrimination firsthand when we answered an advertisement for an apartment. The landlord at the other end of the telephone line said she wanted to ask me three questions. In a very broad Southern drawl, she then said "Are you of the Jewish faith? Are you colored? Do you drink?" In essence, I said that I was neither Jewish nor black, but that I found nothing better than a nice glass of wine to go with a good Sunday dinner. Those answers disqualified me as a renter, but I did not want to qualify under those conditions, anyway.

One day while we were in downtown Atlanta, we saw a few Ku Klux Klansmen distributing leaflets, inviting "all people of good faith" to a public meeting of the Ku Klux Klan in a hotel ballroom. It was the kind of organization whose existence was unthinkable in a postwar Germany that wanted to overcome its past and did not tolerate such open expressions of bias and intolerance. Even though we were aware of the Klan's criminal past, we thought it would be interesting to find out what it looked like from the inside. How did they explain their extreme views and often criminal actions? We could not resist our curiosity and went to the meeting. It was led by the Imperial Wizard, who did not wear a face mask, unlike his fellow Klansmen. The local newspaper, the *Atlanta Constitution*, reported on the event the next day under the headline "Ku Klux Klan seeking uptown status."

Christa and I chose to sit in the back of the room. The meeting started with three prayers, one by a Protestant minister, one by a Catholic minister, and one by a Jewish rabbi. The latter was particularly surprising, in view of the Klan's general attitude toward Jews. The prayers were followed by a series of speeches, all emphasizing the themes of segregation, Southern tradition, nationalism, and anti-Communism. I was particularly shocked, when one of the speakers engaged in a tirade against foreigners and said, "We must stop them foreign exchange students who bring Communism into the country."

It was after the official speeches that the most uncomfortable part for us began. One of the Ku Klux Klansmen asked, "I wonder if there is anybody in the audience who is willing to give one thousand dollars for this great cause." There was no response, but when the request was reduced to five hundred dollars, four or five offers came in. As the amount was gradually lowered, we were almost the only ones left in the audience who did not give at least one dollar. We looked around us; there was a guy with a cane close to us, which did not make us less uncomfortable. We were glad when the meeting finally neared its end. Before leaving, I walked up toward the front of the room and quickly took a picture of the Imperial Wizard. As I returned to my place, someone grabbed me and led me back to confront the Imperial Wizard. He asked me why and for whom I was taking pictures. After I explained that I was only taking them for myself and that I taught at Georgia Tech, he said, "Take as many pictures as you like." However, I was sufficiently shaken that I did not want to take any more pictures. The one I managed to take turned out to be a little bit blurred due to my excitement.

From Atlanta to New Jersey

Our intention had been to come to the United States just for one year, and that was still valid in our minds as I began formalizing my departure from Georgia Tech. I could have remained a professor for the near or long-term future, and the school wanted me to stay. On the one hand, I enjoyed teaching, and was aware that the required effort to prepare lectures and homework would become less time-consuming from year to year. On the other hand, I was afraid that I might have difficulty keeping the knowledge of my field up-to-date. It is essential for a professor to stay in close touch with the application of his field of academic interest, in my case, the electronics industry. There was practically no electronic industry in and around Atlanta at the time; their electrical industry was primarily related to electrical power. It was not until some twenty years later that this changed in the Atlanta area.

Instead of teaching, I thought it might be useful to gain some experience in the industry before returning home—just for another six months. As my time at Tech approached its end, I applied to a few companies for employment. My invitation from Remington Rand Univac in St. Paul, Minnesota, for an interview got me on a plane for the first time ever and I was a little apprehensive. I was surprised when the people who disembarked from the plane I was to take looked so *normal* and did not look like they were in need of recovering from a scary experience.

The Remington Rand interview trip was followed by other interview trips to Microwave Associates in Burlington, Massachusetts, and to Hewlett-Packard in Palo Alto, California. Christa suggested that I should also interview at Bell Telephone

Laboratories in Murray Hill, New Jersey; she had just read an article about their great achievements. So I did.

Following my application to Bell Labs, as the Bell Telephone Laboratories were called, I was invited for a two-day interview. I called them and said that I could only take off one day from my teaching duties. Only later did I learn that the two-day visit was expected for candidates with a PhD. The interview normally started with a talk by the interviewee and was followed by a visit to four departments that expressed interest in the candidate. When I visited Bell Labs on April 6, 1961, and gave my talk about my prior work and my teaching activities, the departments that were present introduced themselves. Their work related to solid state device development, digital transmission, communications techniques, submarine transmission, and the development of the Telstar satellite.

I was asked to express my department preferences. In turn, the visit coordinator later asked each department about their interest in me. Repeatedly I told the coordinator that I was most interested in the Telstar work, but somehow I found no resonance. I learned later that, at the time, the Telstar project was so far advanced that they were only interested in people who had highly relevant experience and who could immediately contribute significantly to the project.

Of the departments that reciprocated my interest in them, the one that impressed me most was digital transmission. This was a new field. Until about 1960, all telephone and television signals across the country had been transmitted in analog form, i.e., as waves. This department was working on a radically new approach that would transmit telephone calls as a string of pulses, or, in a mathematical sense, as a string of ones and zeroes. At the end of my interview, the head of that department, John Mayo, invited me to dinner at a renowned restaurant at the Newark airport.

I had barely arrived home to Atlanta, when I received a call from John asking me what I thought about my visit and stressing the merits of working for his department.

11

Bell Telephone Laboratories

Joining Bell Telephone Laboratories

I decided to join John Mayo's department of digital transmission in Murray Hill, New Jersey, and began my work there on June 30, 1961. The department had just completed the development of the first digital transmission system, called T1, which combined twenty-four telephone calls into a transmission stream of 1.5 million pulses, or bits, per second. The work we had cut out for us was to show the feasibility of going to higher speeds, with the next level having four times the T1 capacity—called T2, and operating at 6.3 megabits per second—by building an exploratory model. The T2 level was also chosen to be used by the Picturephone that was under development in another one of our laboratories. Since one picture phone call was thus equivalent to ninety-six telephone calls, the Picturephone proved later to be too expensive for public use. It did not catch on and was laid to rest, but the T2 transmission level remained as an intermediary level to still higher levels.

The next higher level, T3, combined seven T2 levels and was designed to carry 672 telephone calls at a speed of 45 megabits per second. I was assigned to participate in the exploratory work for combining—technically called "multiplexing"—the lower-level T2 signals to the new T3 level. Later on we began work on a yet higher level, called T4, at which we would transmit 2,688 telephone calls as one single stream of pulses over a coaxial cable, instead of the pairs of individual wires for the lower system, at a speed of 220 megabits per second, or 220 million pulses per second. As an alternative to sending 2,688 telephone calls, two television pictures could be sent over the same pulse stream; it could also support a mixture of voice and one picture. This speed pushed the limit of feasibility for electronic circuits at the time and was considered very exploratory.

I was lucky to have had a slate of outstanding bosses. My direct supervisor, Don Leonard, later became vice president of Bell Labs; my department head, John Mayo, later became president of Bell Labs; and my director became a Bell Labs vice president and was later president of IEEE, the Institute of Electrical and Electronic Engineers. My closest association was with John Mayo, who, after my promotion to supervisor, became my direct superior. John excelled in overall management, technical planning, and leadership. At the same time, he cared and was knowledgeable about the work of everybody, down to our technical assistants. It was obvious to us that he would go places in the company, and he did.

Bell Labs was the research and development branch of the Bell System, which was formally incorporated as the American Telephone and Telegraph Company, or AT&T. The corporation consisted of twenty-two so-called operating companies which owned and controlled the local telephone networks:

Western Electric, which was the manufacturing branch; Long Lines, which operated the long-distance network and oceanic transmission; and the Bell Telephone Laboratories. While there were some 1,300 other independent telephone companies in the United States, the Bell System covered 85 percent of the telephone network in the United States. At the time, AT&T was the largest corporation in the world with about a million employees.

The Bell System certainly underwent a long evolution since the day Alexander Graham Bell spoke the first words into his telephone in 1876, making him the official inventor of the telephone, even though others, like Antonio Meucci, had done similar, but unpatented, work. In 1882, Western Union commissioned a committee of experts to look into Bell's invention. Western Union's blue ribbon panel reported:

> This fellow Bell's profession is that of a voice teacher, particularly a teacher of the deaf. He appears to have had no previous experience with any form of communication electronic or otherwise; yet he claims to have discovered a concept which has been overlooked by hundreds of experts who have spent years in the particular field.
>
> Bell's proposal to place his instrument in every home and business is, of course, fantastic in view of the capital costs involved in installing endless numbers of wires.
>
> We feel that it is unlikely that any substantial number of people will ever buy such a concept in view of the fact that there are telegraph offices now giving efficient round-the-clock service in every neighborhood in even the smallest towns.
>
> In conclusion the committee feels that it must advise against any investment by Western Union in Bell's scheme. We do

not doubt that it might find a few users in special circum-stances—such as between the bridge of a ship and the engine room—but any development of the kind and scale which Bell so fondly imagines is utterly out of the question.[1]

It was only a little more than a year later that Bell founded the Bell Telephone Company.

About 1 percent of the revenue from every telephone call went to finance the Bell Labs. In later years, the company's official name, Bell Telephone Laboratories, was changed to Bell Labo-ratories to reflect the fact that, with the increasing importance of data and image transmission, the telephone was no longer the only component of communication traffic. Bell Labs con-sisted of many subdivisions, called laboratories, some devoted to research and some, like ours, to exploratory development. Other laboratories, at manufacturing locations, developed the final products for manufacture.

With significant funding and a practical monopoly, Bell Labs could afford to engage in truly fundamental work. As a result, our so-called development efforts were devoted to con-ceiving and exploring new communication systems without undue time pressure, to bring products to market. Most of the work at the Bell Labs, done by a total staff of about 20,000 people, led the rest of the world in both research and develop-ment within the fields of communication and electronics. Bell Labs was the source of many inventions, such as sound mov-ies, touch-tone dialing, the transistor, the solar cell, the laser, charge-coupled devices (used today to replace film in cameras and whose inventors received the 2009 Nobel Prize in Phys-ics), speech synthesis, information theory, digital networking,

---

1. T. O'Flaherty, "To Everything a Season," *San Francisco Chronicle,* March 6, 1972, quoted in Julius H. Conroe, Jr., "Retrospectroscope: The Clouded Crystal Ball," *American Review of Respiratory Disease* 114 (1976): 800, http://www.thoracic.org/sections/about-ats/centennial/retrospectroscope/articles/resources/19-TheCloudedCrystalBall.pdf.

digital signal processing, glass fiber transmission, satellite communications, the Unix Operating System, and cellular wireless telephony. Some 30,000 patents have come from Bell Labs, and at least twenty-five items in every household (including your remote control, VCR, stereo, telephone, cell phone, and home computer) depend upon technology developed by Bell Labs' scientists. The labs distinguished themselves with thirteen Nobel Prize winners, sharing seven Nobel Prizes.

The technical standards set by Bell Labs for the telephone system were very high. In order to convert a telephone call into digital form, eight bits of ones and zeroes were generated 8,000 times a second. People in my laboratory did extensive tests to make sure the process did not degrade the quality of telephone calls to any perceivable degree. Similarly, telephone calls at the time were guaranteed to have more than a 99 percent probability of not being dropped. Telephone information operators could be reached in no time, and were trained to provide a requested telephone number in less than thirty seconds. When you compare this with today's telephone or cell phone service, you see that we have made a huge trade-off of high quality for low price.

When Bell Labs first invented and implemented the use of satellites for communication, it planned to send Echo and then Telstar into a medium-altitude, elliptical, and non-stationary orbit in space; Telstar was to circulate the earth about every two and a half hours. Complete global communication capability required fifty to one hundred such satellites orbiting the globe. The alternative to this was to use about three stationary satellites at an altitude of 22,300 miles. But at the time, Bell Labs considered this approach to be inconsistent with the telephone quality required in the Bell System. The key point was that, even at the speed of light, it takes a significant amount of time for your voice to go up to the satellite and down to the receiving person, and then up and down again for your answer, plus some additional processing time. The resulting time delay of almost three-quarters of a second was deemed to degrade telephone conversations unacceptably; yet, stationary satellites were later used because they were very economical.

My wife and I made many telephone calls with our relatives in Germany over the years and we could always tell when a satellite was used. My mother was always confused when it took so long for the person at the other end to react to something she'd said. In later years, the telephone system increasingly used the much faster underwater cable—at least for one direction of a telephone call—unless traffic demands were extremely heavy. Today, as the submarine capacity has increased sufficiently, it seems that communication over satellite is primarily restricted to television use. We can often observe the satellite delay on TV when we notice how long it sometimes takes a remote reporter to begin answering a question from an anchor in a studio.

Working at Bell Telephone Laboratories

One part of my own work within our exploratory transmission system was to develop an electronic circuit unit used commonly in logic and counter circuits, called a flip-flop. A flip-flop can be likened to a push-button light switch that changes between on and off every time you push the button. In the electronic circuit, the output changes whenever a pulse arrives at the input. My circuit had to be able to do this 220 million times a second. It was the fastest such flip-flop in the world at the time. My circuit used twelve individual transistors, made of germanium, each in a little metal can, which was inserted into a socket. It was three by three inches in size. Today a few hundred million transistors are put on a single silicon chip the size of a coin, and my circuit function would only need the space of a few ten thousandths of an inch, squared, which is an area almost a billion times smaller.

Bell Labs actively recruited and, with few exceptions, hired their members of technical staff only from the top 10 percent of students from among the very top colleges. Those who joined the labs and did not have a graduate degree went through a three-year program. The first two years were a part-time program, usually at New York University (NYU), which led to a master's degree. The third year consisted of company-taught advanced courses. I taught a course on transistor physics within this third-year program. In trying to prove to myself the equivalency of two models for the transistor, I came up with my own "charge-control model" for transistors, which I taught to my students. I also presented it at an international conference. I later heard from a professor at the University of Michigan who taught my transistor model.

After my first four years at Bell Labs, I headed a group in the development of the exploratory T4 transmission system at 220 megabits per second for almost three thousand telephone calls or two TV signals. Not only did we show feasibility, but our research and development also led, a few years later, to a commercial system, called T4M, at 274 megabits per second, or 274 million signal pulses per second.

As part of our development, we set up a demonstration system in one of our labs, which attracted many visitors. Very often I had a chance to be the demonstrator, explaining the system and how we convert a continuous signal into individual digital pulses, somewhat similar to Morse code. The word "digital" needed explaining since it was not yet part of everyday language, some forty years ago. We measured the signal strength eight thousand times a second and converted the value of each measuring point into a set of eight yes-or-no pulses. In our demonstration setup, we transmitted the resulting signal over a helium-neon laser through the air. If you held your hand or an object into the laser path, the picture and all the other signals disappeared. Once our publicity department made a movie with me demonstrating the system with the laser interruption. A few days later, the movie had to be shot again, by order of the safety department, since I did not wear safety glasses. However, the laser beam was so weak that you did not even feel it, and it was practically impossible to look into the laser accidentally. When the movie was taken again, I could not see what I was doing because of the darkness of my glasses. When the main local newspaper published an article about the completion of the new Bell Labs building in Holmdel, I had the honor of being featured in a picture that showed me demonstrating our transmission over a laser.

Once we had a major demonstration to give to the Federal Communications Commission (FCC). The visit was so significant for Bell Labs that the president came to the rehearsal. For the actual event, the elevators were converted from automatic to manually staffed. Unfortunately, the FCC head commissioner did not come and instead sent a lower-level delegation. The first question asked by one of the delegates, when he saw the picture of a young woman that we used for the TV transmission, was, "Who is that broad?" His query certainly reduced all tension, as well as our high expectations for the visit.

It was an honor to work at Bell Labs. The requirements were high, both at the time of hiring and later during our employment when the high stakes were consistently evident in the indirect competition between colleagues. This came into formal play at the annual performance and salary reviews. Everybody was ranked against their peers with respect to performance. The rankings would then determine the annual salary increases. Performance review might result in salary differences among peers; one person might get almost no increase and another as much as 10 percent. This type of comparative evaluation started at the lowest group level and continued in increasing ranks.

Educational background became irrelevant at Bell Labs after the hiring phase. I did not know which of my coworkers had a PhD. However, this was different from my later experience in Belgium, where my boss once said at review time, "An engineer with a college degree should always be at a higher salary level than someone who has worked his way up in the industry without such a degree, even if the latter does the same work and performs equally well or better." My Belgian boss reasoned that the former had the better overall background, which would pay off in the long run, but the advantage of practical experience over academic training became increasingly frequent with the advent of computers and software and led to significant changes in classifications at Bell Labs.

We constantly took continuing education courses at Bell Labs, primarily technical or managerial courses. Above all, the work itself was a continuous education. The field of electronics evolved and changed so quickly that your specific technical knowledge typically became obsolete in about five years.

It was also a pleasure and fun to work at Bell Labs. I had very interesting and intelligent people around me. Apart from the colleagues that I interacted with technically, I met many others over lunch. The conversation was usually focused on work, but we also talked about spare time activities; sailing was one of the top items since many of my colleagues sailed. We never talked about politics or other touchy issues that might create conflict. As for myself, I don't think I ever talked about my past experiences in my youth, the Third Reich, or my captivity. You can't do that in a short lunch conversation and with several people at the same time. There was also no reason or desire on either side to do so.

The company provided us with a beautiful environment, with respect to both its campus-like location and its buildings. After four years in Murray Hill, our work was transferred forty miles farther south to a brand new building in Holmdel, New Jersey, which had been designed by the world-renowned architect, Eero Saarinen. The Holmdel building is a rectangular glass building measuring two million square feet, or 185,000 square meters, with room for up to four thousand people. After a later building extension, the building fit up to six thousand people. The building rests in a beautiful 472-acre open setting with two large pools, surrounded by an elliptical internal roadway and beautiful and extensive landscaping. A water tower serving the building became a landmark. Since the concrete water tank rested on three huge concrete legs, it was said that the tower was designed to look like an early transistor.[2]

Inside the building, we had a beautiful self-service cafeteria and a dining room that was set up as a restaurant. Our work was supported by many amenities such as a library; drafting, typing, and copying services; a stock room; a computer center; a branch of one of the local banks; and countless conference rooms.

I remember when our first self-service centers for copying were added in the 1960s. The building had four towers; a small room with a copying machine was set up on almost all of the six floors of the four towers. These machines used a wet process, in which the copying paper rolled through the developer after exposure. A woman was assigned to replace the chemicals every morning. With time, the wet process was replaced by more modern copying machines. We all learned how to un-jam them. Some of the other services also evolved with the advance of technology, like the typing pool that disappeared many years later as we all learned to type on our own computers. Among the other benefits were yearly medical examinations right in the building. For most of our conferences, we could order coffee and danishes. Most of

---

2. Saarinen built a very similar building for IBM Research in Yorktown Heights. The main difference is that the IBM building was curved and used natural stone at the entrance, whereas the Holmdel building was straight and used concrete, to be more in line with its image of being part of a public utility.

these things that helped to create an enjoyable work environment are gone today, not only at Bell Labs, but in many companies.

Apart from these more material benefits, one of the prime assets of working at Bell Labs was the talent of the people around you. Throughout my career at the labs, I was closely associated with many people whose work created not only new communication systems, but also the tools and elements of today's technologies, like integrated circuits, glass fibers, and CCDs, to name just a few. These people were also readily accessible. People's doors were routinely open—unless a special need arose to hold a confidential meeting—and you could approach anybody if you needed or wanted to.

As part of our work, it was fairly important to attend and participate in technical conferences. Unlike the conferences held by many other professions, ours were not held in Hawaii or the Caribbean, but in cities like Philadelphia, San Francisco, or Denver. In those days, Bell Labs realized that attending conferences and contributing to them was an essential part of the work of the members of technical staff. Very often I took advantage of these trips to do some sightseeing or even skiing on a weekend before or after the meeting.

We had many visitors, especially from Japan. They had all done their homework and knew the names of the Bell Labs people they were to meet. I was quite surprised once when one of the Japanese visitors told me that in my earlier years at the labs, I was the one who had done such and such work. I also had some German visitors, especially from the Siemens lab in Munich. Most of them wanted to discuss my work on high-speed circuits. One of them wanted to find out why we were pushing for higher and higher speeds in electronic circuitry, especially when, with time, the electronic circuits had become so dense and small that one could perform electronic processing with several circuits in parallel without going to higher speed. My view was that, some day, a general need for higher speeds would arise, but not until we included the transport of images on a large scale in our bit streams. This became reality in the mid-1990s and, since then, the race for higher speeds is in full swing.

Building Our New Home

As the company announced to us that we would be transferred to Holmdel, we began exploring the new environment. On our first family car trip, we did not find the location where that new building was taking shape. We should have done a bit more homework. The town of Holmdel was marked on the map as only a small intersection of two main streets. Up to that time, Holmdel had been a community of farms with less than one thousand inhabitants. We found out that the new building was some three miles from that intersection. AT&T had owned the land but had only a small shed on it. The center of the town, which consisted of the town hall, the police station, the post office, and schools, would also move to the area where the new Bell Labs building was being built.

Like all of my colleagues, I still had to find a new home. Instead of house hunting, Christa and I went lot hunting. In the end, we found a beautiful wooded lot in a new development of some twelve custom homes, three miles north of the new company location. Each property was about one acre in size, which was the minimum required by the township's zoning ordinance. We talked to Pat, the builder, and decided to sign the contract, but not before obtaining some references from people whose houses he had built; they were quite positive. As time went on, Pat became less and less visible around the construction site. In his stead, we began negotiating with his uncle George, who promised us the world. When we asked him about the possibility of building a contemporary house, for example, he told us that he specialized in contemporary houses. A year later he said he would charge anybody that wanted a contemporary house 20 percent extra. His wife Jean was a great talker; I have rarely met anybody who could twist the truth as well as she could. She was very creative in this art. Unfortunately, our later efforts to change the name of our street to something other than Georjean Drive failed.

Since we had very specific ideas of what we wanted in a house—a lot of light and an open view to the garden instead of the street—we went to an architect, armed with a series of sketches that I had made. He liked one of them and, some three months later, provided us with a set of four drawings and four specification sheets, all for fifteen hundred dollars. We did not hire him for full construction service, but he did step in a few times when we had construction problems with our builder. And we had our share of problems. To cite a few: the basement was excavated two feet too deep, and George had three sets of stairs for the basement delivered until he got it right with the third one. The first was too short for the deeper basement, and at first he wanted to tilt the stairs so that they would fit. It took me a while to convince him that if he did that, the steps would no longer be horizontal. George also began to install our neighbor's glass doors in our house by mistake. A few years after moving into the house, I needed to redo a sinking concrete mini-porch bearing the weight of a corner of the roof. In the process, I found that the corner of the house rested on a pillar, which itself was on three feet of fill, and that the concrete porch had been raised three times during the original construction.

A later rumor had it that George had been in jail for twenty years and that his nephew had suggested he become a builder in his new life, assuring him that he would help him whenever he had serious problems. Having a large set of problems seems to be a normal part of building a house, but we felt that we were exposed to a particularly large share. In our case, George told us that the reason we had so many problems was that I supervised too much. During most of the construction, I already worked in our new facility and I often came to the construction site during lunch time. At our closing in September 1966, I presented a list of over thirty unsatisfactory or unfinished items.

Needless to say, time is the best healer and, with time, we started laughing about our home building experiences with George. I put a lot of work into the house myself. Except for a laundry room and a darkroom, which I considered essential and which was included in the architect's plan, the basement was initially unfinished. So I built a recreation room, a bathroom, and a guest room all by myself, with only some early help from a plumber.

We were very happy in our new house, with its garden and its beautiful view of the Manhattan skyline some twenty-five miles to the north. It became the home for our children, and despite two extended stays overseas, during which we rented out the house, it remained our home for forty years.

The house had the added benefit for me of being close enough to Bell Labs that I could bicycle to work on occasion. Bicycling to work became particularly enjoyable when I did it together with our daughter, Birgit, for one summer while she worked at the labs between two college semesters at Dartmouth.

Holmdel as a township gradually acquired a more suburban character. The new presence of Bell Labs greatly stimulated the growth of the school system. Holmdel got its own high school. I participated on a committee that proposed advanced programs to the school to support the development of specially gifted children. Initially, most of the people moving to Holmdel worked at the labs. It was much later, in the days of McMansions, when builders, buying as much of the available land as possible, no longer built homes that would sell for less than a million dollars, and Bell Labs employees could no longer afford to buy new homes in Holmdel. The new home owners were primarily law-yers, doctors, or financial people who commuted to New York.

Bell Labs Clubs

Another interesting side benefit of working for Bell Labs was the Bell Labs clubs. In each major Bell Labs location, there were some sixty or more clubs, addressing employees' interests, like languages, baseball, chorus, orchestra, hiking, skiing, canoe-ing, flying, Bible study, photography, cinema, Toastmasters, and chess. These clubs could not only use the company facilities, but also received some funding from the company according to their needs and to the number of members that signed up.

I was especially interested in the French and German clubs, which we referred to as the "French and German tables." They met once or twice a week for lunch in the company restaurant or the cafeteria. These two clubs also circulated foreign-language magazines, paid for by the company, among their members. When I was president of the German club, I purchased some flags to put on the table for identification. Of course, I had to be careful that there was not only a German flag but also an Austrian and a Swiss flag, to make sure that it was a German language club without any nationalistic specification. My politi-cal past was still inside me and told me to be careful. For a few years, I was also president of the photography club, in which we organized lectures, exhibitions, and contests.

Another club in which I participated was Toastmasters. I found the experience quite useful, especially in view of the hor-ror that I experienced in my student years with respect to public speaking. My experiences as a professor and my lectures on pho-tography certainly helped me to reach the formal level of "Able Toastmaster."

My wife once pointed to a note in the *Bell Labs News* about a flying club which offered a so-called pinch-hitter course for sixty dollars. It consisted of four lessons in flying theory and four hours of actual flying. The idea was to learn enough about flying that you could safely land a plane as a passenger if the pilot became incapacitated. I thought this might be fun, so I tried it.

The very first flying lesson included taking the airplane into a stall. Its purpose was to experience the flying capabilities and limits of a plane. I indeed enjoyed flying, except a few times when my stomach raised some warning flags, like, for example, when I was instructed to fly an extended series of s-curves. I continued flying the little Cessna 150 after the course and made it to my first solo flight. On my second solo flight, as I was just about to lift off from the grassy air field, another plane came straight toward me from my right side, similar to two cars coming to an intersection at right angles. I squeezed to the left as my plane lifted off. Fortunately, the other plane had lifted off faster than I did. When I complained afterward in the flying office, they told me that I should not worry. The other pilot used the inactive runway to pick up advertising banners to fly along the ocean shore. "He knows what he is doing," they told me. It would have been nice to know this beforehand.

Family and Friends

We had no relatives in our new country, but we gradually made new friends. The years were passing since the time when we had decided to stay just for another half year in the United States. The main reasons for staying were the quality of my work, the ease of living in the United States, and the better pay, which was especially good when measured in terms of the exchange rate from deutsche marks to U.S. dollars. The exchange rate at the time was 4.20 deutsche marks to the dollar, which was about three times better than it would be today, considering the change from deutsche mark to euro and the present exchange rate between the euro and the dollar.

On April 21, 1963, less than three years after our move to the United States, while we were still living in our first home in Murray Hill, a new life and smile came into our family: our daughter Birgit was born. She brought new meaning, new duties, and new happiness into our family. One of my lesser duties was, on the day I went back to work, to give out cigars to coworkers, as was the tradition at the time. The tradition was later modified to also offer candies as an alternative for the increasing number of nonsmokers.

It was somewhat painful for us, and especially for our parents, that we lived so far away from them. We tried to visit there every year or at least every other year. Fortunately, we had the telephone to stay connected. In those days, calling across the Atlantic was almost one hundred times more expensive than it is today. We paid initially about six dollars for three minutes during the day and half of that at night. Back in Europe, telephone customers had a counter of telephone units, with one unit being equivalent to one local call—and local calling was not free. When calling the United States from Germany, this counter tallied one local call every 1.3 seconds during the day and every 1.7 seconds at night. Our own bill here in the States was reduced because I was an employee of the Bell System.

Whenever we visited our hometown of Heilbronn, we were always unsure about how to divide our time between our respective parents. Each set of parents wanted us to stay with them and have our meals with them. The solution was to alternate: on some vacations we stayed with my parents and on others we stayed with Christa's parents. For meals, we might have lunch in one house and dinner in the other.

In our new home country, we did not seek out Germans as new potential friends. Yet it turned out that whenever we met someone from Germany or Europe, we usually had much in common. For us as immigrants, this was especially true in the beginning when it felt good to talk with someone about the things we had problems with or things that we did not like, such as needing the car for every errand, not finding good European bread, or the more superficial relationships one usually had with other people in the States as compared to in Europe. The European culture in which we grew up always stayed with us. Throughout the years, we always felt that we were European to some degree, while, on the other hand, whenever we were in Europe, we felt like Americans (but not American tourists). It is a bit like sitting between two chairs—albeit while hopefully selecting the best of both worlds. Christa and I formed most of our relationships with neighbors and colleagues at the labs.

Among our personal Bell Labs friends, we counted many who had achieved world reputations in science, such as acousticians Manfred Schroeder and Max Mathews, photonics scientist Herwig Kogelnik, and Big Bang Nobel Prize winner Bob Wilson.

We spoke German at home, and that included little Birgit. It was early spring 1966 when Birgit, three years old, played with the children in the neighborhood for the first time. The woman next door once asked to have a talk with Christa and set out to tell her that, by speaking German with our daughter, we were causing her permanent psychological damage, since she was not able to communicate with the other children. I guess our neighbor had never experienced how children of all languages and cultures can play together within a few minutes of meeting each other.

The next addition to our growing family was our son Steffen. His actual birth involved some excitement. We had just moved from Murray Hill into our new home in Holmdel, and Christa had kept her obstetrician from the old location in Murray Hill. On the evening of December 2, 1966, as I was about to drive to a photography club meeting, I backed out of the garage and suddenly heard a big car-crash noise. One of our visitors had left the car's right rear door ajar, and as I moved the car, it hit the garage door post. The car door was bent in the middle at almost a right angle. The car was out of service and was waiting for a major repair. The club meeting was out of question.

Eight hours later, at three in the morning, Christa woke me up to tell me that it was time to go to the hospital in Summit, thirty miles away. She had waited as long as she could, in line with what she considered to be among the most embarrassing things that could happen to a pregnant woman: being sent home by the hospital for being too early. But now it was for real and we had no car. We called our good friend Erich Port, who lived ten miles away, asking him to take us to the hospital. As we arrived at the hospital, almost eighty minutes after our phone call, Christa announced to the hospital staff that helped her out of the car that the baby was coming. She was rushed in and I was ushered to the registration desk to first sign the necessary papers. As I delivered my signatures, Christa delivered our son, as reported in a phone call to the registration desk. I had been looking forward to being present at my child's birth for the first time. It had not been allowed in Birgit's case.

Since everything went so fast, Christa was wide awake when I arrived at her room and asked the doctor to bring her paper cups for the champagne that she had stowed in her hospital bag. Together with the doctor, we toasted the birth of Steffen Dankwart Koehler. My wife and the doctor told me that moments after Steffen was born, the doctor showed Christa the newborn and asked her what the baby was. To make sure she would not be disappointed and with a sense of pessimism, she answered, "A girl" (because she really had wanted a boy). The doctor replied, "Have another look," and she did.

The third arrival from the "stork market" was Kirsten, two years later. Her birth went smoothly, and we enjoyed being a family of five. Kirsten always smiled as a baby and as a child, unless she had a specific problem. She was only nine months old when we moved to Switzerland. When she was almost three years old, she had a serious accident there with a very lucky ending. As we left our car to go to a local park, she suddenly pulled away from her mother's hand and ran toward the park. She was hit by a car as it drove through the parking lot at a fairly fast pace. By the time the car came to a stop, she had been dragged by her shoe by the front wheel of the car. We could later see a twelve foot long trace from her shoe on the road. We took her to the hospital where she recovered from her bruises without any other significant damages. How lucky we were!

Today, all three of our children are glad we spoke German with them, even though the two younger ones usually responded in English. Each of them began to speak German quite well after spending a few weeks toward the end of their high-school years with relatives in Germany. Both of our daughters, neither of whom has a German husband, now speak German with their own children.

12

Switzerland

Joining IBM Research

After having a series of outstanding bosses during my time at Bell Labs, I was at one point disappointed with my new boss. At that time, our work was beginning to move from being strictly "exploratory" to the phase of preparing our system for manufacture, a stage I considered less interesting and therefore disappointing.

I had several friends who worked at the IBM Research Laboratory in Switzerland near Zurich at the time. Some of them had formerly been at Bell Labs. They had suggested several times that I should come work at their lab. Now I began considering it seriously. I visited the IBM Lab during a European vacation and gave a lecture there, the equivalent to an interview visit. Not long after my return, I applied for employment at the IBM Lab. As I was still pondering whether I should accept the subsequent offer that I received, I asked my Bell Labs director if there would be a chance for me to come back to Bell Labs if I desired to later. He said that if he answered my question, it would strengthen my decision to leave and he did not want that to happen. But his answer did strengthen my decision and I accepted the offer from IBM.

In September 1969, we moved to Switzerland. The decision had not come easily, but the lure of living in Switzerland was great and our children had still not reached school age; thus, they would not be as strongly affected by a separation from friends as they would have been in later years. Christa was a full-time mother and was not working at the time. Unlike me, she was not anxious to move. I found that it always took her about two years to get used to a new environment, but once she did, she did not want to go back.

Since we enjoy the outdoors, and especially with Christa's fondness for walking, we soon fell in love with and embraced the Swiss scenery and its mountains. Barely a weekend went by during which we did not explore our surroundings by going on a hike, on a trip into the mountains, or, in the winter, on a ski trip. We lived in a beautiful terraced apartment in Wollerau, about twenty kilometers southeast of Zurich. Our house had a beautiful view to the north over Lake Zurich. As is typical for much of northern Europe, sunshine was more often the exception rather than the rule. Often in winter, we could not see the other side of the lake through the fog and mist, and the sun was rarely visible. But it often required only a fifteen- or thirty-minute drive up the hills to be above the clouds. To make sure people would not "steal" the sun from their neighbors, the zoning laws in our area had stipulations for the north and the south sides of a residential house, making sure, for example, that tall trees on your property would not block the sun for your neighbors south of you.

The IBM Research Laboratory in Rueschlikon, outside Zurich, was relatively small, with just over one hundred employees. Like at Bell Labs, the caliber of the scientists and engineers was very high at the IBM Lab. Two of my colleagues won the Nobel Prize in physics; Heinrich Rohrer, with whom I carpooled to work, received it in 1986 for his work on the scanning tunneling microscope, and Alex Müller received it a year later for his work on high-temperature superconductivity. The lab had three major sections: a mathematics department, a physics department, and a communications department, to which I belonged. Our work involved research on new digital transmission system concepts and on new electronic devices.

One thing that amused me slightly when I started to work for IBM, which I had also noticed on business trips abroad, was the reverence for everything technical that came out of Bell Labs. The game plan that I heard so often at IBM was to beat Bell Labs. My group worked on compression of images with voice for Picturephone, at a time when Bell Labs had already given up its work on the Picturephone. Bell Labs had concluded that it was not yet economical at the time because of its high demand for bandwidth, or, digitally speaking, for bits. My boss proposed that we could beat Bell Labs in the Picturephone game by reducing the required bandwidth by a factor of one hundred without loss in quality. We did meet that challenge, at least to a degree, and obtained some worthwhile results that were useful in applications other than Picturephone. Some ten years later, I found out that the Japanese were still working on the Picturephone without knowing that the rest of the world had lost interest.

There were two sides to my work, however. On the one hand, the work was interesting and the people were of very high caliber. On the other hand, however, there were certain personnel issues that disturbed me. I was in charge of one of the three groups within the communication department. Neither of the other two group leaders in our department was Swiss. This created some hidden, but recognizable, antagonism by the Swiss engineers.

I also found many aspects of the work environment to be in complete contrast to what I was used to at Bell Labs. For example, people kept their office doors closed, and you had to knock to enter. The few people who came from the United States or had worked there for an extended time, were the exception to that rule. You called your colleagues by "Herr" and their last name, with the exception of specific friends and Americans. I did not even call the people with whom I carpooled daily to work by their first names.

The people who worked at IBM in Zurich had a very low allegiance to IBM. IBM paid them to do outstanding work, but in the end, everybody was primarily working to improve their personal image in the scientific community. The goal for many was to establish a scientific reputation that would earn them a position as a chair at a university. This led to much interpersonal competition and occasional discord. Our patent department could handle only about a dozen patent applications per year, and most of us scientists and engineers generated a few patent submissions. Each patent application received a technical review by a colleague, who often would give a low judgment in order to increase the chances for his own submissions.

My boss asked me once to give a presentation about my group's work at a meeting of an IBM-internal committee in the United States. Upon my return from the States, I was criticized by my boss and a member of my group for not having sent my manuscript to this group member for review, since my talk included a description of his work. However, since he was in the midst of his yearly six-week military service somewhere in the mountains of Switzerland at the time, I did not even think this would be feasible.

Our laboratory once conducted a survey of a wide range of topics, from work aspects to employee benefits. The highest score went to the kitchen chef, who got a 98 percent score. The only negative scores for our kitchen came from two people who felt that the food was too good and thus too tempting. Indeed, our cafeteria was like a five-star restaurant. Every Friday we had to sign up for the following week, so the chef could shop for exactly what he needed. He always had a few steaks on the side for guests. In contrast to the cafeteria, many other areas covered by the survey, from leadership to teamwork, rated very poorly. In fact, the survey led to the replacement of the lab director.

We had many visits in the lab from people who came to assess its work. Many visitors were high-level managers from our parent research lab in Yorktown Heights, New York. Others were consultants who were hired to help guide our work. I had the feeling that many of the top-level visitors from the parent lab in the States wanted to have an excuse to visit Switzerland. This idea might already have played a role in the original formation of the lab in Switzerland. One of the hired consultants was a retired former president of Bell Labs. All of the group leaders, including myself, had to make presentations. However, we observed that the consultant was asleep most of the time. Following the poor results of the survey, the number of assessment visits increased with the hope of strengthening the lab.

Swiss Precision

There was another side to Switzerland, which did not cause us any problems, but which still makes us chuckle when we think about it. It is "Swiss precision." Not only are the surroundings clean and the trains always on time—you can set your watch by them—but everything has to be done by the book. Here are some examples:

When our moving van came to unload our belongings at our new domicile, a customs officer appeared to watch the unloading. His duty was to check whether we had imported anything illegally or had anything that might require payment of duty. He looked especially for new items in our possession, which we were required by law to keep for at least six months before possibly disposing of them. When my bicycle was unloaded, he looked for its serial number. It was an inexpensive model and I was quite sure that it did not have a one. But I faked helping the officer look for it, in order to keep him busy while I had arranged for the movers to unload our brand new Head skis—still in their original box—without him seeing them.

The customs officer also recorded that we owned a radio. A few weeks later, we received a notice that we owned a radio, but had not yet applied for or paid for a license to operate it. Most, if not all, countries in Western Europe charge a household between two hundred and four hundred dollars per year to own and operate at least one radio and one TV. The charge is about one-third of that for owning only one or more radios.[1] The good news about this aspect of funding TV is that programs do not get interrupted by commercials; however, special periods between programs are now increasingly used for advertisements.

If we thought that, after we finished our move, we were done with the customs inspection we were mistaken. About five months later, a customs officer came again to our house to check if we still had those items that were recorded as new at the original unloading and therefore had to be kept for at least six months.

We visited our parents in Heilbronn on many weekends. Crossing the border was always associated with a bit of trepidation because of the German and Swiss customs. Once we

---

1. Computers that have access to the Internet, and can therefore receive radio programs, are now considered "novel radios" in Germany and call for the radio fee unless the household already has another radio.

had two pounds of coffee with us instead of the one that was allowed. The German customs made us pay, even though it was the day before Christmas.

The best customs story I've heard was from a German colleague at our lab in Switzerland. When crossing the border back into Switzerland one Sunday evening, the Swiss customs officer asked him if he'd had any work done on his car while in Germany. This question was not unusual since car service and repairs were less expensive in Germany than in Switzerland. When my colleague said no, the officer asked if he could check. To be on the safe side, my colleague disclosed that he'd had some work done the weekend before. "What was it?" the customs officer asked. My colleague said that he'd had new brake linings installed. "Did you pay duty on it?" The answer was no. The officer made him drive the car over to a customs service station. The brake lining was uninstalled, put on a scale to determine its weight, and reinstalled. In addition to the duty for the part, which is determined by weight rather than value, he had to pay the additional cost of uninstalling and reinstalling the brake linings.

At the terrace apartment where we lived, almost everybody was busy on Saturdays washing their cars. Some families had two cars but only one set of license plates, which they would alternate between the "weekday car" and the "weekend car." Registration and insurance were much less expensive for having only one active car at any given time than for two fully registered cars. By having two cars—but one set of license plates—you could save money and show off your status symbol on the weekends. Cars were indeed much more of a status symbol in Europe than in the United States. I heard of a case where somebody in Germany was criticized by his superiors for driving a car to work that was better than that of his boss.

One day, the wife of a colleague and neighbor came to see Christa. She wanted to tell her in confidence that the other neighbors were talking about us, since we did not hang our featherbeds—which we did not have—out the window for airing, thus casting doubt on our standard of cleanliness.

Another time, her husband told me that it was not correct to have my name tag next to the doorbell without my doctoral title. His doorbell with his title was directly above mine and he probably did not want to have people think he was showing off. But it's true that it was customary to put titles on the doorbell.

Life in Switzerland

We had a fair number of friends in Switzerland, most of them colleagues. Even among colleagues, our friends were primarily people who had an American or otherwise international background, or who were Swiss but had spent some extended time in the United States. The main reason for that was probably that we had much in common with them. Furthermore, it is more difficult to make friends in Western Europe than in the United States, and we found it to be especially true in Switzerland. I liken making friends to penetrating the shell of an egg; the shell is particularly hard in Switzerland, but when you have penetrated it, the friendship is all the more deep.

The experience of Harry, an American friend who first worked for Bell Labs and then at the IBM Lab in Switzerland, illustrates this well. One day he rode the train from Zurich to Geneva. In the dining car, he sat at a table across a Swiss passenger and started to talk to him. His table partner obviously was not interested in a deep conversation, Harry told us later, but Harry kept on talking. Toward the end of the journey, Harry not only had cracked the man's shell by engaging him in extensive dialogue, but he was also invited to visit his tablemate at his home. Inviting someone to your home is particularly significant for a Swiss. More often than not, the Swiss entertain friends at a restaurant rather than at home. According to the old sarcastic saying, they do this because "they are hiding their money under the pillowcase." This is probably no longer the case and the renowned Swiss banks are definitely safer than the pillowcases.[2]

We adapted to life in Switzerland and to the idiosyncrasies of the Swiss, and we enjoyed our personal life very much. Birgit, the oldest of our three children, attended kindergarten and subsequently first grade. She had an excellent math teacher who taught what was known at the time as the "new math." He laid the basis for her later interest in science. She also was the one in the family whose Schwizerdütsch, or Swiss German, was the most perfect. It took Christa and me some six weeks until we began to understand this dialect of German, and a much longer time until we could begin to speak it so that the locals were comfortable answering us in Swiss German. They strongly prefer to speak their dialect over what they call the "written German," which they almost treat like a foreign language, even though it is the primary language in school, on the radio, and on TV. The locals usually ask you specifically if they may speak dialect. I must point out that, in addition to the largest German-speaking part where we lived, Switzerland has a smaller French-speaking part and a fairly small Italian-speaking area.

When Birgit attended kindergarten, we joined an organization, equivalent to a mini-PTA. After two groups engaged in a prolonged dispute over the affairs of the school, I tried to settle the disagreement with a compromise, and in the end, became chairman of the organization. I felt proud not so much of this new honor but of the fact that I, a non-Swiss, was chosen.

2. Here's another example of the safety of Swiss banks. I recently signed up for online banking for my Swiss bank account. Not only do I have my own password, but I also received a little tool that looks somewhat like a small pocket calculator. After entering my password in the tool, it waits for me to enter a request code supplied by the bank's web site. The tool then generates another code to be entered into the web site, which then opens the web site access. Both of these codes change with every new access.

While living in Switzerland, we took advantage of the many great things Switzerland had to offer, like hiking, traveling, and good food. These more than made up for some of the idiosyncrasies described above. The Swiss scenery ranks among the most beautiful on this earth. If you live in Switzerland, everything is within easy reach. You can drive to almost every area within a few hours and also have access to excellent public transportation and clean trains. Public transportation is not only accepted but, occasionally, also mandated. For my Swiss tax, I could deduct my expenses for carpooling to work, but the tax law required me to subtract the distance for which public transportation was available from the twelve miles I drove each way. Hence, I could only deduct the short distances of getting from home to the train station and, at the other end, from the train station to the IBM location and vice versa.

We enjoyed the many colorful festivals held in Switzerland, most of which have century-old traditions. One such festival was the annual vote and election in the canton of Appenzell. The voting, which was the privilege of the men, was held publicly in the town square. Approval was expressed by raising a hand. The men were dressed in civilian suits and adorned with swords as a symbol of their status on that day. Appenzell was the last canton in Switzerland to grant women the right to vote. It is said that up to that point, women did not mind not having that right since they told their husbands how to vote anyway.

I once made an interesting observation that seemed to contradict the purity of the Swiss landscape. We had a photography club at the IBM Lab, and there was a darkroom available on company premises. I once did not have enough time to wash my developed and fixed prints for a sufficiently long period in the evening, so I left them in a water tray. When I got back the next day, the prints had several completely washed-out circles in them. The reason for the reaction was that the tap water, which originates from spring water, had bacteria in it, which attacked and ate the photographic emulsion. These bacteria were obviously caused by the dung from the grazing cattle in the hills and mountains.

Skiing

Then there was skiing. We had been skiing before in New Jersey, Pennsylvania, and New England. To ski in New England, we usually went on a bus trip with the Bell Labs Ski Club. What we found in Switzerland was beyond comparison. One of the main differences is that most of the skiing in Europe is above the timberline. You might take a cable car or chairlift in the morning which takes you above the trees, but then you ski above the tree line for the rest of the day. Even in the Rocky Mountains of the United States, skiing is below the timberline, with the exception of only one or two ski areas, such as Arapahoe Basin in Colorado. It may seem surprising that the timberline in the Rockies is at an altitude of around eleven thousand to twelve thousand feet, whereas in Europe it is around an altitude of five thousand feet. Obviously, the trees care more about climate than about air pressure. The ski towns in Europe are also at an accordingly lower altitude than in the Rockies. It is also worth noting that the American East has a continental climate with hot summers and cold winters but, like the American Northwest, Western Europe has an oceanic climate, with moderate winters and summers. It might rain or snow more often in Western Europe but it very rarely comes in the form of a massive snowstorm.

In most European ski areas, being above the timberline offers a beautiful view. For a lunch break in Europe, you usually sit on the terrace of one of the ski restaurants or huts on the mountain, enjoying the view and—hopefully—the beautiful sunshine. Another joy of skiing in Switzerland was the ambience and charm of the ski towns with their beautiful bistros, cafes, restaurants, and hotels.

I have to dispel one myth about skiing in Europe. We often hear people say that they are trying to get the courage together to ski in Europe, indicating that they think skiing there is more difficult than back home. In general, skiing is not more difficult in Europe. Most ski slopes in the European Alps are wide open. You encounter narrower trails through the woods, primarily on your final descent into the valley at the end of the day, and those trails are often too slow rather than too difficult. People in Europe usually ski for fun, not for challenge. Slopes are well marked and well groomed. The Swiss usually groom the slopes so well that moguls, or bumps, are the exception rather than the rule. Sometimes you have a groomed descent on half of a slope and bumps on the other half, even on the so-called black, or expert slopes.

In contrast to this, we found the trails in New England to be narrow, crowded, and very often fairly icy. And many youngsters ski on trails above their ability in order to stay with their buddies, so the trails are sprinkled with fallen skiers. In New England, I used to see someone being taken down on a sled by the ski patrol typically once per hour; in Europe, it's perhaps once per week, often by helicopter. However, that is New England. When I compare the Rockies with Europe and New England, I would rank them, with respect to accidents, about halfway in between the two. On the other hand, the snow in the Rockies is usually more reliable and often more abundant than in Europe, where the winters are much less predictable.

I once consulted a physician in New Jersey—whose name happened to be Dr. Stitch—about the problem I still had with the foot that I had broken twenty-four years earlier. It started swelling and gave me pain whenever I danced for a long evening or when I skied. It was probably the image that skiing in the eastern United Stated is "a sport for youngsters" that led Dr. Stitch to tell me that, at my age of forty, I would be giving up skiing soon anyway. I am still skiing at more than twice that age, and I have even gotten better in recent years. Christa and I are not quite what you call expert skiers, but we both have been moving fairly close to that level.

To Leave or Not to Leave

About a year after our move to Switzerland, I met my former Bell Labs director at a conference in Munich. He was the one I had consulted about whether the door to Bell Labs would be closed by my move to Switzerland. At the time, Christa was still not very happy living in Switzerland. I indicated to my former director that we might possibly be interested in moving back to the States.

Over a year later, I received a call from another director at Bell Labs in Murray Hill, offering me an attractive position with him. I was shocked. By now, we, and especially Christa, enjoyed living in Switzerland. On the other hand, the work atmosphere at Bell Labs was a much better match to my interests and well-being than was the tension I experienced in the IBM Lab. A negative factor with this new offer was that the job was in Murray Hill, New Jersey, requiring a daily thirty-mile commute from our house in Holmdel, which we still owned. The real estate market had taken a big dip just at the time we left for Switzerland, which was why we decided to temporarily rent our house, rather than selling it. The present decision to leave or not to leave was even harder than the decision to move to Switzerland in the first place. Finally, one day in June 1972, I went to work with my notice in my hand, still undecided about whether to hand it in or not. A few hours later, I did.

We had been in negotiations to buy a small building lot in Switzerland, even though we had no direct intentions of building there at the time. A few days before we left Switzerland, the front page of the Zurich newspaper published the full text of a new law that foreigners could no longer buy property in Switzerland. We went to the respective town office to, hopefully, finalize the purchase. They said that their county had not yet received the new law officially; therefore, they did not yet consider it valid.

One little hitch came up during the signing. We wanted to have the lot listed in both of our names, but we were informed that including my wife on the deed would require approval by a guardianship court, since she was "only" a woman (I hope that today this requirement has changed.). We had zero time left. The property transfer was made to me. At the time, there were very few houses on the hill surrounding our new lot and most of the surrounding land belonged to a farmer who lived further up the hill. When we sold the property recently, it was the only vacant lot left on the entire hill.

Immediately after we left the closing, we went up the street to another town office to report the termination of our residency, a legal requirement.

13

Return to the United States

Back at Bell Labs

The movers came. Our goods were packed, and I flew back to New Jersey. Christa and the children stayed with her parents in Germany for a few weeks and then had an enjoyable voyage to the States on the SS *France*.

I was back in Murray Hill, where I had started out my initial Bell Labs employment in 1961. Because we had moved back into our house in Holmdel, I had to commute the thirty miles from Holmdel to Murray Hill every day. The work in my group was in the field of electronic components. Some of our effort was devoted to "magnetic bubbles," a Bell Labs invention for generating magnetic memory devices that kept their memory even without power. The technology was initially very promising and many in the scientific community predicted it would replace semiconductors to some degree, but it died around 1980 because high-density hard disks proved to be technically and economically more advantageous for memory storage and semiconductor technology was rapidly advancing.

Our department also carried out technical and economic studies to provide the vice president of the components area with input that would help him guide future work within his responsibility. One of our studies tried to answer the question of whether Bell Labs should spend more effort on semiconductors based on gallium-arsenide instead of silicon. Silicon was, and still is today, the generally used semiconductor material.[1] Another one of our studies detailed the increase in equipment cost to manufacture semiconductor chips, which seemed to go through the roof.

My work was quite interesting. I also participated in many special task forces. I became involved in modeling the yield of the manufacture of semiconductors, which led to my becoming one of several contributors to a book on silicon integrated circuit technology, although the royalties did not make me rich.

Given the long distance from home to work, I was happy to find someone to start a car pool with me. My partner was Fabian Pease, who was a pioneer in photolithography, the technology that inscribes the patterns on the semiconductor chips; he later became a professor at Stanford. At one time, we publicized in our building that we were looking for one or more people to join our car pool. Karen joined us; she found out afterward, and was a little shocked, that both Fabian and I had passed her office inconspicuously to take a first look at her before inviting her. We were embarrassed.

Later, we had a young female engineer from Iran join our car pool. She asked us one day if we had any idea what she could give her fifty-year-old boss for his birthday. Another new member of the car pool, who had just joined Bell Labs after twelve years of service in the military, said, "A young girl." He

---

1. Germanium, of which the first commercial semiconductors were made, was already abandoned by the time we did that study.

obviously was not yet groomed with respect to politically correct language and remarks. The young woman said that her boss was "much too old for that." In the ensuing conversation, she voiced the opinion that a person had lived long enough when he or she reached forty. The statement reminded me of my childhood, when we considered another child, four years older than we were, to be *old*. Everything is relative.

The Lure of a University

Our stay in Switzerland not only restored our appreciation for living in Europe, but also renewed our connection with old friends from college and from my early work at Telefunken. So I was not overly surprised when, in 1975, three years after our return to the States, I received a letter from a friend from my college days. He suggested that I apply for a full professorship, a chair, at the University of Dortmund where he and another former colleague of mine were full professors. Such an application would go to a so-called *Berufungskommission* (a nomination committee), whose function it is to screen the application and to invite the top applicants for a visit and lecture at the university. The committee then submits their hiring recommendation to the minister of education of its state. The minister then decides who receives the "call" for the chair.

The open chair at the University of Dortmund was in the field of electronic systems, an area not directly along the lines of my experience and specific interests, but the holder of a university chair has some leeway to interpret a field widely and thus to find appropriate and interesting research tasks.

The city of Dortmund is in an area that was not at the top of my list. It is in the heavy-industry area of Germany, in the Ruhr Valley. The electronics faculty was divided into electric power engineering and communication engineering. The former was dominant, and the relationship between the two factions was less than perfect. I soon found out that this was one of the reasons my friends wanted me to join the faculty. They were looking for an ally. I later learned that some professors' wives exchanged nasty letters with the wives of professors in the other faction.

On my first visit, Christa visited the university with me. My good friend hosted our visit. He asked me at the outset to not use our first names or the corresponding informal *du,* while on the campus, lest others find out we were friends.

Several months after my visit, I was informed that I was choice number two for the position. Not much later I heard that number one had declined; hence, I moved up to the top candidate position. The next step was my negotiation with the ministry of education for the state of North Rhine-Westphalia in Düsseldorf. I combined my trip with a business trip to Europe.

The negotiation with the ministry was successful in the sense that I was indeed offered the chair. The ministry's representative explained to me that because I had just reached the age of fifty, I could not receive all of the financial benefits that full professors normally enjoy, such as a later pension at 75 percent of their salary (until a few years earlier, it used to be 100 percent for full professors), or comprehensive health benefits. These benefits contribute significantly to the attraction of the position of a full professor. At the time I first submitted my application to the university, I was still forty-nine and would have qualified, but not now.

In the end, the combination of the subject of the chair, the unfriendly atmosphere among the professors, and the financial reduction by the ministry of education made me decide not to accept the position.

I'd like to tell a little side story. At the beginning of my trip I had a chance to visit my parents briefly. As I usually did on such trips, I took my photographic gear with me, but, alas, I left my good macro lens with my parents. I called my mother and asked her to send the lens to the ministry of education in Düsseldorf so they could hold it for me until my visit. When I arrived there, I immediately asked about the lens. They explained to me that they had the package but that they had given it to the police who performed a "minor implosion." My mother had only put the business address of the ministry and my name on the package, with no other explanation. In those days, a terrorist underground organization, called the Baader-Meinhof Gruppe was active in Germany, which led to widespread precautions. The plastic case into which the lens was screwed was fractured but, fortunately, my lens was not damaged.

Changes at AT&T

After about eight years of commuting, I decided to accept an offer from the Bell Labs department I used to work for in Holmdel, where we were still living. When I had first started out in the Laboratory for Digital Transmission at Bell Labs in 1961, we packed ninety-six telephone calls into a digital pulse stream; now that number was approaching a quarter million, and the transmission was over glass fibers instead of copper wire pairs or copper cables.

AT&T, as a public utility, had to provide telephone service to all customers in their territory, even to the remotest corner of the United States. Now a new company, MCI, was beginning to provide competitive service. MCI chose to provide service only on a specific high-density route from Chicago to St. Louis, Missouri, and planned to offer similar services between other major cities. They needed connection to the various local networks, and AT&T was neither anxious nor particularly cooperative. MCI filed an antitrust suit in 1974, claiming that AT&T impeded their service efforts and stifled competition. Jokes circulated at the time that MCI had more lawyers than landlines or that MCI was a law firm with an antenna on the roof.

As a result, the Department of Justice initiated a lawsuit against AT&T, which went on for ten years. The findings were that the AT&T leaders purposely slowed down the process of connecting MCI, and later some other competitors, to its network. MCI also claimed that AT&T impeded competition by subsidizing the long-distance telephone market with the local telephone sector, i.e., the sector with people who owned black telephones,[2] which later was proven to be untrue.

The Bell System was broken up on January 1, 1984. The local telephone service, formerly in the hands of twenty-five AT&T subsidiaries, was separated from AT&T into seven separate new phone companies. AT&T kept the operation of the long-distance telephone network, the manufacturing branch of the original company, and Bell Laboratories. The general view in Washington was that competition is good at any price.

Against expectations, prices in telephone service did not come down until some fifteen years later when new technologies like cell phones (another Bell Labs invention) and the Internet started competing with conventional telephone service. But at what price? What followed was the loss of tens, if not hundreds, of thousands of jobs and the disappearance of basic research at Bell Labs. The latter was a trend that spread throughout the entire American industry, especially in sectors related to technology. Basic research began moving partially back to the universities, where it had historically been. Yet the universities now began to carry out their research in cooperation with industry, which was leading to short-term goals instead of basic long-term research. America's world dominance in many areas of basic research, especially those related to technology, began its downturn.

In our own work at Bell Labs, we felt two direct financial consequences of the divestiture. One was that we could no longer spend much time on exploratory investigations and

2. Customers had to pay a fee at the time to have a telephone set in color. The simplest form of telephone service was therefore referred to as the "black telephone."

development. The other was a push to bring systems to market much faster than before.

Even in the part of Bell Labs that we had labeled "research," the concept of research was changing. In my earlier years at the IBM Research Laboratory in Switzerland, I thought a lot about what we should call "research" as opposed to "development." To define research, I think we need to think in terms of two numbers. What is the probability of making money, and how many years will it take to make money? In the old Bell System, the work in our basic research departments involved investigations that had perhaps a probability of 10 to 20 percent for making money in ten years. The exploratory development that I was involved in, which we did not call "research" at the time, typically had a probability of, let's say, 70 to 80 percent, for making money in four years. Today these numbers are different: the people whose work is now considered "research" at Bell Labs are expected to bring revenue in about two to three years with a 90 percent chance of success. This latter definition may now apply to many or most other companies, and, in many smaller companies, it might have applied all along to what they called their company's research.

Another aspect that kept affecting the work environment at Bell Labs was affirmative action. The basic idea of not only making discrimination illegal but also of positively supporting minorities is without question the right thing to do. Affirmative action, however, says that you must choose the minority for hiring or promotion, if he or she is qualified, regardless of who is *more* qualified. To follow this literally makes sense in a large part of the work environment, including AT&T in general as a public utility. But it seemed to be in some conflict with Bell Labs' past tradition and its goal of hiring only the best, in order to be a leader in research and development. In this case it is impossible to set a defined threshold for minimum qualification.

I felt, and still feel, that Bell Labs pushed the concept too far toward its literal interpretation. The performance evaluations of our management included an assessment of their attitudes and actions with respect to affirmative action, which led to actions that were only taken to better their own salaries. Initially, affirmative action related primarily to black employees. We had only a few black engineers and engineering assistants, and it turned out that, specifically in our laboratory, they were not among our better performers. Yet practically every year, upper management came back to us and asked us to reduce the raises of everybody by a certain amount, since we did not treat our black employees well enough—which would affect their own personal performance reviews negatively.

Affirmative action later included other categories of people like women, Hispanics, and Asians. Since, on average, we had very few black engineers available for hiring, let alone promotion, affirmative action concentrated on females and Asians. This had the effect that white males had almost no chance of being hired and, even more so, that promotions came to a practical standstill for white males. It is true that, especially when software became a dominant activity, many Asians were highly qualified and it made sense to find good candidates among them. In my last years at Bell Labs, I had the impression that about one third of the employees in my building were Asian women, mostly Chinese.

You had to be careful at work not to open or hold a door open for a woman, because she might consider it discrimination. You could only do so if she had some difficulty opening the door, for example when she was carrying something, and if it was obvious that you would have done the same for a man. On a more humorous note, I became so conditioned from our work environment and our annual affirmative action workshops that I had to pause whenever I used or heard the word "girl" in reference to a young girl of, say, eighteen years or younger. I had to reassure myself that, in this case, it is a correct expression.

Some Special Activities

In addition to my regular work with my group, I became involved in a few interesting side activities during these years. One of these was my participation in the accreditation of the electrical engineering departments of four colleges between 1982 and 1986. For a college or university to be accredited in an engineering discipline, it needed to be judged by ABET, the Accreditation Board for Engineering and Technology. I volunteered through Bell Labs to participate in the program as an accreditation visitor.

An accreditation team consisted of about six people who visited a given college for one and a half days. Each team member was responsible for one of the engineering and technology departments. The school provided us with information on all aspects of their instruction, such as course hours, course content, textbooks, examinations, homework, and teachers. We also had access to information regarding the curricula, class sizes, finances, class schedules, and professor's salaries. We could interview any professor or student that we wanted. In some of the four schools that I visited, the head of the department vacated his office and put it at my disposal. On the last afternoon of a visit, each of us presented our findings on the respective school department to the president of the school. Our team leader indicated what the overall preliminary recommendation of the ABET team was, according to our deliberation the night before.

Accreditation is usually given for six years, but sometimes it is only temporarily granted for three years, pending resolution of any shortcomings that were found. Of course, accreditation can also be denied. It is not infrequent that a well-known college receives less than the full accreditation. The better colleges sometimes take gaining accreditation for granted, in contrast to some of the lesser known colleges, for which accreditation is essential to their existence and which therefore make huge efforts to satisfy the requirements.

Another interesting activity for me was to participate in the organization and paper selection committee for a major electronics conference, the International Solid-State Circuits Conference. I was in charge of international arrangements. This yearly conference was typically attended by some fifteen hundred professionals. It was held first in Philadelphia in 1954, later alternated between Philadelphia and San Francisco, and is now held every year in San Francisco.

At one of these conferences in San Francisco—it was probably in 1978 or 1980—a group of Chinese engineers came to see me before the start of the conferences and introduced themselves as the Chinese delegation. To my knowledge, this was the first time that we had seen conference attendees from the People's Republic of China. They had two questions. One was whether we had a delegation from Taiwan at this conference, in which case their delegation would not attend. The other one was whether they could present a technical paper at the conference. Before giving them a definite answer, I consulted with the chairperson of our organizing committee. I then told the Chinese that every conference attendee was here as an individual and there was no such thing as a delegation. We had no idea how many people had come from Taiwan. It seemed that the Chinese accepted that answer. On the issue of presenting a technical paper, we explained that all technical papers were submitted months before the conference to our selection committee, which had strict quality criteria for accepting a paper and that all submitted papers had been thoroughly reviewed. Furthermore, all accepted papers were now printed in the conference digest. Apart from this procedural aspect, we found that the paper which the

Chinese wanted to present was about four to five years behind current technology. Since the conference had many panel discussion sessions in the evening, we offered them an opportunity to present their paper at the most appropriate of these sessions. Needless to say, they did not show up at the session.

For one of the evenings, the conference committee asked me to arrange a dinner with the Chinese visitors on the top-floor restaurant of the hotel. When I arrived there, the restaurant knew all about me and the visitors. It turned out that the FBI was present all over the conference to monitor the Chinese "delegation." Since I had no security clearance, I was not officially informed about any details, but it became obvious to me.

In contrast to the Chinese visitors, the presence of Japanese attendees at our technical conferences had been a common sight for many years. The number of Japanese papers also increased from year to year. In the late 1960s and early 1970s, we had great difficulties understanding the "Japanese English", since their accents were quite severe. Lew Winner, the conference administrator, organized tutoring sessions for all Japanese speakers in the hope of making their presentations more understandable. Over the years, their pronunciation became better. Many of them had more difficulty understanding the questions in English than presenting their well-rehearsed talks. It appeared that many had a series of answers to potential questions written down beforehand and, when questioned, searched for which of their cases might suit the question best.

In the earlier years of the conference, Japan was still in the copying mode with respect to American technology. At many visits to Bell Labs, we noticed that they had voice recorders in their pockets. At the technical conferences, it seemed they often came in teams, with one person absorbing the content of a talk, another one recording the sound, and a third one taking pictures of the screen. I was amused when sometimes they used a flash on their camera when taking a photograph of a slide, resulting in pictures of a white screen. Over the years, the Japanese moved from the copying mode to becoming strong contributors and technical competitors.

I was glad that my work at the labs gave me the opportunity to do a fair amount of traveling. I am not talking about the countless one-day or two-day flights to our factory in Merrimack Valley, north of Boston, but about the flights to conferences in more interesting places. Very often I combined the flights, especially the ones to San Francisco, with a stopover for a skiing or sight-seeing weekend in the Rocky Mountains.

On one of these trips, one of my colleagues and I rented a car in Denver to go to Vail to ski. As we got closer, it became quite cold in the car and we concluded that our car heater did not function properly. We later realized that the cold outside was simply stronger than the heater. The pilot had told us before landing that the temperatures were falling in Denver. It was about two o'clock when we arrived in Vail. If we changed quickly we could still get in some skiing. We hurried to the registration desk at the lodge and to our rooms to change. For security, I padded some full-length pajamas under my long johns, and off we went to the slopes. Our chairlift stopped once or twice on the way up, which was very uncomfortable, given the cold. We started our first run. When we stopped to catch our breath, we looked at each other. We both had white rims around our eyes and mouths—frostbite. A quick warm up at mid-station and then down. The temperature was -22°F plus wind chill. Even the next morning, the temperature was still at 0°F. I chose to look at the mountains instead of skiing them, at least until the afternoon.

My most exciting business trip was to Japan in October 1983. A group of engineers at one of the Western Electric manufacturing locations in Kearney, New Jersey, was involved in the design and development of power supplies. One day, I received a call from this group. They explained that they were about to submit a paper to a technical conference in Tokyo relating to the field of power supply circuitry. The circuit design that they wanted to present was based on an algorithm that I had developed and published internally within the company, and they thought it would only be fair to have me as a coauthor. In the end, the paper was accepted, but none of the original authors received permission to attend and present the paper. The reason was that all of their bosses wanted to go to the conference in Japan themselves. Hence they offered me the opportunity to present the paper.

The question was who would pay for my expenses. The people in Kearny would not. So I went to my director. As expected, he said that this particular conference was not along the line of work and interest of his laboratory. When I asked if the laboratory would at least pay the local expenses, he declined, saying that it was either all or nothing, and his decision was nothing.

Some five years later, I told the story of my trip over lunch at work and also mentioned the refusal of my director to finance it. My new director took me aside afterward and told me that it was wrong for me to discredit a decision by one of my superiors. As an employee, I had to accept my bosses' decisions without recounting, let alone complaining about it, to others.

I found a small travel agency in New York that sold me a low-cost flight to Tokyo with Korean Air. When I asked whether my flight happened to be Korean Air flight 007; they answered affirmatively. Only six weeks earlier, that particular flight had been shot down by the Russians when it strayed into Russian territory. To my benefit, nobody dared to fly Korean Air flight 007 anymore, and on my trip I had three seats for myself. Since the theme of the conference was outside my field, I attended the conference for only the one day on which I presented our paper. Then I enjoyed four additional days of sightseeing in Japan.

In Kyoto, I called Klaus Blech, a friend of mine, whom I had last seen at the University of Berkeley when we both were exchange students in the United States. He was now the German ambassador to Japan.

He invited me to lunch. Since I am not particularly fond of Japanese food, I was looking forward to a good German lunch. Klaus explained to me that, since they constantly had to eat big formal meals, he kept it simple for the day and made some shrimp. Unfortunately, shrimp was not on the top of my list, but I kept silent. One reason for my dislike was that the shrimp we often ate at the fraternity house at Georgia Tech usually had a funny smell. I guess getting them at low cost had been more important to the fraternity than getting them fresh. Nevertheless, I had an enjoyable visit at the embassy. Following his assignment in Tokyo, Klaus Blech became the German ambassador to Moscow and held that position during the time the East German wall came down.

Klaus suggested that I rent a bicycle on my forthcoming sightseeing trip in Kyoto. This proved to be an excellent suggestion and was much better than the bus tour I took on my first sightseeing trip from Tokyo, which never gave me enough time to do my photography as I wanted. Once, when the group was re-boarding that bus, a man arrived late. When he was told that everybody had waited for him, he pointed at me and said, "I thought he is always the last." After that excursion, I chose my subsequent trips by studying the folders at the hotel that offered tours, but I did them on my own.

On the last day before my flight back home, I decided to take a bus to Lake Kawaguchi in the Mount Fuji area. After my arrival in the area, I met someone from New Jersey who lived in Japan. He suggested that I take the train home instead of the bus, to avoid rush hour problems. So toward the end of the day I went to the train station. Nobody spoke English. I made clear that I wanted to get to Tokyo as we looked at the time table. When going over the individual listing in the table they gestured to me that some were "no good." On the others they implied a "yes" answer, combined with a mysterious additional explanation. I selected one of the latter cases. After about two hours on the train, I again had a beautiful view of Mount Fuji. I was obviously back at the same point where I started. In one train station the train had reversed direction. That was where I should have gotten off and changed trains. Needless to say, I was somewhat scared and was thinking I might miss my flight the next morning. Now I did what I should have done in the first place, namely talk to some well-dressed young men on the train. Most educated young Japanese spoke some English. They were eager to help and also said "thank you" at the end of the conversation for honoring them with your question. I was saved, changed trains at the right point and got safely back to Tokyo in the evening.

On the bus to the airport the next morning, I sat in the front of the bus, since only the first four rows were reserved for non-smokers. The woman next to me on my Korean Air flight 008 also started smoking. She did not want to hear from the flight attendant that she was not allowed to smoke in that section. In contrast to my 007 flight, Korean 008 was packed full.

Our Children Are Growing Up

Since our return from Switzerland, all of our children had attended the public schools of Holmdel. Because of the dominance of Bell Laboratories employees in the population of the former farming town, the school system rapidly evolved into a first-class source of education. A high school was added to the existing elementary and middle schools. I participated in a parents committee to lobby for special math education for gifted children. All of our children did quite well in the Holmdel schools. Due to the many extracurricular activities, from ballet to music to plays, we parents had our share of the typical chauffeuring.

The children were not the only ones to go to school; their mother also became a student. As I explained earlier, in Germany, only one of the three possible school branches leads to the Abitur, the stringent high school diploma. Christa had chosen as a teenager to pursue a practical career instead, beginning with an apprenticeship in textile retail. Therefore she did not have a high school diploma when she came to the United States. She decided to take the high school diploma examination and then set out to study toward a college degree. To this day, I am still surprised with her choice of field of study: accounting. She took a test to evaluate her abilities and interests, which suggested accounting as the best choice. The reason for my surprise is that she is the opposite of the prototype of an accountant. Whatever she does, be it shopping, housekeeping, cooking, or any other activity, she does it conscientiously but quickly and without getting too hung up in the details. Other than for social reasons, for a change of scenery, or simply to give Christa a break from cooking, I usually don't have a huge interest in going to restaurants. I have the best one at home. Above all, Christa also deserves all the credit I can give for raising our children and making them into the personalities they are today. Not that I did not do my share, but much of the time, I was at work. I could rely on her and could see the fruit of Christa's influence and education of our children.

Despite her full-time duties at home, Christa managed to make up for her shortened education. For almost ten years, she drove twice a week in the evenings to Rutgers University in New Brunswick, New Jersey, taking care of our three children during the day. In the end, she received her bachelor's degree in accounting.

Like their parents, all of our children were somewhat involved in music. No one in the family was a musical genius, or close to it, but we all enjoyed and are still enjoying music. Birgit learned the piano; Steffen learned the oboe, saxophone, and guitar; and Kirsten played the clarinet. Kirsten later got involved in a singing group that participated in some public singing events. She also was a cheerleader and a drum majorette. A significant extracurricular activity for all three of our children was performing with the high school theater group in plays as well as musicals. It taught them music, team spirit, self-esteem, and was fun. We parents enjoyed the performances as much as a professional performance. This was not because they were equally good, but because our children were part of it—and because the level and quality of the productions were astonishingly high and far from being amateurish.

Birgit developed into a more mature child than the other two, comparing them as they were at the same ages. She was more than three years older than Steffen and had many of the traits of a single child, perhaps also due to her more serious nature. The two younger ones were much closer in maturity and interests. This showed up both positively and occasionally negatively. For some time, there was a fair amount of fighting between Steffen and Kirsten. Once we were even notified by the school that they had been fighting there. As a punishment, we made them write—under the threat of a TV-watching ban—a one-page essay on "why I should not fight with my sister/brother in school," which they considered a cruel punishment. But just a few years later, when both had left the paternal coop for college, the two always consulted each other first before asking their parents for advice or opinions.

Birgit was the first to leave home to go to college. She received credit for almost a full academic year when she entered Dartmouth, which is a testament to the quality of the education in

Holmdel's high school. She chose a double major in chemistry and physics. Chemistry was what she had always wanted to do, and the choice of physics might have been influenced by her work at Bell Labs during one summer, where everybody told her that "physics is much better than chemistry." After graduating from Dartmouth, she went on to Stanford for a PhD. We were happy to see her receive a scholarship during that time from the National Science Foundation, because it was both an honor and a financial relief. Following her graduation, she did postdoctoral research at SRI (formerly Stanford Research Institute) and later at the University of Colorado at Boulder. Her research field was atmospheric chemistry, in particular the chemistry of the ozone hole.

Steffen's professional choice surprised me. He never really discussed his desires and intentions with us, just as he always did his high school homework entirely on his own. He liked to engage in logical arguments and debates and, for some time, told us he wanted to study law. He never showed any practical talent or inclinations when it came to repairs or other mechanical work. In the high school theater group, however, he was part of the lighting team, which of course had to do with electricity. One day he told us that he wanted to study electrical engineering—like his father. The field certainly had changed since I'd studied at the Technische Hochschule in Stuttgart. There were no requirements for stints of practical work in factories or electrical stores for Steffen. The theory stayed the same, but the computer had entered the field. Steffen went to Cornell for his undergraduate study and then went on to the University of Southern California for a master's program, which evolved into a PhD program.

I do not know if I influenced Kirsten in her choice of field of study. I once explained to her that I really would have liked to study architecture. It became her choice, combining her logical and her artistic talents. She attended and graduated from the

University of Virginia, with its beautiful campus and famous buildings designed by Thomas Jefferson.

Today all of our three children are married. Birgit married Mark Nutcher, a graduate student in economics, whom she met in Boulder. After spending a few years as a chemistry professor at Williams College in Williamstown, Massachusetts, Birgit, with Mark and their two children, Cory and Sasha, moved to Portland, Oregon. Birgit accepted a position there with the Bonneville Power Administration based on her interest in environmental aspects, in particular, the mitigation of climate change. Birgit's family became the magnet that made Christa and me move from Holmdel, New Jersey, to Portland after our retirements.

Steffen married Cathy Priest, a neurobiologist with a PhD from UCLA, and they live in San Mateo, California. Kirsten is married to Michaël (Mickey) De Lathauwer, a partner at Goldman Sachs who hails from Belgium. The two live in London, as Mickey was transferred there on their wedding day from Hong Kong. I'd like to add that their wedding was especially memorable for Christa and me since they chose to be married in the same town hall and the same church in Heilbronn that we were married in, some forty-three years earlier. The reception was a grand affair in a castle outside the city. The two now have three children: Annika, Emeline, and Leyli.

In a sense, we are an international family, and we like to travel. A friend of Mickey's told me recently that he still remembers what I said when I gave a slide presentation at Mickey and Kirsten's wedding: "A family who skis together, stays together." Indeed we are thankful to have a beautiful harmony in the family. Over the last years and decades, whenever some of us meet somewhere, the others try to be part of the get-together. Almost all of our major ski vacations were family vacations and, to the degree possible, still are.

Travel

Travel was always written with big letters in our family. Our first travels took us back home to our parents in Germany in the 1960s.

After we came back from Switzerland, we began to go skiing once a winter for a whole week, either in the American West or in Europe. The crowded, and often icy, New England destinations fell out of favor with us. Courchevel in France became one of our favorites, even though it is a prime destination for the French jet set. We liked it because 90 percent of the hotels and chalets in the top resort, called Courchevel 1850, are higher than the base station and are scattered along the slopes, thereby offering what is called "ski-in, ski-out." We preferred to go skiing toward the end of February or early March when the deep cold of the winter was usually over and the snow was still good. With very few exceptions, we never felt really cold during our ski vacations and instead could enjoy the warmth of the sun that reminded us of the approaching spring.

A few times we looked for a more direct escape from the winter by going to the Caribbean. Our first Caribbean trip was to Barbados and Jamaica. Some years later, when I went by myself to the Caribbean, I chose to go to a Club Med location, Guadeloupe, where the fixed price included everything from meals and wine to sports. The latter gave me an opportunity to learn windsurfing, sailing, golfing, and to take tennis lessons. On my last Club Med trip in 1996, I went with our daughter Kirsten to Turkoise in the Turks and Caicos Islands, since she wanted to go scuba diving, and this location was particularly well known for that.

Among my favorite travel destination are the Rockies and the American West. Most of my trips were either for hiking or, as far as my personal interests were concerned, for photography. Especially when I am by myself, photography gives me a purpose to be outside and to be active. It gives me an incentive to observe and enjoy the world around me.

Among our most interesting trips were our trips to Asia. The first of these was in November 1989 with a German travel organization called Studiosus in Munich, which offered cultural and hiking tours. It took us to Nepal. Even though we found that the extensive explanations of the many Buddhist and Hindu temples that we visited on our hikes took much—to Christa's thinking, too much—time away from hiking, the trip was a most interesting experience. The hikes were mainly in the hilly five-thousand- to six-thousand-foot high mountains. Much of the time, we had a fabulous view of the nearby Himalayas. Our main hotel in Kathmandu featured woodwork on the doors and windows that was hundreds of years old. The owner and the architect bought it from people in town who they caught tearing it down for firewood. At the end of our trip, I participated in an exciting sightseeing flight with Buddha Air to Mount Everest, flying at an altitude of twenty-five thousand feet, only about four thousand feet lower than the peak.

When our daughter Kirsten moved to Hong Kong in 1999 to join her friend and future husband, it gave us another incentive to travel. Not only did we get to see Hong Kong the next year, but from there we traveled to Thailand and Cambodia, most of the time with Kirsten and Mickey. Friends had told us that it was not worth visiting Bangkok, since it was "just a dirty and busy city." We found that there was much truth in this, but Bangkok is nevertheless an exciting city with its Royal Palace, canals, and interesting surroundings. During the following visit to Chiang Mai, we stayed at the Regent Hotel, with its beautiful individual villas surrounding a huge area of rice fields and exotic plants and flowers. It was certainly an unforgettable experience. Nowhere did we eat better fruit than in Chiang Mai. We had been warned about the many beggars imposing on you in Cambodia, but we found this was not excessive, and that the visit to Angkor Wat was worth every effort and pain.

In between our more exotic trips, we traveled to Germany almost every year. During some of these trips, I could attend some high school class reunions, organized by some of my former school mates. One of these meetings was especially memorable for me. It was a reunion of those of us who were together as high school students in the antiaircraft battery. Of the original eighteen, nine attended. Five were killed in the last days and weeks of the war; some had died since then. Since it was our first meeting after more than forty years, each of us spent five to ten minutes describing our lives since the last year of the war. I only wish I could have had a tape recorder. Each of these stories was fascinating and different and would have been worth printing. Each of us had different experiences in those last months of the war and began a different new life. Only about three of these life stories were what you might call success stories. One of the success cases was an executive at Zeiss in Germany with an honorary doctorate. Another one, who had to take a fair amount of teasing as a student for a nasal twang in his voice, had a good position at the European Union in Luxemburg and came with his impressive-looking wife. Others in our group had what you might call "normal" but nevertheless very interesting careers and a few of my classmates were still struggling with their lives, especially economically.

One of my school friends, Werner Haag, in fact, the only one who, like I, immigrated to the United States after the war, told us about his trouble finding his own first class meeting. It was in the restaurant of our famous town hall in Heilbronn. The restaurant had four different meeting rooms. Werner looked into the first room and found a meeting of some old men. Then he went to the second, the third, and the fourth without finding his meeting room until he realized that those "old men" were his classmates.

14

Photography

Interest in Photography and Successes

After my teenage introduction to photography via my father and his 9-by-12-centimeter glass-plate camera, I got a 35-millimeter camera, which I continued to use while I was in the antiaircraft and the pre-military National Labor Service in Poland. I also had it with me initially in the army, but I lost it during the days of combat.

After I came back from captivity, I acquired a Zeiss Ikon camera, which had bellows and took 2¼-size pictures. My first extensive use of the camera was when I was an exchange student at Georgia Tech. I joined the camera club there and submitted some of the pictures that I had taken on my vacation travels. Some of these photographs earned me my first ribbons, which helped to foster my interest in photography.

Membership in photography clubs helped me both to stimulate my interest in photography and to continue learning through the feedback I received there. After we moved to Holmdel, I joined the local Shore Camera Club. In my darkroom at home, I enjoyed experimenting with different techniques that I had read about in photographic magazines. At the Shore Camera Club, one of the older members, who had been a former president, kept criticizing us younger members for our experimental approaches to photography. He submitted his thirty-year-old photographs in the contests and preached that "real photography is only when you mix your own chemicals for the darkroom." In the end, a group of us left the club, primarily due to these critiques.

I heard of a new club being formed in Matawan, New Jersey, much closer to where I lived than the Shore Camera Club. I joined their first meetings and realized that the founder had good intentions but no plan to go forward. A few weeks later, the new club folded. Armed with a list of the ex-members, I decided to start a photography club of my own. I happened to meet two people who said they would like to help me, and we found a potential meeting place in Hazlet, New Jersey. Thus, in November 1979, the Hazlet Camera Club was born; its name later changed to Monmouth Camera Club, to reflect the name of our county. The club grew into what is now probably the largest camera club in New Jersey, with about one hundred members. As I said good-bye when moving to Portland, Oregon, years later, the club not only made me a life member, but also announced the creation of a yearly prize for the best photograph of the year, which is called the Dankwart Koehler Award.

In addition to the camera clubs, I increased my photographic expertise through articles in photographic magazines and through my own experimentation. With respect to more formal education, in 1984, I took a course on portrait photography at the New School in New York and participated in photography workshops in France and the American West. The workshops in France in 1989 and 1990 were part of the Rencontres de la Photographie in Arles, France, which is considered by many to be the premier photography festival in the world. The workshops I selected were on figure photography; the first of these was led by Lucien Clergue,[1] who had founded the Rencontres in 1969 and is one of the most renowned photographers in Europe in this field.

One of my memorable workshops involved photographing the slot canyons in Arizona, in particular the Upper and Lower Antelope Canyons. It is one of the most amazing photo opportunities in North America. Several years later, I attended another workshop to photograph the Wave, a sculptured band of rock formations, not far from Antelope Canyons, at the border between Arizona and Utah. It was good to have a guide since the main point of interest is off the beaten path and can only be reached after a ten-mile drive on a dirt road and a two hour hike. A guide also helps you in finding your way back, which not everybody succeeds in doing. Because of the fragility of the rock formations, only ten people per day receive permits to go there.

On one of my Antelope Canyon trips, we had lunch outside a canyon with our workshop leader and the owner of a local tourist office, who sold tours and souvenirs, as well as transcendental and spiritual items. The woman suggested that I eat some of the grasses where we sat. She said that this kind of grass had special powers, which the American Indians had first recognized. She said that the grass had an energy of 400 hertz. Of course, I could not let this go and tried to explain that 400 hertz did not represent energy, but instead meant that something oscillated four hundred times a second and could possibly create an audible sound, whose pitch equals that of the A above middle C, which is tuned to 440 hertz.

---

1. UCR/California Museum of Photography, "Lucien Clergue," http://www.cmp.ucr.edu/exhibitions/signs/bio.html.

Bryce Canyon is another location that has always fascinated me. I often recommend it to visitors from Europe, since its fairytale landscape is something that exists nowhere else in the world, let alone Europe. Its expanse is small enough that, unlike the Grand Canyon, you can experience it in a few easy and short hikes. But you must explore them by walking rather than taking a bus tour around the rim.

I vividly remember one of my visits to Bryce Canyon. I got up very early at Ruby's Inn to experience sunrise at the canyon. The magical scenery was embedded in somber twilight until the moment the sun appeared. Within a few seconds, the canyon was filled with bright sunlight. I was used to sunlight building up more gradually at sunrise because of haze. But here, the air was crisp. I had the sensation that God had turned on the lights for the stage of his beautiful world. What I saw was too breathtaking to leave and return to my motel. Instead, I walked farther and farther down into the canyon, surrounded by bizarre red rock formations. As I resurfaced three hours later at the canyon rim, someone asked me a question, and I realized that I could not immediately speak due to the dry air and my parched throat. I was glad I had followed a common rule for photographers: photography should be done in the morning and evening instead of the middle of the day.

To *make* a photograph rather than to *take* a photograph requires time. Therefore I normally can only engage in serious photography when I am by myself or with other photographers. Christa, on the other hand, is a passionate walker and does not want to stop when she is on the go. She rarely waits next to me while I take a picture, but often walks some fifty or one hundred yards farther than I and waits there. Photography also has given me a purpose and an objective when I am traveling by myself. And it helped me to see the world around me more intensely.

A photographer does not take a photograph simply because something worth photographing is in front of him or her. If you put a group of photographers into a closed environment and ask each one to take some pictures, you will find that they are all different. Every serious image is a reflection of the photographer's personality. A friend of mine, who was a psychology professor, occasionally gave photography lectures in our club. At some of these, he asked us to participate in an experiment. He asked people to bring a group of their photographs. The experiment was for us to discuss and guess what kind of a person the photographer was. And indeed, the pictures revealed a lot. Some photographers try to depict the ugly and disturbing, which is normal in photojournalism, but in photographic art, the work usually reflects in some way the mental state of the photographer.

Speaking of the photographer as the creator of an image reminds me of a little joke that I heard. It is much more than a joke and is very illustrative. It is about a photographer who was invited to dinner and was asked to show some of his pictures. After his show, the hostess praised him for his photography and said, "You must have a very good camera." Upon leaving, the photographer said to the hostess, "This was a fantastic dinner; you must have very good pots and pans." The point is that it is not the camera but the photographer who creates a good photograph. The camera is just a tool.

My own pictures are characterized by simplicity and order. In addition to this, I have used my technical interests to experiment with many known and lesser known darkroom techniques, more recently followed by digital computer techniques. But above all, I have always looked for beauty, big or small, in the world around me. For my most recent solo exhibit here in Portland, I chose the title, "In Search of Beauty."

I can say that I was fairly successful in many of the contests that I participated in. I recently counted the ribbons and awards I have received and arrived at a number higher than five hundred.

Through the Photographic Society of America, I participated for a while in international slide contests, where I received twenty-four acceptances, one of which earned me the top gold medal in an international salon. In New Jersey, I joined a list of people who volunteered as judges and lecturers in New Jersey photography clubs. I have also judged in international contests and given lectures at the annual convention of the New England camera clubs. The topics I presented in my lectures included composition, night photography, special effects, close-up photography, and darkroom techniques. I most recently presented a lecture on composition at the annual conference of the Photographic Society of America in West Yellowstone. I also had a few publications in photographic magazines. In one of these, I described a technique that I had developed, entitled "Still Life in Ice," where I froze plants and flowers in a tray during the winter.[2]

Over the years, I've had the opportunity to exhibit my prints in a number of solo and group shows. In New Jersey, I could exhibit regularly at the gallery of the Guild of Creative Art, an art group of which I was also a board member.

Like almost all of today's photographers, I have switched to digital photography and digital processing. My collection of some forty thousand slides and ten thousand negatives is now being augmented by an increasing number of digital files. I use Photoshop to optimize my digital images, as well as to create new digital combinations and transformations. As for my cameras, I have for some time now settled on Nikon and am currently using a Nikon D300.

Loss of Photographs

When my twin sister Ursula was teaching pottery, she had a student, whom I will call Greta, to protect her identity. Greta was

---

2. Dankwart Koehler, "Still Life on Ice," *Petersen's Photographic*, December 1983, 54–56.

a good-looking young woman who seemed interesting, but a bit eccentric. On one of my trips to Heilbronn in 1982, I asked her if she would like to have a photo session with me and she agreed. She lived with a friend in a new suburban house. When I arrived, I found that the house was located at the precise spot where I had been stationed with our antiaircraft battery during the war, near Heilbronn.

At one point in our session, she agreed to have some topless pictures taken. I need to remind American readers that Europeans have a different attitude toward nudity than Americans do. In Europe, you can find topless pictures in public magazines, even on the cover page, displayed openly in your grocery store. You might also see topless pictures on posters in the streets. Also, in those days, many young women had started going topless in Europe's public outdoor swimming pools. When I participated in the above-mentioned workshop by Lucien Clergue in Arles, a Belgian TV crew came to make a documentary about him and his work. We were in the middle of a shooting session in his backyard. They asked our four female students if they would object to be filmed as they were posing for us nude. None of them did.

Needless to say, Greta later wrote me a very complimentary letter for my pictures, including the topless images, and said that she regretted that she could not show those special pictures around.

About six years later, she asked me to send her all of my pictures and negatives of her, since they were in the way of her forthcoming engagement. I did not feel compelled to do so, since I considered the photographs my property, but I returned most—though not all—of the topless negatives and prints.

Not much later, she wrote that her fiancé had torn up all the pictures and asked me whether I had any more. I answered that I might have a few more prints. Within a few days, she called to say that she was interested in coming to the States and visiting us, thereby taking the opportunity to discuss the remaining prints with me and obtain some of them. We invited her to our house in Holmdel, and she accepted. On the day of her arrival, I picked her up at the airport.

Since both Christa and I went to work during the day, Greta was alone in the house. On her third day in the States, Greta received a call and told us that her grandmother, with whom she was close, was ill, and that she needed to depart quickly. I reminded her that we had not yet gotten around to talking about the photographs. As I looked for them, I found that she had already gone through all my prints, slides, and photography files, and that a fair amount of photographs and file cards were missing. Before she left, we took her to the police station, not to file a complaint, but to document her presence in Holmdel.

Two months later, I received a threatening letter from her fiancé, a lawyer in a little town in the Black Forest. He claimed that I had used pictures of Greta in camera club contests and art exhibits. I did not answer the letter. Another two months later, on August 10, 1988, while I was at a workshop out of town, Christa called me to say that the window in our basement guest room was broken. Some boxes were strewn on the floor. She had called the police, who came to the conclusion that it must have been caused by the wind

When I got home two days later from my workshop, I immediately made a shocking discovery: Greta had broken into our house. A rock near the front entrance had been turned over. In the past, we used to hide the front door key under the rock and we had told her so on her prior visit. But we later changed its location. Hence, she obviously could not find the key and therefore broke the basement window to the guest room to get into the house from there. On the floor of the guest room was an empty box in which I had kept all my correspondence with her and the remaining prints I still had from our photo session.

Upstairs, a box with some eight thousand negatives, including all the family negatives from the prior ten years, was missing. So were four boxes, each holding about eight hundred slides, including several lectures that I used to give to camera clubs.

Our neighbor told us that she had seen a fairly new car, which was probably a rental car, parked during the time of the break-in in an unlikely parking spot between our two properties. A mustached man had been inside. Our neighbor had considered calling the police but decided against it. We now went to the police and had fingerprints taken in the house; however, the police said the case was not serious enough to initiate an international legal action.

I called my nephew in Germany, who checked with Greta's father. He said that she was with her fiancé on a trip but would not say where they had gone. He also said that she had recently removed all photographs of herself that she could find in her parents' home, which to me sounded somewhat pathological.

One month later, I filed a criminal complaint against Greta through a lawyer friend in Germany. I received a notice from the court asking me when I might be in Europe to be a witness in the trial. By the time the trial took place, which was fifteen months later, we had moved to Belgium, but I was never invited. The case was heard by the German court in January 1990. I later hired a lawyer to obtain the court proceedings.

The police had searched the house of Greta and her fiancé, the lawyer. Of course, he was smart enough to make sure none of my photographs or file cards could be found or recognized. The only witness in the court hearings was the fiancé, who confirmed all of Greta's statements. I found out from the court proceedings that the two made some thirty incorrect or deliberately false statements to the court. The fiancé said that he was on business in New York during the time of the burglary, but had no reason whatsoever to go to Holmdel, since everything had been resolved. Greta also said that she had paid for the photography session, that I had returned all the pictures, and that she was satisfied, none of which was true. She even invented a story that I had tried to embrace her in the basement under the pretense of showing her my photographs. The entire proceedings read like a fairy tale.

They told the judge I made up the whole story as an insurance fraud on my part. The fiancé had investigated and found that I filed a claim with my insurance for the loss of the photographs. (In reality, I was only insured for the small material value of the film.) Greta's fiancé also told the court that Greta never called him during her first visit to Holmdel. My phone bill showed that she had called him and not her grandmother as she claimed. Like most Europeans, she did not know that our telephone bills in the United States listed every phone call in detail, rather than simply counting billing units as was the case in Germany at the time. Greta was acquitted due to lack of evidence.

Needless to say, it took me many years not only to get over the loss of so many photographs, but to recover from the emotional stress. Because of the experience, I became more careful to obtain photographic releases, no matter my intended use of the photograph, artistic or commercial, and no matter whether a release was legally required.

15

Three Years in Belgium

AT&T Expatriate

The evolution of the long-distance communication system kept moving on. When I joined Bell Labs in 1961, we assembled some hundred telephone calls into a bit stream of six megabits per second to be transmitted on a single wire. Twenty-eight years later, we were working on a bit stream of 1.7 gigabits per second, which could transmit a quarter of a million telephone calls in the form of light over a single glass fiber as thick as a hair. The new system was called SONET, even though this word seems to have its roots in sound rather than light.

AT&T acquired a development laboratory and factory in Holland. One of their missions was to adapt the SONET optical transmission system to the European communication network and its specifications. When I heard that my bosses were looking for a group leader to work on the development of integrated circuits that could be used in both the American and the European systems, I let them know that I was interested, and they agreed to have me lead the project. The systems development was in Holland, but the integrated circuit chips were to be developed in Belgium. For three months, beginning on May 1, 1989, I stayed in Holland to become familiar with the system, and then moved to Belgium to lead the chip development. The assignment was meant to be for about one and a half years; therefore, Christa came with me to Belgium. Our children had flown the coop, but for the first year, Kirsten, twenty-one at the time, was still in the age range where the company paid for her to visit Belgium yearly.

It was a marvelous time for both Christa and me. The company rented a one-family house for us in Waterloo, a small city bordering Brussels in the south. The work was interesting and challenging; everything was new for me. The people in my department were required to speak three languages: Flemish (i.e., the Belgian version of Dutch), Walloon (the Belgian version of French), and English, the official company language. The conversational language in our meetings was the primary language of the city of Brussels, namely French. Only when we had a U.S. visitor did we switch to English.

Having these two official languages is a major issue in Belgium. Before leaving the United States, I received a set of instructions about what to do and what not to do as an expatriate in Belgium. One of the instructions was that, while in Belgium, I should never enter into a discussion regarding the conflict between the Flemish and the Walloons. Needless to say, I violated the rule on my second day. Many conversations on the topic followed. The animosity between the Flemish and the Walloons goes back to the early years when Belgium received its independence from Holland in 1831. The country was made up of the predominantly Catholic French-speaking Walloons in the southeast, and the Dutch-speaking Flemish in the northwest; the capital, Brussels, was a buffer between the two. At the time the country was formed, the Walloons were economically dominant with their wealth in mining and other heavy industries. Today the roles are reversed with the emphasis shifted toward trade and service in the economy, dominated by the Flemish. In contrast to many, if not most other conflicts in the world today, the Belgian problem is less based on religion than on language and historic development. Belgium also has German as a third official language since it received some territories from Germany after World War I, but that part of the country is very small and its language and culture are being gradually absorbed by the Flemish surroundings.

I recently heard someone arguing on a radio station that we should have both English and Spanish as official languages in the United States, just like the Belgians and Swiss have more than one official language. But it does not appear to me that having that heritage is a blessing in either of the two countries.

On a French-speaking radio station in Belgium, I once heard someone report about a festival in the French-speaking part of Belgium at which he said Flemish beer was flowing like water and that this should never happen again. After all, Belgium, with its over 125 breweries, has enough of them in Wallonia. It came as no surprise to me that the darkroom of our camera club in French-speaking Waterloo was as much used for storing beer to be consumed during the meetings as for developing and printing photographs. The animosity towards the Flemish also found its expression once when the club's president reported about a Belgian contest where all three judges were Flemish and said that we should no longer submit entries to that contest.

When you look in the Belgian telephone book for a government office, you find offices duplicated; there is always a Dutch-speaking and a French-speaking office for the same function, with separate telephone numbers. Since the Belgians have a fairly extensive bureaucracy, even without this duplication, about every fifth Belgian works for the government. To pay for it, the Belgian taxes are accordingly high. When we were in Belgium, the top tax rate for the upper middle class was close to 70 percent.

We experienced an example of non-language-related Belgian bureaucracy when we registered our car. We took Christa's Volkswagen with us to Belgium. AT&T would not have paid for the transfer of a car on its own, but since it fit into the moving van, the transport came for free. We had eight weeks to register the car in Belgium after our arrival. Toward the end of those eight weeks, we went to the respective office, but ran into two little obstacles. The first one was that the engine number in the import papers was different from the number the Belgians found on the car. They use a number from the engine block, where the last three digits are still X's, before the factory finalizes the number and puts it on a different spot above the engine compartment, whereas our papers showed the full number. We were finally able to convince the office that the two numbers referred to the same car.

The other obstacle was that the car papers were in the name of Christa Koehler. But Christa was registered with the town of Waterloo as Christa Ischebeck, since women in Belgium keep their maiden names. (Switzerland, in contrast, used both last names, hyphenated, for both partners.) The car registration office told us that they needed the sales document proving Christa Koehler had sold the car to Christa Ischebeck.

"Don't you understand that the two are the same person? That there was no such sale and hence there is no such document?" we said.

But the woman was adamant. "Without that sales document—no registration!" she said. "C'est la loi" (That's the law).

We were approaching our deadline. After another visit to the office, another woman there suggested that we come to her home; she might be able to fix it. And so we did—and, in the end, the car became registered. We thought that she found some ingenious way to overcome the bureaucracy. A few days later it dawned on us that we should have paid her some money and that this was the whole purpose of her offer. We sent her some New York T-shirts for her children, but no money.

When it came to the art of driving, the law was not as rigidly observed. It had only been a little over fifteen years since driver's licenses were introduced in Belgium—and it still showed. Making a rough mental count, I found that, on my way to work, I typically observed at least one serious traffic infraction, such as passing on the right shoulder or sidewalk, or driving through a filling station to avoid a traffic light. On a two-by-two lane highway with heavy traffic into Brussels, I once saw a guy overtaking a dozen cars by using a lane for the opposing traffic and then positioning himself in front of the first car, ahead of the white line and already in the intersection in order to wait for the light to turn green.

One of my colleagues told me that he never used his rearview mirror, since the traffic behind him was the responsibility of the car behind him and not his. People told me at the time that the police had no time to give tickets for traffic violations, because they were much too busy taking care of traffic accidents.

We did find one instance where Belgian bureaucracy worked to our advantage: on one of our weekend trips to Germany, we stopped in the little Belgian town of Arlon. We fed our parking meter, only to find that the stores were closing half an hour later, at noon. So we did a little sight-seeing instead of shopping. When we came back to our parking meter, shortly after two o'clock, it showed only half an hour of elapsed time. Not only was the town asleep for two hours but the parking meter also took time out and continued where it left off before its lunch break.

Most streets and quarters of Brussels had a French and a Dutch version of their names. We often saw street signs where one of the two languages was smeared out with graffiti. When our director at the AT&T lab sent an announcement to the staff, it was always on two pages, one in Dutch and one in French. You were not supposed to find that one language was dominant. One of my Belgian souvenirs is a copy of a company calendar. It looked like an intricate checkerboard, alternating between French and Dutch lines and words. Considering the pattern and the type size, nobody could claim that either of the two languages had been given priority.

Most of the Dutch and Belgian engineers on our project were formerly associated with Philips. Their background and experience was European, and they were proud of it. Very few had ever been to the United States. These people had an attitude similar to the one I had encountered back at IBM in Switzerland: AT&T was their employer on paper, but they did not feel deeply connected to the company. This meant the Europeans didn't want the Americans to simply tell them what to do, as their American colleagues on the other side of the ocean often tried to do. I had the advantage of an American background, but at the same time, I was accepted in Belgium as a European who understood them—and I don't mean their language, as much as their feelings, their culture, and their pride. My Belgian boss did not have much management experience and I found myself very often making suggestions to him on how to handle certain situations, which he usually accepted. All in all, I really enjoyed my time working in Belgium. Since our development was a joint development with my home laboratory in the United States, I traveled about every other month back to the United States, with the privilege of flying business class.

Christa was increasingly enjoying her stay in Belgium, too. She joined the American Women's Club of Brussels and took part in many of their activities, including museum visits and trips. We also undertook a number of trips on our own within Europe, many of them, of course, to Germany. One particularly interesting trip was a visit with a friend, who was originally a director at Bell Labs but was now a retired professor in Göttingen, which was close to the East German border. In June 1990, seven months after the fall of the Berlin Wall and four months before the formal reunification of East and West Germany, we traveled with him into East Germany. The border guards were still in place but were scheduled to disappear a week later. In contrast to their days in the Communist regime, they were very friendly, yet we almost did not get admitted because our car still had New Jersey license plates. Only Germans were allowed to cross the border. Luckily we had West German passports. Our friends had American passports, but since they had German license plates, their passports were not checked.

We enjoyed visiting a few famous landmarks such as the Wartburg castle and the room where Martin Luther was incarcerated, where he translated the Bible. But the most interesting aspect of the trip for us was seeing East Germany from the inside. It was shocking to see that the houses and stores looked like time had stopped some fifty years earlier. No sign of house painting, repair, or reconstruction could be seen, except on a few official buildings.

Since Christa was still a German citizen at the time we were in Belgium, she was allowed to accept work in Brussels. A year after our move, she began to work for a small oil equipment company whose office was in a small castle in a city park. A part of her salary was paid "under the table," as it was one way the Belgians coped with their high tax rates. AT&T also helped us as expatriates with our tax situation, by refunding some of the taxes but not by hiding income illegally.

In the summer of 1991, my boss asked me at my performance review how old I was. This would have been an illegal question in the United States, and I was not sure at first if I should answer it. I did anyway, and told him that I was sixty-five. He jumped up and said that it was against Belgian law for me to work beyond my sixty-fifth birthday. He needed to confer with the head of the personnel department. My originally planned one and a half years in Europe had grown to over two years, but there was still much development work to be done. My boss came back later that day and said that, because of the work, I could stay for another five months, until December 31, under the label "consultant." I begged them not to make me move on Christmas, and they agreed to let me stay until early February.

We took the opportunity to undertake two more vacation trips while still living in Europe. The first one was to Morocco in November 1992 and the second one was to Egypt, which we started a few days after our belongings had left our house in Waterloo with the moving van. Both trips were with Club Med. They were extremely well organized and focused on the cultural aspects. Our Moroccan vacation, during which we stayed in Marrakesh, included a trip in Land Rovers over the Atlas mountain range with visits to the homes of some Berber families. The trip to Egypt was organized around the usual boat trip up the Nile, with visits to the many exciting sites and temples along the way. One day, when we were in the Valley of the Kings next to the entrance to the tomb of Tutankhamen, someone tapped me on my shoulder. It was Christa's brother Wolfram, who had spotted me when I went on a roof to take a photograph. He was also touring Egypt with his wife, but none of us knew of the other's presence in Egypt. Since we had not seen each other for a while, we visited him on his Nile boat for a drink in the evening.

16

Back Again in New Jersey

Bell Labs Continues to Change

When I had left for Belgium, my department had made a commitment to take me back at the end of my assignment. Back in my prior laboratory, work pressures had increased, both on an individual level and for Bell Laboratories as a whole. The climate in the electronics industry was changing; competitive technologies threatened to outdate conventional telephony, and new competitive companies were entering the market. Companies like AT&T could no longer afford to do much basic research or to devote years of work to perfecting the technologies for their new products before bringing them to the market. People in research shifted their horizons from basic research to exploratory development, and those of us who used to do exploratory development shifted to short-term development for manufacture.[1]

---

1. Narain Gehani, *Bell Labs: Life in the Crown Jewel* (Summit, NJ: Silicon Press, 2003), 228–231.

There is no doubt that AT&T, which grew out of a public utility, was a very bureaucratic company, partly due its huge size. It had a lot of inertia when it came to responding to the market and to staff inefficiencies. There was no question that the laboratories also needed to change to adapt to the new communications and electronics markets. One could say that, in the prior years, Bell Labs developed and put on the market what could be conceived and achieved technically. Now the new and widely proclaimed mission was to develop what the market needed, something that is not easy to determine, if at all. Very often you only think that you need something after you have it. And if something is new and unknown, how can you know that you need it? Did you know you needed a cell phone before you knew what a cell phone was?

It was not easy to strike a good balance between the old world and the new world. On top of that, the president of AT&T at the time, Bob Allen, was a financial person, whose vision, in my mind and the minds of most Bell Labs people, ended with the current financial year. It is my reading that he had no interest in advancing technology and preserving the value of Bell Labs as a leading research and development institution. It was under his leadership that AT&T began its deadly decline. How much of this was caused by mismanagement of the company and how much was a consequence of the evolution of American life, enterprise, and market forces is hard to tell. CNBC named Allen in its list of the "worst American CEOs of all time."[2]

Rumors started about a new breakup of the Bell System. Top management felt—or was it an excuse?—that the systems and manufacturing part of the company could sell their products to many other communications companies if they were not tied to the long-distance part of AT&T. The plan emerged to separate the company into two entities: an equipment-manufacturing

---

2. Portfolio.com, "Worst American CEOs of All Time," CNBC.com, http://www.cnbc.com/id/30502091?slide=10.

and -development part, which would be called Lucent Technologies, and a long-haul systems-development and -operation part, which was to keep the name AT&T. Most of Bell Labs was assigned to Lucent Technologies and was allowed to keep the name, but about one quarter of the Bell Labs people whose work was aligned with the mission of the new AT&T, were to become AT&T Labs.

Even before this split, a first wave of suggested, yet voluntary, retirements began. Employees were offered a retirement package, generally known as a "golden handshake." The value of the package increased with the employee's age, salary level, and years of company affiliation.

At the end of 1995, after this first wave of golden handshakes, I was sixty-nine years old and told my boss that I planned to retire. Only a few weeks later, AT&T offered a substantial retirement package to forty thousand people. Fortunately, my planned retirement announcement had not gone beyond my direct bosses and was not yet official; I was still eligible for the package. I found myself to be the seventh oldest person on the Bell Laboratories list. I was offered a nice golden handshake, consisting of almost one year's salary. An additional bonus was included if you signed an agreement not to sue the company for age discrimination, even though the package could rarely be interpreted as implying age discrimination. There was a further bonus in the form of a stimulus of ten thousand dollars if you started a new business. Needless to say, I took the package.

Shortly after I retired, the split into AT&T and Lucent took effect. Even though I retired from AT&T, I officially became a retiree of Lucent.

The series of retirement packages has continued ever since. Companies like AT&T and Lucent used the mechanism as a means to improve their bottom line for the current year with the result that they became smaller and smaller. It was, and still is, very painful to see the Bell Laboratories sinking from one of the foremost research facilities in the world to a small development institution.

I can only image what a forward-looking, technically oriented management could have done with the human resources of Bell Laboratories and AT&T, especially in the form of entering new businesses. Why couldn't they form new sub-entities within the company and become the next Microsoft, Yahoo!, or Google? When a dominant technology becomes obsolete, a company must reinvent itself, not shrink until nothing is left.

As I reflect about the differences between AT&T and IBM, I remember how, every year, we employees in IBM research were asked to brainstorm about possible new businesses and products, large or small, that IBM could and should go into. Our proposals were then transmitted up the ladder and considered by the respective people at the top. This was a process foreign to AT&T top management. It is no wonder that now, in 2009, IBM has about 400,000 employees worldwide.[3] It had 406,000 in 1984 and 220,000 in 1997 (their downsizing concerned only poorly performing divisions).[4] On the other hand, when Lucent was spun off from AT&T in 1997, the part that remained as AT&T had 49,000 employees in 1997, 32,000 in 2001, and 14,000 in 2005,[5] whereas Lucent's number of employees went down from 153,000 in 1996 to 30,000 in 2006.[6] In 1984, Lucent and AT&T together had about 230,000 employees.[7] To

---

3. IBM. "About IBM," http://www.ibm.com/ibm/us/en/.

4. Lamia Abu-Haidar, "IBM Offering Employees Buyouts," *CNET News*, October 17, 1997, http://news.cnet.com/IBM-offering-employees-buyouts/2100-1001_3-204361.html.

5. Communications Workers of America, "SBC/AT&T Merger Is Good for Employees and Consumers," news release, http://files.cwa-union.org/National/CommunicationsPolicy/Other/SBC-ATTMergerGood.pdf.

6. Answers.com, "Lucent Technologies," http://www.answers.com/topic/lucent-technologies-old-company.

7. Abby Goodnough. "The Downsizing of America: A Crack in the Bedrock," *New York Times*, January 14, 1996, http://www.nytimes.com/specials/downsize/resource-0114.html.

say this in more simple terms: The number of IBM employees went down to about one half of its peak size and recovered fully, whereas AT&T, after 1984, went down to about a quarter of its size and seems to have recovered relatively little. Given the small number of active employees today, Lucent naturally has great difficulties in supporting their financial pension and health care obligations to the huge rank of retirees. My chances of ever seeing a cost-of-living adjustment to my pension are as a good as non-existent. The medical benefits that we retirees started out with are shrinking—and the premiums rising—from year to year. The company's premium contributions for my wife already went to zero.

The beautiful Lucent building in Holmdel where I worked for much of my career was once occupied by some 5,600 Bell Labs employees.[8] The little extras that added to the pleasure of working at this research facility quickly disappeared. Gone were the library, the Bell Labs clubs, employee travel, the stock rooms, and so forth. Since 2007, the building has been empty, and it was recently sold. Negotiations are under way between the township and the buyer about the fate of the building. All or part of it may be torn down, since it is not well suited to house many smaller companies, but there are strong movements under way to preserve it as a national landmark. Lucent Technologies merged with French Alcatel in 2006, even though it was more an acquisition than a merger, and AT&T was purchased by SBC, one of her former seven daughters. Ironically, it almost appears as if the breakup of AT&T is being undone.

---

8. Antoinette Martin. "Pastoral Site of Historic Inventions Faces the End," *New York Times*, June 14, 2006, http://www.nytimes.com/2006/06/14/realestate/commercial/14bell.html?ex=1307937600&en=9ceb237dc7596dc8&ei=5090&partner=rssuserland&emc=rss.

17

Retirement Life

The Date Is September 11, 2001

Even though we enjoyed our stay in Belgium very much, it was good to be back in our own home in New Jersey. I enjoyed doing the things I wanted to do in my retirement, with photography at the top of my list. I took advantage of one of the offerings in my AT&T retirement package, namely a financial contribution to starting a new career. With the package money, I founded a two-person photography company in New Jersey, DK-Images, LLC, with Christa as the second member. Christa was still at work in the accounting department of our nearby hospital at the time.

On September 11, Christa was on a business trip by car in Northern New Jersey. I was at home. We normally do not watch television during the day, but at some point in the morning, I happened to turn it on and see the terrible images of a plane striking the World Trade Center in New York. I looked out the window and saw the smoking World Trade Center twenty-five miles away over the Raritan Bay.

My first thoughts went to Kirsten and Mickey. They were both in New York; Mickey had come from London for a business meeting. After watching the horrific events, I received a call from Kirsten saying that she could not reach Mickey, who was supposed to be in the Goldman Sachs building in lower Manhattan. Fortunately Kirsten's call was soon followed by a second call. Mickey had walked down some forty-three flights and was now crossing downtown on the way to his hotel, on Seventy-Eighth Street. He was together with Claire, a colleague who happened to be a former school friend of Kirsten. The decision to evacuate the Goldman Sachs building was made quickly since, as Mickey told us later, it was one of the southernmost buildings in Manhattan, and it was feared that it might become a next target. Finally, the two made it safely to the hotel, but not before Claire bought herself a new pair of shoes to replace the pair she wore out from walking.

Moving to Portland, Oregon

It has been more than a decade since I said good-bye to daily work, and I almost feel I am as busy now as I was before. I don't know where I found the time to go to work. Admittedly, I am not on a hectic schedule and may not be getting up as early in the morning as before. Yet I have not felt boredom, except perhaps during the minutes it takes my computer to find something or to reboot.

In 2006, we moved to Portland, Oregon, where our oldest daughter lives with her husband and two children. Christa once said that, during all of her married life, she always had to move where I wanted to move, but now it was her time to choose. We have not regretted the move, even though we still do not have many friends here. We like the house we bought, even though it is bigger than our former house in New Jersey. We have ample space for our respective interests in photography and quilting, and for guests, especially our grandchildren. We were not actually looking for a large house but primarily for a house that was well lit, close to some shopping, and, if possible, had a view. Indeed, we found a house on a hill in the section of southern Portland called Hillsdale, with a beautiful, almost 180-degree view. As I wrote in our first Christmas letter from Portland, "We moved from the hills of Holmdel to our new home in Hillsdale."

It is true that the computer plays a significant part in my use of time. It has become an indispensable tool, not only for photography, but also for most of my daily activities. I also maintain some web sites. In the past I maintained the web sites for the art guild in New Jersey and for the Monmouth Camera Club. I also set up a web site for the Infinity Photo Art Group, a photography club that I joined, in Beaverton, Oregon. And, of course, I also have my own photographic web site.

Looking Back

Like my father, I am not a person who seeks or likes conflict, let alone violence in any form. I believe in the power of compromise. Very often I find that when intelligent people have opposite opinions, the truth or solution can be found somewhere in between. Of course, this is not the case when these opinions are shaped by personal advantages or by outside dictation, as is often the case with, for example, extremist political or religious beliefs.

As I look back over my life, I see it filled with countless memories. Some of them are beautiful, and some I would like to erase, but I can't. Very often, my past experiences, such as scenes from the war, come back in my dreams.

I went through hard times and was rewarded with a subsequent long string of good times. I always tried to do the right thing as my parents raised me to do. I don't regret many decisions that I made during my life. We might tend to do that in hindsight, but all we can do is always try to make the right decision from the choices available to us at the given moment.

Being Grateful

Christa and I have continued our string of travels, and the winters so far still see us on skis. It appears that we are traveling more than ever and are enjoying our frequent flier "elite status." We enjoy many of these vacations together with our children, and we sense that our children like to be with us, as well. Similarly, we joyfully observe that when two of our children get together somewhere, the third one tries to be there too, and we parents always feel welcome. We just celebrated our golden wedding anniversary with all our children and their families in Bettmeralp, a little town in the Swiss Alps, followed by a "golden honeymoon" on a Greek isle. We think that we are a "normal" family when we enjoy the togetherness with our children, their marriage partners, and, of course, our grandchildren. However, when we hear or read of so many other families experiencing discord and divorces, we begin to wonder whether our "being normal" is really normal.

I am happy and proud to have helped create and be part of such a wonderful family, and as I look back over my life of over eighty years, I see its beginning in the equally happy family of my parents. I also see its following years of war and hardship and a return to happy days. You can look for the positive or the negative in your life. As it is reflected in my photography, I prefer to find myself "in search of beauty."

Appendix A

Personal Thoughts on Selected Topics

Human Memory

I would like to put some thoughts to paper, relating to the human memory. I cannot prove these thoughts scientifically; they are derived from my own observations and logical reasoning. The particular topic that always interested me is the longevity of memory. I always get a little upset when I read about us having two memories: long-term and short-term. It is as if at two o'clock in the morning or so, our brain transfers what it learned during the day from one part of the brain to another.

We do not observe that we remember some things for only a short while and others for a long time. I believe there is a continuous spectrum in between. The length of how long we remember something can have any duration. I am theorizing that all our initial impressions last only fractions of seconds unless we reinforce the memory immediately, for example by dwelling on what we see, hear, or read. The reinforcement needs to be repeated. Every time we reinforce a specific memory event, it becomes a longer-term memory. To me this makes all the more sense, when we consider that much of what goes on in the memory is an electro-chemical process, which is likely to be subject to continued modification and also degradation. I do not know whether the underlying process is a strengthening of the synapses, a growing of dendrites, or something else. The question is how fast this degradation, or loss of memory, takes place. My assumption is that every time we refresh an element of memory, it moves into a state of longer-term retention or slower rate of degradation. In mathematical terms, we would say that we increase the time constant of the decay.

This is best illustrated with an example. Every time we look around us or listen, our brain gets bombarded with a huge amount of information; in technical language, we'd say it's bombarded with gigabytes, terabytes, or even petabytes of information. If we pay attention, we can pick out something more specific from the image, like a face, a tree, a sign, or a name. If, a few minutes later, we try to remember what we experienced, we can still do so but for only a small fraction of what we saw originally. In doing so, we reinforce our earlier memory for the part we now remember. The decay rate has moved from a fast rate of fractions of a second to seconds, to minutes, and on to hours and more. If we reinforce this memory after a few hours or days, we can retain it for weeks or months. If we repeat the process after that time, we might never forget that memory again. I played with these thoughts with Christa and a friend as a game last year; we tried to remember an unusual name of someone we met briefly and who otherwise was not of interest to us. We reinforced our memory after increasing intervals and now Christa and I have no difficulty remembering that name.

Very often people have difficulty remembering something, especially a name. If, however, we try to think of something else that our memory stored at about the same time and in the same context, such as the names of other people from the same time period and surroundings, all of a sudden the forgotten name pops up. I conclude from this that our memory works with associations; related memory elements are linked together as if they were stored right next to each other.

I wonder if we will ever really understand the miracle of the human mind.

Legal Issues

While I am reminded of some legal issues, I would like to use this opportunity to voice some of my reflections related to the American legal system and to some other topics. These issues have nothing to do with the events in my personal life but are things that have kept going through my mind or about which I have some strong opinions. In Part I, I already addressed one such general issue, relating to music.

Our lives are increasingly controlled by laws. It looks like we went from the industrial age to the communication age and have now entered the legal age.

- Some time ago, a photography club's existence, and possibly the existence of all such clubs, was threatened because an officer of the club was sued for one million dollars when another member slipped while delivering some photographs to the officer's home. Obtaining the necessary insurance would go far beyond the means of any small club.
- A woman was awarded 4.2 million dollars after spilling hot coffee on her lap and scalding herself at a McDonald's drive-thru. (The award was reduced twice and she later settled for $ 89,000.)

- A woman in Oklahoma City received 1.75 million dollars and a new Winnebago because her motor home crashed after she set the cruise control at seventy miles per hour and left to make sandwiches; the owner's manual did not say you needed to remain in the driver's seat when putting the vehicle in cruise control.

When I read or hear about court cases, I often have the impression that they are, in the first place, professional battles between the prosecutors and the defense attorneys, rather than attempts to arrive at the truth. For example, if the prosecution or defense obtains proof illegally, it is thrown out of court. Why not punish the person or group that committed this illegal act, instead? Is it not more important to find the truth and punish the guilty and free the innocent, if that illegally obtained proof establishes it?

A somewhat related problem exists with respect to the application of the concept "beyond a reasonable doubt." How many people are convicted unjustly because the majority of a jury felt or guessed that it was reasonably likely that it was this or that way, even though no proof existed and the majority of the jury persuaded the minority so they could go home? The result may be either freedom or life in prison—and nothing in between. On the other hand, there are many cases where no doubt is left about the crime. Yet, no distinction is made between these two situations. There are infinite shades to the word *reasonable*. Maybe there should be at least two levels of doubt and the sentencing should be made accordingly.

The amounts of the awards given in many cases often appear ridiculous to me. They would not be possible in many other countries—even though I can only speak about Germany, where the court fees are related to the jurisdictional claim amount. I assume it is similar in other countries.

Hypocrisy

There is one issue that often gets to me. It touches on the afore-mentioned issue of nudity. Certainly it is a private topic and every person must decide how far he or she wants to go. What I cannot understand are the cases of women's public persecution for having nude pictures taken. Vanessa Williams lost her Miss America crown for having nude pictures taken for *Playboy* magazine. Miss Nevada recently lost her crown for the same reason. Had these women slept every night with another man in the pageant hotel, that would probably have been okay, but nude photographs were not.

Having sex before marriage is completely accepted in our society today, but having yourself seen by others is a sin. What kind of hypocrisy is that? I am glad that Michelangelo painted the Sistine Chapel at the Vatican in 1512 in Italy and not today in the United States. If he had, Michelangelo could have found himself in serious trouble, and perhaps the Pope would have been in trouble, too. An art teacher in Texas was recently fired because she took her students to an art museum where they were "exposed" to seeing an antique nude sculpture.

Appendix B

Summary of *Zeugen des Abendlandes* (Witnesses of the Western World) by Franz Goldschmitt

In very factual form and with much added statistical information, Franz Goldschmitt describes the conditions in the concentration camp from its beginning in 1933 as an indoctrination camp for Communists and socialists through the war years and finally to its liberation by the American troops. About 228,000 people lived in or passed through the camp. Close to 3,000 clerics were in the camp. While Dachau was not an extermination camp like Auschwitz and Buchenwald, the indescribably inhuman treatment of the Dachau prisoners, from tortures to executions, especially up to the summer of 1942, became part of the worst aspects of human history. The conditions in the camp improved in 1942 for the regular inmates, but the camp also served as a transit station to the other concentration camps.

In the summer of 1942, the German government officially forbade bodily punishment. The prisoners could even buy beer in the camp. The clerical prisoners, for whom Goldschmitt became the spokesman, were housed together in one block and saw a significant improvement in their treatment. The SS guard troop now treated Father Goldschmitt with a certain amount of respect, which he utilized to the benefit of the prisoners. He received many packages with large amounts of food, tobacco, and even French liquor from his family, which he shared with his fellow prisoners and used for occasional strategic bribes for the SS guards. As the liberation of France progressed in the second half of 1944, the communication with his family, including the packages, stopped. The more the war approached its end, the more the situation in the camp became catastrophic and intolerable. Berlin ordered many other camps to be closed. Prisoner transports constantly arrived in Dachau, thousands dying on the way or after arriving. In the end, Berlin ordered that no prisoners should be left for the approaching troops. Fortunately, at the last minute, the SS troops fled and the deadly chaos came to its memorable end.

Bibliography

Abu-Haidar, Lamia. "IBM Offering Employees Buyouts." *CNET News*, October 17, 1997. http://news.cnet.com/IBM-offering-employees-buyouts/2100-1001_3-204361.html.

Answers.com. "Lucent Technologies." http://www.answers.com/topic/lucent-technologies-old-company.

Communications Workers of America. "SBC/AT&T Merger Is Good for Employees and Consumers." News release. http://files.cwa-union.org/National/CommunicationsPolicy/Other/SBC-ATTMergerGood.pdf.

Fulbright Commission. "The First Class of Fulbrighters." Berlin: German-American Fulbright Commission, November 2003. http://www.fulbright.de/fileadmin/files/commission/program/downloads/first_class_fulbrighters.pdf.

Gehani, Narain. *Bell Labs: Life in the Crown Jewel.* Summit, NJ: Silicon Press, 2003.

Goldschmitt, Franz. *Zeugen des Abendlandes.* Saarlouis, Germany: Felten Verlag, 1947.

Goodnough, Abby. "The Downsizing of America: A Crack in the Bedrock." *New York Times*, January 14, 1996. http://www.nytimes.com/specials/downsize/resource-0114.html.

Grass, Günter. "How I Spent the War." *New Yorker*, June 4, 2007.

Heck, Klaus. *Before You Cast the Second Stone.* Dillsboro, NC: Western North Carolina Press, 1979.

IBM. "About IBM." http://www.ibm.com/ibm/us/en.

Köhler, August. *Durchs Augenglas der Liebe.* Bad Cannstatt, Germany: Cantz, 1961.

Koehler, Dankwart. "Still Life on Ice." *Petersen's Photographic* 12, no. 8 (December 1983): 54–56.

Martin, Antoinette. "Pastoral Site of Historic Inventions Faces the End." *New York Times*, June 14, 2006. http://www.nytimes.com/2006/06/14/realestate/commercial/14bell.html?ex=1307937600&en=9ceb237dc7596dc8&ei=5090&partner=rssuserland&emc=rss.

Max Kade German-American Research Institute. "Who Was Max Kade?" Pennsylvania State University. http://www.maxkade.psu.edu/kadeinfo.html.

Portfolio.com. "The Worst American CEOs of All Time." CNBC.com. http://www.cnbc.com/id/30502091?slide=10.

Selig, Robert. "Armseliges Deutschland: War Defeat, Reparations, Inflation, and the Year 1923 in German History." *German Life*, October/November 1998. http://www.germanlife.com/Archives/1998/9810_01.html.

UCR/California Museum of Photography. "Lucien Clergue." http://www.cmp.ucr.edu/exhibitions/signs/bio.html.

Vrba, Rudolf. *I Escaped from Auschwitz*. Fort Lee, NJ: Barricade Books, 2002.

My parents' wedding in Heilbronn, August 18, 1921

Narrow street, downtown Heilbronn, 1921. (Photograph by Gebr. Metz, Tübingen. Photograph courtesy of the Fotosammlung Stadtarchiv Heilbronn.)

Old street in Heilbronn; upper floors extend outward over the street to gain space. (Photograph by Fritz Abelein. Photograph courtesy of the Fotosammlung Stadtarchiv Heilbronn.)

My parents, Uli, Volker, Ursula, and I

My twin, Ursula, and I with our toy cow

The house in Heilbronn that I grew up in,
Solothurnerstrasse 21, on a national holiday

In our garden at the house in Heilbronn. Our weather station is in the background.

My father, early in the war

Hitler Youth leaders. I was always one of the smallest. Next to me is my friend, the pianist Hans–Günther Bunz, June 1941

Hitler Youth hike. We missed the last train. I am on the right, next to the mailbox.

My parents during father's leave

The four of us during the war years. Uli was on
leave from military service in France.

Our 88-mm antiaircraft battery near Heilbronn

Luftwaffenhelfer, 1943

In the National Labor Service
(Reichsarbeitsdienst) in Zychlin, Poland

Im Namen des Führers und Oberſten Befehlshabers der Wehrmacht
verleihe ich
dem

G e f r e i t e n
Dankwart K ö h l e r
1./Div.Füs.Batl.1559

das

Eiſerne Kreuz 2. Klaſſe

Div.Gef.Stand , den 17.April 1945

Generalmajor und
Divisions-Kommandeur
(Dienstgrad und Dienststellung)

Form. 1094. Din A 5. Druckerei Gen.Kdo. V Stuttgart

Document awarding me the Iron Cross Second Class

Heilbronn center after air raid on December 4, 1944.
(Photograph by Hermann Eisenmenger, Heilbronn.)

Kilianskirche after the air raid. (Photograph by Hermann
Eisenmenger, Heilbronn.)

Left, view of downtown Heilbronn after the air raid; right, Heilbronn after the postwar reconstruction. (Photographs by Hermann Eisenmenger, Heilbronn.)

The city's memorial for the December 4, 1944, air raid, with the inscription by my parents

My United States prisoner of war registration

My design for a wood-carved picture stand, featuring the church of Le Val d'Ajol in France and that of my hometown in Germany

My 1946 Christmas letter from captivity

The heads of the accounting department during my
last—and better—year of captivity in Sarralbe

POW in Sarralbe, France

My father, around 1965

My mother, around 1962

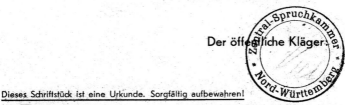

Auf Grund der Angaben in Ihrem Meldebogen sind Sie von dem Gesetz zur Befreiung von Nationalsozialismus und Militarismus vom 5. März 1946 nicht betroffen.

Der öffentliche Kläger

Zentral-Spruchkammer
Nord-Württemberg

Dieses Schriftstück ist eine Urkunde. Sorgfältig aufbewahren!

Denazification document showing that I was not implicated by the respective law

Celebration of my doctoral promotion with my coworkers at the Telefunken Research Laboratory

My wedding with Christa Ischebeck on July 11, 1959

Our departure for America at the Heilbronn train station with our
parents and two of Christa's brothers

Teaching electromagnetic theory at Georgia Tech

Christa, July 1963

The Imperial Wizard. Taken while attending a "public" Ku Klux
Klan meeting in Atlanta with mixed feelings.

John F. Kennedy in Newark, New Jersey, October 12, 1962

Christa with Birgit at the zoo, about 1965

Birgit at Turtle Back Zoo, about 1965

Airview shows Bell Laboratories' new glass and concrete building with parking lots and pools holding eight million gallons of water for the structure's central air conditioning.

IN GRAND STYLE

Bell Labs Opens Big New Building

HOLMDEL TOWNSHIP—The Bell Telephone Laboratories officially opened its recently completed $34 million building yesterday in a style to match the grandeur of the concrete and glass structure.

More than 40 persons attended the press tour of the Research and Development Center. The building was designed by the late Eero Saarinen and was one of the final achievements of the noted architect. He died in 1961 before the first phase of construction was completed.

Mrs. Saarinen was to have presented a sketch of the building to company officials but was unable to attend because of illness. Kevin Roche, an architect and associate of Mr. Saarinen, made the presentation.

The 1,200,000 - square - f o o t building, located on 460 acres off Crawfords Corner road has about 650,000-square feet of work space.

Started in '59

The four-building c o m p l e x was started in August 1959 and completed recently in two phases. The building houses about 4,000 employes and has capacity for 5,300, a third of the laboratories' work force.

Dr. Dankwart Koehler, Holmdel Township, tests pulse code modulation transmission over a laser beam section in a new Bell Laboratories' research laboratory. (Press Photo)

Newspaper article in the Asbury Park Press about the opening of the new Bell Laboratories building in Holmdel, New Jersey. The text reads: "Dr. Dankwart Koehler, Holmdel Township, tests pulse code modulation transmission over a laser beam section in a new Bell Laboratories' research laboratory."

My design of an electronic flip-flop circuit. It was the fastest such circuit in the world, operating 220 million times a second. Also shown is one of the twelve transistors used in the circuit.

Our new architect-designed home
in Holmdel, 1966

With our daughter Birgit at the new
house in Holmdel, 1966

With little Birgit on my shoulder

Sample of my photography: "Bison in Yellowstone Park"

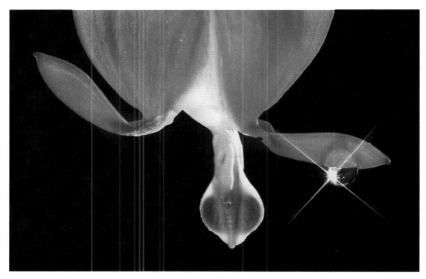

Sample of my photography: "Bleeding Heart"

Sample of my photography: "Frosted Tree in Bavaria"

Sample of my photography: "World of Dreams." Darkroom combination of female figure on beach and window frost.

Sample of my photography: "Horse and Tree with Moon."
Darkroom effect called "solarization."

Sample of my photography: "Antelope Canyon, Arizona"

With our five granddaughters at an exhibition
reception in Portland, 2008

The entire family, 2008. Back row: Steffen, Cathy, Mark, Birgit, Leyli,
Christa, Dankwart, Kirsten, Mickey, and Emeline; front row: Sasha,
Cory, and Annika.